Configuring Value Conflicts in Markets

Configuring Value Conflicts in Markets

Edited by

Susanna Alexius

Research Fellow, Stockholm Centre for Organizational Research, Stockholm University and Stockholm School of Economics, Sweden

Kristina Tamm Hallström

Associate Professor in Management, Stockholm Centre for Organizational Research and Lecturer, Stockholm School of Economics, Sweden

Edward Elgar
Cheltenham, UK • Northampton, MA, USA

Published by
Edward Elgar Publishing Limited
The Lypiatts
15 Lansdown Road
Cheltenham
Glos GL50 2JA
UK

Edward Elgar Publishing, Inc.
William Pratt House
9 Dewey Court
Northampton
Massachusetts 01060
USA

A catalogue record for this book
is available from the British Library

Library of Congress Control Number: 2013951849

This book is available electronically in the ElgarOnline.com
Business Subject Collection, E-ISBN 978 1 78254 447 0

ISBN 978 1 78254 446 3

Typeset by Servis Filmsetting Ltd, Stockport, Cheshire
Printed and bound in Great Britain by T.J. International Ltd, Padstow

Contents

Contributors

Susanna Alexius holds a PhD in management from the Stockholm School of Economics. She is a research fellow at Stockholm Centre for Organizational Research (Score) and lectures at Stockholm School of Economics, Uppsala University, and for a number of executive education programmes including IFL where she is a programme director. Alexius is interested in how organizations respond to demands from their institutional environment. She has recently published on the topics of organizing for and against professional standardization of management consultants, responsibilization of consumers, value-complexity of organizational hybrids, and the translation and commercialization of sustainability.

Sebastian Botzem is a research fellow at the Social Science Research Centre Berlin. He studied political science and holds a PhD in business administration. His research focus is on transnational standardization in accounting, regulation of financial markets, and the role of organizations in international political economy. Botzem's recent publications include *The Politics of Accounting Regulation: Organizing Transnational Standard Setting in Financial Reporting* (2012, Edward Elgar).

Daniel Castillo holds a PhD in sociology from Stockholm University and is currently a research fellow at Stockholm Centre for Organizational Research (Score), Stockholm University. His research interests include the relation between state and market, with a focus on phenomena related to corruption, as well as how the state organizes new markets. Castillo has recently published the dissertation *State Boundaries in Transition: A Study of Sponsoring, Corruption and Market Relations*.

Jenny Cisneros Örnberg holds a PhD in political science and is Director of the Centre for Social Research on Alcohol and Drugs (SoRAD) at Stockholm University, Sweden. Her research interests include the interaction between domestic and European policy-making in the field of public health, specifically in the policy areas of alcohol, gambling, tobacco and pharmaceuticals.

Matilda Dahl holds a PhD in business administration and is a researcher in management at Stockholm Centre for Organizational Research (Score) where she has been working in the 'Organizing Markets' programme, studying processes of organization in the financial sector. Her research is focused on international organization, transnational governance, and various processes connected to a growing audit society. Dahl also works as an assistant professor at Gotland University.

Christina Garsten is Professor of Social Anthropology at Stockholm University and Chair of the Executive Board of Stockholm Centre for Organizational Research (Score). She recently joined Copenhagen Business School as Professor of Globalization and Organization. Her research involves globalization processes in corporations and markets, with a current focus on the role of think tanks in setting agendas for global governance and in influencing political priorities. Earlier works have focused on transnational organizational culture, on organizational visions of transparency and accountability for transnational trade, and on policy changes towards flexibility and employability in work life.

Ingrid Gustafsson is a PhD student at the School of Public Administration, University of Gothenburg. Her thesis work is on the increasing use of international standards and standard compliance mechanisms such as accreditation in Swedish public administration. Swedac (the Swedish Board for Accreditation and Conformity Assessment) is used as a case to understand the complex system of standards, certifications and accreditations. Gustafsson's main interest is in the organizational implications such systems have for public sector organizing.

Martin Gustavsson is an associate professor in economic history and a researcher at Stockholm Centre for Organizational Research (Score) and Sociology of Education and Culture (SEC), Uppsala University. His research focuses on the interplay between economics, politics and culture in a historical perspective. He has studied different markets, all deeply embedded in social, political and cultural settings: for example the art market in Stockholm 1920–1960, the market for exclusive furniture in Sweden 1935–1955, the Swedish market for media technology 1973–2000, and the market for local shopping centres in the suburbs of Stockholm 1943–2000.

Andrea Mennicken is an associate professor in accounting at the London School of Economics and Political Science (LSE) and a research associate at the Centre for Analysis of Risk and Regulation (LSE). She received her doctorate from LSE in 2005 for a thesis entitled *Moving West: The Emergence, Reform and Standardisation of Audit Practices in Post-Soviet Russia*. She holds a master's degree (LSE) and German diploma degree (Bielefeld University) in sociology. Her work has been published in both

English and German, for example in *Accounting, Organizations and Society, Financial Accountability and Management, Foucault Studies* and with VS Verlag für Sozialwissenschaften. Her research interests include social studies of valuation and accounting, transnational governance regimes, processes of marketization, standardization, and public sector reforms.

Anette Nyqvist holds a PhD in social anthropology. She is a researcher at Stockholm Centre for Organizational Research (Score) and a lecturer at the Department of Social Anthropology at Stockholm University. Nyqvist's research interests concentrate on issues of power at the nexus of statecraft and market-making. Her publications include *Opening the Orange Envelope: Reform and Responsibility in the Remaking of the Swedish National Pension System* (2008) and *Organisational Anthropology: Doing Ethnography in and among Complex Organisations* (co-authored with Christina Garsten, 2013). Her forthcoming book is a monograph of her current research on the financial and political strategies of institutional investors.

Martin Rosenström is a PhD student in management at Stockholm Centre for Organizational Research (Score) and Stockholm School of Economics. His thesis work is on aspects of organization in the construction of the European market for CO_2 emission allowances, with a focus on the Swedish context and on the practices of measuring CO_2 emissions. His research revolves around the organization of markets, with a special interest in how the forms of 'market' and 'organization', as forms of coordination, can co-exist.

Adrienne Sörbom is an associate professor in sociology, a research director at Stockholm Centre for Organizational Studies (Score) and senior lecturer at Södertörn University. Her research interests may be termed 'political sociology', and include the organization of global politics among different types of actors, such as trade unions, social movements and global think tanks. Sörbom's work has been published both in Swedish and English, for example, in *Statsvetenskaplig tidskrift*, *Critical Sociology*, with Edward Elgar.

Kristina Tamm Hallström is an associate professor in management at Stockholm School of Economics and a research director at the Stockholm Centre for Organizational Research (Score). She has conducted research about legitimacy and authority in transnational standard setting and about the emergence and legitimization of certification and accreditation as audit practices. She has published several articles, chapters and books with international publishing companies. Tamm Hallström is currently conducting research on trust in eco-labels, as well as on the power and consequences of classificatory work in the context of management accounting and control in both private and public organizations.

Renita Thedvall holds a PhD in social anthropology and is active in the field of policy and organizational anthropology. Thedvall has a particular interest in how policies around, for example, quality in work or fair trade are developed, shaped and framed via indicators or standards. She is currently working on how the Lean Management model is negotiated, discussed, implemented and operates in public preschools. Renita is a senior lecturer and Director of Studies at the Department of Social Anthropology and a senior research fellow and Deputy Director at Stockholm Centre for Organizational Research (Score) at Stockholm University.

Karolina Windell holds a PhD from Uppsala University's Department of Business Studies. She is research scholar at Stockholm Centre for Organizational Research (Score). Her main research interests concern the relationship between news media and organizations and, in particular, how the media creates, disseminates and legitimizes ideas about responsible organizational behaviour. Her studies include news production, corporate communication, reputation management, and corporate social responsibility (CSR).

Acknowledgements

This volume is a product of inspirational discussions and collaborative work between the contributing authors and many other colleagues over the past two years. The idea of writing a book on the theme of value conflicts in markets was born in early 2010 at a Score workshop organized in Saltsjöbaden by the research directors of the Organizing Markets programme. Among the topics that came up during the first plenary session, value conflicts turned out to be particularly engaging and attracted a large number of participants for the scheduled sub-group discussions.

As editors, we are grateful to research directors Nils Brunsson, Christina Garsten and Göran Sundström for their immediate support and encouragement to invite in authors from our partner research centres. The positive response received resulted in a number of co-authored chapters in which empirical findings from two or more markets were compared. As expected, this comparative approach brought with it a few challenges, but it also prompted us to engage in constructive, fruitful dialogues that we feel have greatly enriched both the comparative analysis within and between chapters, and the overall theoretical contribution of the volume.

We would like to thank Riksbankens Jubileumsfond (Bank of Sweden Tercentenary Foundation) for the generous grant that made this book possible. We are also grateful to The Swedish Foundation for International Cooperation in Research and Higher Education (STINT) for funding three international workshops in 2010–2012. The purpose of these meetings was to discuss the ongoing work and to give each other critical feedback and constructive input. We extend special thanks to Göran Ahrne, Patrik Aspers, Lotta Björklund Larsson, Nils Brunsson, Marie-Laure Djelic, Staffan Furusten, John Meyer, Mats Jutterström, Yuval Millo, Rune Premfors, Rita Samiolo, Linda Soneryd and Göran Sundström, whose valuable comments and suggestions on various drafts of chapters greatly improved the final product. We also extend our thanks to our colleagues at SoRAD, Stockholm University, and the Department of Business Studies, Uppsala University, who generously invited us to give seminars on the book, which helped us to refine the arguments. We are also grateful to the two anonymous reviewers who on behalf of Edward Elgar provided constructive comments on an early version of Chapter 1, and finally, to our language editor Kelly V. Olsson for her much appreciated flexibility and efficiency.

It has been a stimulating journey to experience first-hand how the collaborative approach of this project has evolved, enabling us to share, compare, complement and learn so much from each other while drawing on our different experiences and materials. We are proud of the outcome and wish to extend an invitation to the reader to take part in further exploration of the timely yet ageless subject of value conflicts in markets.

Susanna Alexius and Kristina Tamm Hallström
Stockholm, July 2013

1. Value work in markets: configuring values, organizing markets

Susanna Alexius and Kristina Tamm Hallström

FAR-REACHING CONSEQUENCES OF VALUE WORK

Why are certain commodities, like gambling or prostitution, illegal in one country and legal in another? Why are certain markets, like those of prison services or pharmaceutical retail, privatized while others remain in the hands of state monopolies? Why do certain commodities, like coal and alcohol, continue to be openly contested for centuries although for very different reasons in different time periods, while other commodities, like personal insurance and certification, are far less frequently struck by conflicts?

In this volume, we provide both an analytical framework and a number of case studies which suggest that, in order to answer the questions above, we must look further into the processes and consequences of value work. We define values as criteria that direct our actions to that which we perceive as important, meaningful, desirable or worthwhile (Suchman 1995; Graeber 2005). We define value work as attempts to influence the value set-up of a market and/or to influence the ways in which different market values are configured, in the sense of arranged or ordered. And by organization of markets, we mean the addition of elements of organization such as regulation, sanctions, supervision, hierarchy and membership (Ahrne and Brunsson 2011).

The empirical case studies drawn upon in this volume help to demonstrate how the plurality of market values at stake in a market often poses great challenges to sellers and buyers, to other market organizers, and to the wider society. We further analyze how value plurality and potential value conflicts are responded to through different kinds of value work. 'Missionary' work done by social movement organizations is a straightforward example of value work, whereas the use of seemingly neutral experts, accounting tools and management models are examples of less obvious but highly influential value work. And, as argued above, we suggest that value work may have a considerable impact on the way markets are regulated, supervised or in other ways organized. By empirically scrutinizing the interrelations between value work and market organization, we thus aim to help to explain why and how markets are organized.

SCRUTINIZING MARKET VALUES IN THE PLURAL

Value analysis is a fruitful path to a better understanding of any social setting – a family, an organization, or society at large (Ahrne 2007).

A general assertion is that it is value plurality – clusters of values – rather than single values that govern behaviour (Liedtka 1989). The co-existence of numerous and at times conflicting values is part of society as we know it. Drawing from over a dozen market studies – in which market values are defined inductively and pragmatically as values perceived to be at stake in everyday market life – the authors of this multidisciplinary volume demonstrate that the economic value so strongly associated with market exchange is far from the only kind of value that individuals and organizations in and around markets have to consider and attempt to shape and configure. Just as there is a plurality of values at stake in any organization, there is a plurality of market values at stake in any market setting. The different chapters highlight the diversity and dynamics of markets values such as sustainability, safety, decency, integrity, environmental concerns, transparency, independence, public health, democracy and fairness.

It goes almost without saying that every decision and action that takes place in a market setting cannot be governed by money, or at least not by money alone. Markets are not only about economic values and profits. Yet, as a result of economic theories and models that help to make up markets, the term 'market value' has become closely associated with valuation and pricing and the economic worth of goods (Callon 1998a, 1998b; Callon and Muniesa 2005; MacKenzie et al. 2007; Fourcade and Healy 2007; Beckert and Aspers 2011; Moeran and Strandgaard Pedersen 2011). For example, in economic theory on so-called 'negative externalities', 'missing markets' and 'market failure'[1] (Dahlman 1979), social and environmental values connected to pollution that causes damage to public health and the environment are described in economic terms as 'social costs'[2] (Carande-Kulis et al. 2007). Putting a price tag on clean air or estimating the economic value of public health or long-term environmental soundness are prime examples of what we call 'harmonious modes' of attempts to hide or neutralize potential value conflicts in markets – see below.

We do not view markets as strictly corresponding to a single market value domain, system or logic, a view that is captured in its essence in the following quote from Harvie and Milburn (2010: 633): 'What is valued within the value system of the global market is [economic] market value and market value alone'. Thus, we take a critical stance toward how economics has come to dominate popular notions of market value (in the singular), and we argue for a more holistic view of market values (in the plural), where the value analysis is not limited to a monetary scale of valuation but involves other symbolic values as well. Although economic values no doubt shape markets, so too do values such as the above-mentioned – sustainability, safety, decency, public health and democracy. More specifically, we wish to contribute by further problematizing the view that there is little value plurality in most markets – that every decision and action taken in a market setting can be translated or exchanged into a price or a cost.

THE VALUE WORK OF MARKET ORGANIZERS

One assumption uniting us in our collaboration has been that the 'invisible hand' (Smith 1776) needs ample support from a wide range of individuals and organizations struggling to configure values and organize markets in a variety of ways. It is reasonable to assume that, in all markets, the value plurality at hand is being shaped by a large number of market organizers and their activities. Following the Scandinavian neoinstitutionalist tradition, with its comparatively greater emphasis on agency, we take an interest in how market organizers – individuals and organizations involved in market formation and market reform – attempt to engage in value work in order to make a difference in bringing about and configuring market values and, at times, take part in initiating organizational reforms in response to market contestation.

In addition to mutual adjustment (Lindblom 2001) and cultural processes (Aspers 2011), markets are admittedly made up and continuously shaped by sellers and buyers, but also by individuals and organizations not directly involved in the exchange situation, such as regulatory agencies and standard setters, social movement organizations, researchers, ranking institutes and consultants (Helgesson, Kjellberg and Liljenberg, 2004). While states are likely to become involved in the organization of markets that have become constructed as contested (Brunsson and Hägg 1992; Fligstein 1996, 2001), the degree and modes of state involvement tend to vary over time and space in response to both local conditions and global governing trends.

It can also be expected that various non-state organizers are involved in processes of value configuration and market organization, for example, through 'soft' governing structures such as voluntary standards, certification schemes, codes of conduct, guidelines, and so on, which have been analyzed as a new form of regulation that compensates for the declining or at least changing capacities of nation-states (Rose and Miller 1992; Jacobsson 1993; Brunsson and Jacobsson 2000; Haufler 2001, 2003; Higgins and Tamm Hallström 2007; Bartley 2007; Tamm Hallström and Boström 2010). We can thus expect several types of market organizers – both state and non-state organizations – to engage in the organization of markets. To understand how market values play out in local market contexts, as well as how they change, are conditioned by, and influence market reform, we have studied a wide range of such market organizers who cooperate harmoniously at times, but also struggle and get into conflict (Helgesson et al. 2004).

Although we distinguish between various types of market organizers, we do not presume that a certain value is necessarily linked to a certain actor category (Wicks 1996 and Wood 1996 as cited by Gurney and Humphreys 2006: 94–95). Rather, we find that organizations and individuals in and around markets have the capacity to act as plural actors (Lahire 2010/2011) who must cope with plurality and tensions between different values, and can negotiate their way through a number of different value domains (Graeber 2005: 441; Thévenot 2001; Boltanski and Thévenot 1991/2006). It is accordingly our belief that any ideal typical ideas of a priori 'global market value', 'civic value', 'domestic value' and so on, must be treated with caution – or better yet, be put under scrutiny.

Sometimes contestation drives the organization of markets to the point where the legal market is shut down and market exchange is prohibited. Current examples of such highly contested commodities that are prohibited in most countries today are child labour, human body parts, sexual relations, addictive drugs and votes (Radin 2001; Ertman and Williams 2005; Satz 2010). In other cases, the legal trade of the contested commodities continues but under strict state supervision and regulation such as alcohol and gambling as discussed in this volume.

It has been noted in previous research on the value plurality/complexity of markets that how market values 'co-exist', 'dominate', 'compete' are 'combined', are 'entangled' or 'interwoven' matters (Thornton and Ocasio 2008: 107; Browne and Milgram 2009). We elaborate on these findings and contribute empirical and analytical nuance to help explain how values are temporarily configured as a result of value work performed by individuals and organizations in different market settings.

Another important source of theoretical inspiration in analysing these processes has been studies of value plurality within or between organizations (Kraatz and Block 2008; Pache 2011). As suggested by Thévenot (2001: 410), organizations lend themselves well to being theorized as 'arrangements which have been specifically designed for compromised complexity'. The literature provides an extensive list of organization studies on how value plurality may be and is dealt with within and between organizations, through strategies of compromise, negotiation or balancing (Oliver 1991; Tamm Hallström 2004; Boltanski and Thévenot 1991/2006; Dahlberg 2010), decoupling (Meyer and Rowan 1977), hypocrisy (Brunsson 1989), prioritization or colonization (Abdallah, forthcoming), sequential prioritization (March and Simon 1958; Cyert and March 1963), or the delegation of responsibility to other organizational levels (Ahrne and Brunsson 2008; Jacobsson and Sundström 2009; Fries 2011) or to consumers in processes of responsibilitization (Shamir 2008; Williams 2007; Alexius 2011). Finally, yet another strategy found in organization studies is to change the organizational form and ownership (Brunsson 1994). As a whole, this previous work has inspired us in our endeavour to study the value work performed by organizations and individuals attempting to influence and reconfigure the set of market values at stake, and the framing of values in harmonious or conflictual terms, at a certain time in a certain market context.

To distinguish our studies empirically from studies of value complexity within and between organizations, we have taken particular interest in cases where the value complexity at hand concerns the market at large, that is, value complexity that is experienced by a large number of market actors – although not necessarily experienced and approached in a similar fashion. We demonstrate how the plurality of market values plays out in practice and often poses great challenges for market actors, market organizers and wider society. We also demonstrate that value work and value configurations have a considerable impact on the way markets are regulated, supervised, or in other ways organized. By empirically scrutinizing the interrelations between value configurations and market organization, this volume thus contributes to explaining why and how markets are organized.

CONTESTATION IN TRANSITION

The set of market values at stake in a certain market is neither given nor stable. As demonstrated in the empirical chapters, the values at stake change over time, clearly influenced by the value work performed by various market organizers. As noted earlier, while economists primarily have been interested in the economic value of markets, we are inspired by previous research by sociologists and anthropologists who have studied value complexity without first reducing it (Zelizer 1979, 1985, 2005; Fourcade and Healy 2007; Thévenot 2001; Boltanski and Thévenot 1991/2006; Browne and Milgram 2009; Stark 2009; Graeber 2005). As an example, in her historical process studies of the commodification of life insurance, children and intimacy, Zelizer (1979, 1985, 2005) highlights the role of values and ideologies in the struggles of market making. Her studies demonstrate how extensive value work over the course of decades, mainly on the part of life insurance companies, recategorized profiting from death into a morally justified investment (Zelizer 1979). In terms of consequences, she also suggests that the 'value compatibility' of a product innovation such as life insurance can explain whether the innovation is adopted or rejected by buyers (ibid.). Zelizer's work describes both legitimation (ibid.) and illegitimation (Zelizer 1985) of products as a continuous process of struggles to shape market culture and market values.

Many authors who have written on the theme of value complexity in markets – including Zelizer (1979, 1985, 2005), Fourcade and Healy (2007) and Brown and Milgram (2009) – are primarily interested in the morality of markets (see also Hirschman 1982). For instance, in their literature review, Fourcade and Healy (2007) set out to search for the 'kind of moral order capitalism rests upon' and propose a view which they call 'moralized markets', a view that 'sees markets as cultural phenomena and moral projects in their own right' (p. 1). Although we share Zelizer's and Fourcade and Healy's constructionistic approach and interest in the 'work necessary to produce, to sustain or – conversely – to constrain the market' (Fourcade and Healy 2007: 27), the primary aim of this volume is not to analyze markets as moral projects. It is not our intention to normatively judge degrees of morality, but rather to study value work that may result in markets being perceived as more or less moral.

Furthermore, we do not share the widespread notion that certain markets are more value-laden than others; an idea that value plurality is a particularity of certain special cases, so-called 'contested' markets (Radin 2001; Hong and Kacpercyk 2007; Satz 2010). We think this idea is misleading, since what is contested, and why, changes over time and space (Fourcade and Healy 2007: 21; Zelizer 1979, 1985). The empirical case studies of this volume contribute to further demonstrating that most markets could, at least at some point in time, to some degree be labelled 'externality markets', 'risk markets' or 'immoral markets', for instance. By bringing in or highlighting values such as safety, public health, life, integrity, equal rights and human rights, previously uncontested market exchanges may be framed as concerning a complex plurality of values

– more than simply a delivery of products or services to customers and economic value to owners (Friedman 1970). As a result of such value work, previously uncontested markets may also rather suddenly be viewed and treated as immoral, illegitimate, risky or 'dirty', due to their failure to address the complexity of values brought about.

The trading of slaves, for example, was once a legal business, whereas there are strict regulations prohibiting this type of trade today due to long-time efforts to highlight values relating to human rights. The trade of bananas, coffee and cacao beans are other examples of products that were not particularly contested some decades ago, but which today are critically evaluated according to 'fair trade' values. The reverse situation, a transition from previously contested to less contested as a consequence of value work also occurs. One such example is the highly contested 19th century US life insurance market where, at the end of the 1800s, it was neither morally justified to establish monetary agreements relating to life and death, nor to set a value on the 'priceless' child (Zelizer 1979). Today, however, it is almost the other way around: it has become difficult for parents, at least in the global north, to justify not insuring their children (see Chapter 6 in this volume).

An historical comparison of formative moments in the market for gambling also offers ample evidence of changes to the value set-up of markets (Alexius, Castillo and Rosenström, 2011). In the 1920s, the values of leisure, sports and modernity were added to the value set of the Swedish gambling market through value work that neutralized the perceived value conflict and opened the way to a normalization and legalization of gambling. However, following successful attempts to counter this development through the addition of values such as safety/anti-fraud, protectionism and charity, the value conflict was revived and the Swedish state managed to justify its continued monopoly (ibid.; see also Chapter 10 in this volume).

CONFIGURING VALUES – ORGANIZING MARKETS

It is an empirical fact that when a market or elements of it – for example, the commodities, the sellers or the buyers – become contested, such contestation tends to spur organizational initiatives such as regulation, sanctions and supervision, or an increasing level of hierarchy or use of membership (Ahrne and Brunsson 2011). Contestation has organizational consequences. As Fourcade and Healy (2007: 22) put it: 'The appropriate classification of goods [. . .] is often the subject of conflict. Objects or relationships may move back and forth across boundaries in response to

Value work

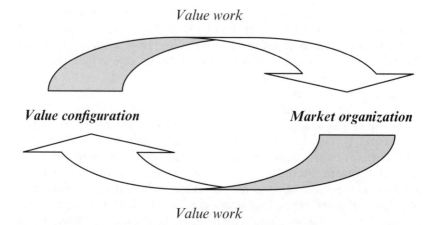

*Figure 1.1   The loop: the two-way relationship between value
              configuration and market organization*

technological change, the mobilization of interested groups, or the efforts
of moral entrepreneurs'.

Contested markets are, however, neither organized in the same way
nor to the same degree (Ahrne and Brunsson 2011). Our main theoretical proposal is that organizational outcomes in terms of market regulations and so on can be explained in part by the value work behind value
configurations, that is, the arrangement and rearrangement of the set of
market values at stake. As noted, the purpose of this volume is to further
our understanding of the dynamics of market organization by studying
how value work brings about different value configurations, which in
turn influence the organization of a market (see Figure 1.1). We also
demonstrate how the organization of a market in turn influences value
work creating, hence, a two-way relationship or loop between market
organization and value configurations. A fundamental finding illustrated
by the market studies of this volume is that value configurations matter
to the organization of markets, and that we should therefore pay more
attention to them if we wish to explain the various degrees and nature of
market organization.

A reflexive approach is needed when studying value complexity
(Fourcade and Healy 2007: 27). As social scientists we are well aware
of the duality of agency and structure (Giddens 1984). One of the core
premises of the institutional logics approach to the study of the values
of individuals and organizations is that these values are embedded in
prevailing institutional logics (Thornton and Ocasio 2008; Thornton et

al. 2012). Market values are no exception. Markets are also embedded in cultural and institutional contexts influenced by politics and ideologies that in turn affect the way they are realized, the expectations that are raised about them, and the individuals and organizations that participate in their shaping.

Although we recognize the influence of this more top-down macro approach literature on institutional embeddedness (Thornton and Ocasio 2008; Thornton et al. 2012), we agree with its proponents that to further our understanding of the influence of logics and values in markets we need bottom-up micro studies of the dynamics and influence of market values to complete the empirical picture. In this volume, we therefore theorize markets as arenas for political struggle where values are negotiated and value conflicts arise and are configured in various ways (Fligstein 1996, 2001; Schneiberg and Bartley 2001; Yakubovich et al. 2005). More specifically, we argue that in order to understand and perhaps even be able to predict how decisions will be made concerning what products may be legally produced and sold or not, who the legitimate sellers and buyers may be, and where the exchange may take place, we must not limit ourselves to a top-down approach of institutional embeddedness, but must rather complement this fundamental line of research with more bottom-up, micro-process studies of value work in market settings.

Moreover, since market values, value configurations and value conflicts are not essential in any sense, but rather constructions that change over time and space, we have applied a process perspective that has allowed us to capture the activities and struggles of market organizers behind such value transformations. The empirical studies presented in the following chapters were all conducted using an inductive approach. Wherever possible, a close-up, bottom-up approach was chosen to allow the empirical case studies speak to for themselves. We have also aimed to stay alert not only to value conflicts that are openly articulated, but also to any hidden controversies or conflicts that might be expected based on historical accounts of, or on conflicts in, similar markets. With our holistic definition of values described earlier, values may just as well show up in individuals' feelings and desires, organizations' objectives or in market discourse and regulation. Our aim throughout has been to trace and describe the transforming value configurations and their implications for the organization of markets.

To sum up, when viewing markets as organized, we assume that markets are shaped and governed not solely by mutual adjustment, networking and price mechanisms, but foremost by elements of organization such as regulation, sanctions, supervision, hierarchy and membership (Ahrne and Brunsson 2011). We argue that the processes of value work that bring about value configurations help to explain how markets become organized (Abolafia 1996; Callon 1998a; MacKenzie 2009; Aspers 2011). We also demonstrate that the nature and extent of such market organization in turn drives and influences further value work (see the 'loop' in Figure 1.1).

HARMONIOUS OR CONFLICTUAL MODES OF VALUE CONFIGURATION?

The authors have identified, described and analyzed two general modes of value configuration resulting from various efforts of value work, which in turn may add nuance to our understanding of the organization of markets. In some cases, values are configured in a harmonious mode that seems to neutralize or otherwise downplay a potential value conflict. In other cases, values are configured in a conflictual mode, that is, in ways that bring about a reinforced and sustained conflict.

We find that market crises and drastic changes bring increased attention to value plurality and that, during such formative moments, a window of opportunity opens for new modes of configuration. Sometimes value conflicts become visible when the conditions of market exchange undergo substantial change. Examples of substantial change include deregulation, technical innovation, or a more general market crisis. However, value conflicts may also be the result of long-term proactive and at times less obvious efforts, by social movement organizations or by scientists, for example, to frame and promote certain values.

Generally, we propose that the more a market is perceived as having value plurality and value conflicts, the higher the expected level of organization in that market. Although further and more systematic research is needed, we find it reasonable to assume that some market organizers opt for a conflictual mode of value work as they benefit from creating or enhancing a sense of value conflict, since a higher perceived degree of contestation is likely to result in a higher degree of organization of the market at hand. Following the same logic, we find it plausible that market organizers who want lower degrees of organization, typically a deregulation of some kind, will opt for a harmonious mode of value work, which has the potential of concealing possible value conflicts behind popular concepts such as transparency, independence and 'win–win', for example.

In the following, we elaborate on the two general modes of value configuration identified. As noted, one characterizes a harmonious value plurality, and the other represents a more conflictual value plurality. Among the market cases analyzed in this volume, we find examples where the value plurality at stake is configured in terms of a peaceful co-existence, as an alignment, or – in popular business rhetoric – as a 'win–win' situation. We discuss how such value work may justify self-regulation or facilitate decisions about privatization reforms and market deregulation. We also demonstrate that if, on the other hand, values are actively polarized to reinforce or sustain a perceived value conflict, such value work may help to justify stricter regulation and contribute, for example, to protecting state monopolies. We believe that the value configuration framework proposed in this introduction, together with the findings of the market studies presented in the following chapters, provide a fruitful avenue for further examination and analysis of the interrelation between value work and market organization. In particular, it would be interesting to further elaborate on the conditions under which value conflicts are configured in markets. Although the present volume presents some general propositions regarding the two-way relationship between value configurations and market reform, future research could investigate more systematically whether there are patterns to be found in the market organizers who are involved in attempts to achieve a certain configuration and in the organizational reforms that follow the arrangement of a certain configuration.

Harmonious Modes of Value Configuration

Several value work activities observed in our market studies can be classified as activities of a harmonious mode as they concerned attempts to 'gloss over', conceal or neutralize value conflicts. For example, in Chapter 4, Sebastian Botzem and Matilda Dahl discuss the bank and stock exchange markets in the Baltic countries and describe how widespread claims of trust relating to the value of transparency have helped criticized market actors and market organizers get through the recent financial crisis, though in somewhat different ways. In Chapter 5, Kristina Tamm Hallström and Ingrid Gustafsson describe how the value of independence has been used in a similar fashion in verification markets. The authors go on to discuss how some values and value conflicts in their respective markets are overshadowed when other, more abstract value conflicts are highlighted. Through the organization of accreditation, that is, accreditation being a control of the verification of companies that serves to assure the value of independence, the authors demonstrate how the economic dimension of the business of verification is neutralized (Chapter 5). In Chapter 6, Martin Gustavsson similarly explains how various value conflicts are hidden and downplayed by insurance companies through the establishment of a complex, private 'legal system' that, at least superficially, shows several similarities with the public legal system. Examples of value work that examine what a harmonious value

configuration mode has to do with value convergence or value alignment is discussed by Anette Nyqvist and Renita Thedvall in Chapter
8, and by Christina Garsten and Adrienne Sörbom in Chapter 9. The
authors describe how market intermediaries like the FLO (Fairtrade
International), KPA (a Swedish pension fund) and the World Economic
Forum organize with the purpose of changing the notion of a value conflict into a notion of a necessary and positive interrelation between values
such as economic profits on the one hand and sustainability and social
responsibility on the other. We find that such reinforcement of the popular
notion of 'win–win' may alternatively be interpreted as yet another means
of 'glossing over', concealing or neutralizing a value conflict at hand.

Alignment and convergence are thus configurations arranged in an
effort to obtain a (seemingly) harmonious relationship between market
values. In this respect, these modes differ from cases where the plurality of market values at stake is perceived as a value conflict or potential
value conflict. In the great majority of these cases, the value conflict is
perceived as a 'problem' or 'threat' in need of a 'solution' or 'resolution'.
The authors point to 'struggles', 'tension', 'value battles' and 'crises', and
describe the urge of organizations and individuals to shape and control the
value complexity at hand, often by attempts to close or conceal potential
value conflicts.

A third set of examples illustrating a harmonious, or at least not openly
conflictual mode, can be found in Chapter 2 in the market for prison
services and in Chapter 4 in the pharmaceutical retail market. In Chapter
2, Andrea Mennicken describes how potentially conflicting values such
as decency versus economics, or rehabilitation versus punishment and
security, were configured as a hierarchy, in a process of value hierarchization. Following the escapes of high security prisoners in the mid-1990s,
an inquiry argued that the prison service put too much emphasis on the
values of care, decency and rehabilitation, in relation to the values of security, discipline and control. Private-sector accounting instruments such
as key performance indicators (KPIs) were then introduced, resulting in
a hierarchization of values. But as Mennicken describes, when faced with
criticism, the same instruments were then used as a 'catalyst of problematization' in an attempt to flatten the hierarchy and rebalance values in order
to bring the less prioritized concerns about the quality of care and the
prisoners' decency and rehabilitation back onto the agenda. In Chapter
3, Jenny Cisneros Örnberg describes another case of value hierarchization, in the pharmaceutical retail market, in which the value of customer
satisfaction came to be prioritized over the value of patient security as a
result of strategic value work. Once again, we see how the configuration
of value hierarchization is unstable and characterized by an ongoing

problematization and attempts to rebalance the values hierarchized. Finally, the market for online newspapers, discussed by Karolina Windell in Chapter 7, may be mentioned in this respect. The author shows how market actors strive to balance economic and professional values, but a possible value hierarchization that prioritizes economic values is reinforced through the use of electronic evaluation devices used to track reader preferences and frequency of articles.

Conflictual Modes of Value Configuration

On the other side of the continuum we find more conflictual modes of value configuration that feature value work that aims at sustaining (rather than resolving) value conflicts. Although most of the chapters describe markets where attempts are made to resolve value conflicts, as discussed above, there are a few exceptions worth closer examination. From an organizational reform perspective, it seems rather expected that value conflicts can be used to justify a higher degree of organization of a market, that is, the introduction of market reforms of various kinds. As seen in chapters 8 and 9, through efforts of value convergence and value alignment, a plurality of values may be represented in terms of a peaceful co-existence. However, for other market organizers, the notion of peacefully co-existing values poses a threat to their existing market positions. In Chapter 7, Karolina Windell describes how value plurality seems to be highlighted and even deliberately constructed as a conflict, by newspaper companies but also by journalists and representatives of their professional associations. In doing so, these market organizers help to justify their future press subsidies and protect their positions that are under threat from the increasingly online newspaper market. In Chapter 8, Anette Nyqvist and Renita Thedvall describe how FLO and KPA, who generally 'mission' the convergence of market values, simultaneously act to uphold the notion of value conflicts in their own respective markets of Fairtrade labelling and pension funds. Through the use of 'polarizing tools' such as standards, criteria, screening instruments and labels, these market organizers contribute to the polarizations 'good' and 'bad', 'ethical' and 'unethical', 'fair' and 'unfair', and so on, in order to stake out a favourable position for themselves as 'good', 'ethical' and 'fair' sellers in their respective markets. In Chapter 10, Susanna Alexius, Daniel Castillo and Martin Rosenström employ historical accounts of value configurations and market reforms of the alcohol, gambling and coal markets to illustrate that in certain highly contested markets, value work helps to sustain rather than resolve contestation. More specifically, they demonstrate how value conflicts have been re-intensified and contestation of the commodities sustained for centuries in processes characterized by attempts to add values to the conflict, to expand the scale of contestation (for example from local to global) and to relocate the scope of contestation (for example from the commodity to its consumption).

OUTLINE OF THE BOOK: CHAPTER ABSTRACTS

In Chapter 2, *Accounting for values in prison privatization*, Andrea Mennicken studies the roles that seemingly mundane and apolitical accounting instruments for prison rating and performance measurement play in the organization of value complexity in prison privatization. Focusing on the case of prison privatizations in England and Wales, she unpacks different values and risks at stake, and raises the question of the extent to which accounting can play the role of a 'mediating instrument' in cases where conflicting values are at stake. Mennicken shows that the introduction of private sector-based performance measurement can, on one hand, facilitate value hierarchization, where worries about organizational reputation management and concerns about process, cost and security come to the fore. On the other hand, accounting instruments for performance management do not only contribute to value hierarchization. In the case studied, the performance measurement instruments that were introduced oscillated between value hierarchization and value balancing. Because of their ambivalent nature and the criticism they attract, the instruments themselves functioned as an important catalyst of problematization and a platform for debate about prison values and reform. The chapter concludes with a discussion of the implications of these findings for our understanding of the relationship between market organization, quantification and value configuration.

In Chapter 3, *Customer satisfaction over patient security? Value hierarchization in pharmaceutical retail*, Jenny Cisneros Örnberg looks at how values in the pharmaceutical retail market in Sweden have been reconfigured over the past 20 years; a process that contributed to the privatization, in 2009, of the formerly state-held monopoly on pharmaceutical retail. The chapter shows how a reconfiguration of values has taken place – from an emphasis on patient security and health, to customer satisfaction values such as availability, efficiency and customer service. An advancement of values associated with open competition and a free market has been prioritized over other values such as security, control and health. There is, however, a possibility that a new value configuration will develop if the assumed outcomes for the customer, of lower prices and improved availability and service, are not met. A future of increased value conflict may also be expected if state expenditures increase at the same time as private pharmacies profit, or if the privatization leads to increased or inappropriate pharmaceutical consumption and use.

In Chapter 4, *Trust in transparency: value dynamics and the reorganization of the Baltic financial markets*, Sebastian Botzem and Matilda Dahl offer their explanation of the changes in value configurations in the Baltic financial sector. Comparing banks and stock exchanges and how these market organizers reacted to the financial crisis, the chapter focuses on transparency in economic development and processes of 'financialization'. It tracks changes in the Baltic financial sector and argues that we are witnessing changing values at multiple levels. Transparency emerges as a core underlying value in both fields but plays out in different ways. Following the crisis, banks have strengthened their internal risk management, while exchanges benefitted from an image of being a neutral trading infrastructure rather than a collective set of actors. While contestation of core values at the market level continues, the changes to date remain within the neoliberal paradigm. A closer look, however, reveals the importance of organizational activities in changing value configurations that centre around transparency.

In Chapter 5, *Value-neutralizing in verification markets: organizing for independence through accreditation*, Ingrid Gustafsson and Kristina Tamm Hallström look at how third-party verification markets are expanding, despite being inherently fragile and value-laden, into more and more areas of social life. Based on a study of two such markets – the management system certification market and the recently deregulated motor vehicle inspection in Sweden – the authors note that the organization of these markets can be characterized as a constant quest for authority. The dilemma behind their fragility has to do with verification as a profit-making business in service of the paying customer, and verification as a governance tool to protect values such as the safety, quality and sustainability of products and services exchanged in other markets. Although these markets are fundamentally different in scope, Gustafsson and Tamm Hallström examine the emergence and use of a similar hierarchical meta-governance structure in terms of state-based accreditation based on international standards. They discuss how this structure – although containing also other dilemmas – can explain how the requisite independence of verification auditors is legitimized, which in turn provides them with authority. The meta-governance structure helps to neutralize the problematic economic values involved in the business of verification. The authors thus conclude that there is a neutralizing value configuration that supports this particular organization of verification markets.

In Chapter 6, *Harmony or hidden conflicts? Proactive self-regulation in the personal insurance market*, Martin Gustavsson studies the case of the personal insurance market, a market historically marked by recurrent value conflicts. Concentrating on the period 1870–2011 in the first part of the chapter, he looks at central values at stake in debates and battles in the Swedish personal insurance, and organizational measures that public and private market organizers have used to deal with the value conflicts in focus. A high degree of private self-regulation has been particularly notable. In the chapter's second part, Gustavsson discusses how the self-regulatory apparatus that was established at the industry-wide level in the 1940s, and supplemented with bodies at the level of specific enterprises in the 1970s, came into use during the 2010s. Disputes on child insurance – a particularly controversial type of personal insurance in Sweden – receive special attention. Does corporate self-organization affect the issues addressed in the media? Articles about child insurance in the Swedish press 1982–2011 are studied. Successful use of the proactive self-regulatory bodies explains why many of the values that are potentially at stake have not generated debate or radical organizational changes. The chapter thus illustrates the two directions of the book's main model, the 'loop', of the impact of value configurations on market organization and vice versa.

In Chapter 7, *'The word' and 'the money': balancing values in the online newspaper market*, Karolina Windell analyzes the increased friction between journalistic ideals and financial performance in today's changing media landscape. Situating her study in the Swedish online newspaper market, Windell describes the values articulated by online newspapers, and how values of independent news reporting to serve democracy are balanced with commercial values. The chapter demonstrates how the introduction of new technology – that makes it possible to track readers' reading preferences online – makes it difficult to separate 'the word' from 'the money' in the online newspaper market, and thus how values about independent news reporting and commercialism have become blurred.

In Chapter 8, *Polarization* and *convergence of values at the intermediary position*, Anette Nyqvist and Renita Thedvall show how economic, social and environmental values are arranged and rearranged in value configuration processes. The empirical examples used by the authors are Fairtrade International (FLO) and the Swedish pension fund company KPA – two organizations that sit in an intermediary position in their respective markets. The chapter sheds light on how such intermediary positions in the marketplace open the way to value configurations in the form of both polarization and convergence, and how both FLO and KPA continuously and strategically use value configurations with the outspoken object of both making money and changing the world.

In Chapter 9, *Values aligned: the organization of conflicting values within the World Economic Forum*, Christina Garsten and Adrienne Sörbom examine the guiding values of the World Economic Forum (WEF), values that represent different and sometimes contradictory positions. The authors analyze how the WEF as an organization works to align some of these values. More specifically, the authors examine how different sets of sociological values are articulated and balanced at the WEF. Here, the value of 'economic growth' is fundamental. Equally important is the value of 'social development'. In the explanation offered in the chapter, Garsten and Sörbom discuss how WEF's mission, to 'improve the state of the world', builds on the idea that the values of economic growth and social development are interlinked and interdependent. The value of social well-being is not seen as running counter to the value of economic growth. The initiatives and activities of the WEF build on this alignment to mobilize and gain support and leverage.

In the tenth and final chapter, *Contestation in transition: value configurations and market reform in the markets for gambling, coal and alcohol*, Susanna Alexius, Daniel Castillo and Martin Rosenström apply an historical approach in their analysis of how value conflict discourses and organization have evolved from the 1800s onward in three long-contested commodity markets. Situated mainly in the Swedish context, the three case studies demonstrate that the values at stake, as well as the organizational arrangements brought forth in response to underlying value conflicts, have changed significantly over time in all three markets. The commodities have remained contested, but for different reasons. Analysing a dozen transformative moments in total, the authors conclude that if there is an underlying value conflict, how this value conflict is configured matters to the organization of a market. The chapter theorizes and illustrates three processes by which the value conflicts of the three contested commodity markets are found to have been shaped and altered by adding values to the conflict, by expanding the scale of contestation (for example from local to global) and by relocating the scope of contestation (for example from the commodity to its consumption).

NOTES

1. In its broader meaning, the term 'market failure' refers to a situation in which a free market without intervention makes the market economically inefficient.
2. According to economic theory, whenever there is a divergence between private and social cost in a market, that is when the mutual adjustment and private contractual arrangements between sellers and buyers do not seem to absorb certain social costs thought to be associated with market interaction and exchange, there is said to be a 'market failure' of the

invisible hand. When brought to light, such a 'market failure' typically brings with it calls for reform, often in the form of organized efforts to somehow 'internalize' the social costs otherwise not dealt with by anyone – that is bringing the social costs back into the realm and calculations of sellers and buyers. Taxation, financial disincentives and property rights legislation are examples of mechanisms discussed as 'corrective measures' to 'internalize' the social costs assumed to be motivated by, and concerned with, economic profits only.

REFERENCES

Abdallah, L. (forthcoming). Fostering gender advisors in the new economy: The wandering of gender equality to enhance growth. In Garsten, C. and Lindvert, J. (eds), *Sway: Balancing economic and social values* (working title).

Abolafia, M. (1996). *Making Markets*. Cambridge, MA: Harvard University Press.

Ahrne, G. (2007). *Att se samhället*. Malmö: Liber.

Ahrne, G. and Brunsson, N. (2008). *Meta-organizations*. Cheltenham, UK and Northampton, MA, USA: Edward Elgar.

Ahrne, G. and Brunsson, N. (2011). Organization outside organizations: The significance of partial organization. *Organization*, 18: 83–104.

Alexius, S. (2011). Making up the responsible gambler – Organizing self-control education and responsible gaming equipment in the Swedish gambling market. Paper presented at the NFF Conference, Stockholm University, 22–24 August 2011.

Alexius, S., Castillo, D. and Rosenström, M. (2011). *Contestation in Transition: Value-conflicts and the organization of markets – The cases of alcohol, gambling and coal*. Score Working Paper Series, 2011: 2.

Aspers, P. (2011). *Markets*. Cambridge: Polity Press.

Bartley, T. (2007). Institutional emergence in an era of globalization: The rise of transnational private regulation of labor and environmental conditions. *American Journal of Sociology*, 113(2): 297–351.

Beckert, J. and Aspers, P. (eds) (2011). *The Worth of Goods. Valuation and pricing in the Economy*. Oxford: Oxford University Press.

Boltanski, L. and Thévenot, L. (1991/2006). *On Justification: Economies of worth*. Princeton, NJ: Princeton University Press.

Browne, K.E. and Milgram, B.L. (eds) (2009). *Economics and Morality. Anthropological Approaches*. Lanham, MD: Altamira Press.

Brunsson, N. (1989). *The Organization of Hypocrisy: Talk, decision and actions in organizations*. Chichester: Wiley.

Brunsson, N. (1994). Politicization and 'company-ization': On institutional affiliation and confusion in the organizational world. *Management Accounting Research*, 5: 323–335.

Brunsson, N. and Hägg, I. (eds) (1992). *Marknadens makt*. Stockholm: SNS Förlag.

Brunsson, N. and Jacobsson, B. (eds) (2000). *A World of Standards*. Oxford: Oxford University Press.

Callon, M. (ed.) (1998a). *The Laws of the Market*. Oxford: Blackwell Publishers.

Callon, M. (1998b). The embeddedness of economic markets in economics. In Callon, M. (ed.), *The Laws of the Market*. Oxford: Blackwell Publishers.

Callon, M. and Muniesa, F. (2005). Economic markets as calculative collective devices. *Organization Studies*, 26: 1229–1250.

Carande-Kulis, V.G., Getzen, T.E. and Thacker, S.B. (2007). Public goods and externalities. A research agenda for public health economics. *Journal of Public Health Management and Practice*, 13(2): 227–232.

Cyert, R.M. and March, J.G. (1963). *A Behavioural Theory of the Firm*. Englewood Cliffs, NJ: Prentice-Hall.

Dahlberg, C. (2010). *Picturing the Public – Advertising self-regulation in Sweden and the UK*. Doctoral thesis in sociology, Stockholm University.

Dahlman, C.J. (1979). The problem of externality. *Journal of Law and Economics*, 22(1): 141–162.

Ertman, M.M. and Williams, J.C. (eds) (2005). *Rethinking Commodification*. New York: NYU Press.

Fligstein, N. (1996). Markets as politics: A political-cultural approach to market institutions. *American Sociological Review*, 61(4): 656–673.

Fligstein, N. (2001). *The Architecture of Markets*. Princeton, NJ: Princeton University Press.

Fourcade, M. and Healy, K. (2007). Moral views of market society. *Annual Review of Sociology*, 33: 285–311.

Friedman, M. (1970). The social responsibility of business is to increase its profits. *The New York Times Magazine*, 13 September 1970.

Fries, L. (2011). *Att organisera tjänstesektorns röst*. Doctoral thesis in business economics, Stockholm: Stockholm School of Economics.

Giddens, A. (1984). *The Constitution of Society: Outline of the theory of structuration*. Cambridge: Polity Press.

Graeber, D. (2005). Value: anthropological theories of value. In Carrier, J.G. (ed.), *A Handbook of Economic Anthropology*, pp. 439–453. Cheltenham, UK and Northampton, MA, USA: Edward Elgar.

Gurney, P.M. and Humphreys, M. (2006). Consuming responsibility: The search for value at Laskarina Holidays. *Business Ethics*, 64(1): 83–100.

Haufler, V. (2001). *A Public Role for the Private Sector: Industry self-regulation in a global economy*. Washington, DC: Carnegie Endowment for International Peace.

Haufler, V. (2003). Globalization and industry self-regulation. In Kahler, M. and Lake, D.A. (eds), *Governance in a Global Economy: Political authority in transition*. Princeton, NJ: Princeton University Press.

Harvie, David and Keir Milburn (2010). How organizations value and how value organizes. *Organization*, 17(5): 631–636.

Helgesson, C.-F., Kjellberg, H. and Liljenberg, A. (eds) (2004). *Den där marknaden. Om utbyten, normer och bilder*. Lund: Studentlitteratur.

Higgins, W. and Tamm Hallström, K. (2007). Standardization, globalization and rationalities of government. *Organization*, 14(5): 685–704.

Hirschman, A.O. (1982). Rival interpretations of market society: Civilizing, destructive, or feeble? *Journal of Economic Literature*, 20: 1463–1484.

Hong, H. and Kacpercyk, M. (2007). *The Price of Sin: The effects of social norms on markets*. Princeton, NJ: Princeton University Press.

Jacobsson, B. (1993). Europeisering och statsförvaltningen. *Statsvetenskaplig Tidsskrift*, 96(2): 113–137.

Jacobsson, B. and Sundström, G. (2009). Between autonomy and control: Transformation of the Swedish administrative model. In Roness, P.G. and

Saetren, H. (eds), *Change and Continuity in Public Sector Organizations*. Bergen: Fagbokforlaget.

Kraatz, M.S. and Block, E.S. (2008). Organizational implications of institutional pluralism. In Greenwood, R., Oliver, C., Sahlin, K. and Suddaby, R. (eds) *The Sage Handbook of Organizational Institutionalism*, pp. 243–275. London: Sage.

Lahire, B. (2010/2011). *The Plural Actor*. Cambridge: Polity Press.

Liedtka, Jeanne M. (1989). Value congruence: The interplay of individual and organizational value systems. *Journal of Business Ethics*, 8: 805–815.

Lindblom, C.E. (2001). *The Market System: What it is, how it works and what to make of it*. Yale: Yale University Press.

MacKenzie, D. (2009). *Material Market: How economic agents are constructed*. Oxford: Oxford University Press.

MacKenzie, D., Muniesa, F. and Siu, L. (eds) (2007). *Do Economists Make Markets? On the performativity of economics*. Princeton, NJ: Princeton University Press.

March, J.G. and Simon, H.A. (1958). *Organizations*. New York: Wiley.

Meyer, John and Rowan, Brian (1977). Institutionalized organizations: Formal structure as myth and ceremony. *American Journal of Sociology*, 83: 340–363.

Moeran, Brian and Jesper Strandgaard Pedersen (2011). *Negotiating Values in the Creative Industries*. Cambridge: Cambridge University Press.

Oliver, C. (1991). Strategic responses to institutional processes. *Academy of Management Review*, 16(1): 145–179.

Pache, Anne-Claire (2011). *When Competing Logics Enter Organizations: The politics of organizational responses to conflicting institutional demands*. Working Paper, ESSEC Business School, Cergy, France.

Radin, M.J. (2001). *Contested Commodities: The trouble with trade in sex, children, body parts, and other things*. Cambridge, MA: Harvard University Press.

Rose, N. and Miller, P. (1992). Political power beyond the state: problematics of government, *British Journal of Sociology*, 43(2): 172–205.

Satz, D. (2010). *Why Some Things Should Not Be for Sale – The moral limits of markets*. Oxford: Oxford University Press.

Schneiberg, M. and Bartley, T. (2001). Regulating American industries: Markets, politics and the institutional determinants of fire insurance regulation. *American Journal of Sociology*, 107: 101–146.

Shamir, R. (2008). The age of responsibilization: On market-embedded morality. *Economy and Society*, 37(1): 1–19.

Smith, A. (1776). *An Inquiry into the Nature and Causes of the Wealth of Nations*.

Suchman, M.C. (1995). Managing legitimacy: Strategic and institutional approaches. *Academy of Management Review*, 20(3): 571–610.

Stark, D. (2009). *The Sense of Dissonance – Accounts of worth in economic life*. Princeton, NJ: Princeton University Press.

Tamm Hallström, K. (2004). *Organizing International Standardization. ISO and the IASC in Quest of Authority*. Cheltenham, UK and Northampton, MA, USA: Edward Elgar.

Tamm Hallström, K. and Boström, M. (2010). *Transnational Multi-Stakeholder Standardization. Organizing fragile non-state authority*. Cheltenham, UK and Northampton MA, USA: Edward Elgar.

Thévenot, L. (2001). Organized complexity: Conventions of coordination and the composition of economic arrangements. *European Journal of Social Theory*, 4(4): 405–425.

Thornton, P.H. and Ocasio, W. (2008). Institutional logics. In Greenwood, R., Oliver, C., Sahlin, K. and Suddaby, R. (eds), *Handbook of Organizational Institutionalism*. Thousand Oaks, CA: Sage.

Thornton, P.H., Ocasio, W. and Lounsbury, M. (2012). *The Institutional Logics Perspective: A new approach to culture, structure and process*. Oxford: Oxford University Press.

Wicks, A.C. (1996). Overcoming the separation thesis: The need for a reconsideration of business and society research. *Business and Society*, 35(1): 89–118.

Williams, T. (2007). Empowerment of whom and for what? Financial literacy education and the new regulation of consumer financial services. *Law and Policy*, 29(2): 226–256.

Wood, D.J. (1996). Reconciliation awaits: Dichotomies in business and social theory. *Business and Society*, 35(1): 119–122.

Yakubovich, V., Granovetter, M. and MacGuire, P. (2005). Electric charges: The social construction of rate systems. *Theory and Society*, 34(5–6): 579–612.

Zelizer, V.A. Rotman (1979). *Morals and Markets: The development of life insurance in the United States*. New York and London: Columbia University Press.

Zelizer V.A. (1985). *Pricing the Priceless Child*. Princeton, NJ: Princeton University Press.

Zelizer, V.A. (2005). *The Purchase of Intimacy*. Princeton, NJ: Princeton University Press.

2. Accounting for values in prison privatization

Andrea Mennicken

INTRODUCTION

This chapter studies values and risks at stake in prison privatization.[1] In so doing, the intention is not to provide yet another study on the pros and cons of prison privatization. Several detailed and valuable studies have already been carried out in this respect, with mixed results (see for example Gaes et al. 2004; Harding 1997; James et al. 1997; Logan 1990; Moyle 2000; NAO 2003). Instead, the chapter investigates the organizational processes and calculative instruments by which different, potentially conflicting values and rationalities are mediated and dealt with. It examines the roles that seemingly mundane and apolitical accounting instruments, in particular instruments of prison rating and performance measurement, play in the organization and management of value complexity in prison privatization. Focusing on the case of prison privatization in England and Wales, during the years before the first private prison was opened in 1992 and the years that followed, the chapter explores processes of value reconfigurations through the lens of changed accounting practices. It examines the extent to which accounting instruments can play the role of a 'mediating instrument' (Miller and O'Leary 2007) where conflicting values are at stake.

Since the 1980s, in the UK, market-oriented, private sector-based management and accounting frameworks have been introduced into the public sector in an attempt to increase efficiency in the allocation of financial and human resources, to enhance managerial accountability, and to aid experimentation with mixed public–private organization (Hood 1991; Humphrey et al. 1993; Kurunmäki and Miller 2011; Pollitt 1993). In England and Wales, prisons have been at the forefront of such reforms. The first private prison (Wolds Remand Prison) was opened in 1992 (James et al. 1997). Today, the UK has Europe's most privatized criminal justice system (Nathan 2003a). Of the current 133 prisons in England and Wales,[2] the management of 14 has been contracted to private companies such as Sodexo Justice Services, Serco and G4S Justice Services.[3]

The prison privatizations are part of wider processes of market-oriented, governmental reform (Hood 1991, 1995; Miller and Rose 2008). Under the Thatcher government, the privatization of prisons was seen as a 'test case' for neoliberal, market-oriented public policies (James et al. 1997: 1). Private prison contractors were believed to be able to deliver 'better value for money' because of being 'under fewer constraints about the way in which tasks are tackled' than the public sector (Home Office 1988: 8). It was envisaged that the recruitment and deployment of staff would be more flexible and cost-efficient in private prisons (ibid.). Further, it was thought that private contractors would be able to make use of experience gained in other fields 'to apply methods which simply would not have occurred to the existing providers of the service' (ibid.).

Numerous studies have shown, on the other hand, that the profit orientation of contracted-out prison management can run the danger of losing sight of traditional prison values, such as rehabilitation, prisoners' decency, safety and security, prison staff morale and job satisfaction (see for example Coyle et al. 2003; James et al. 1997; Liebling 2004; Moyle 2000; PRT 1994, 2005; Taylor and Cooper 2008). Globally operating security corporations, like G4S Justice Services, Serco and Sodexo Justice Services, which run private prison establishments in England and Wales today, are interested in economic gains. They think about prisons in terms of organizations governed according to a market logic: competition, economic calculation and objectives of profit making (Cooper and Taylor 2005; Moyle 2000; Nathan 2003a, 2003b; Taylor and Cooper 2008). With the private security corporations, new stakeholders have entered the picture, including investors (for example banks) and shareholders. As James et al. (1997: 44) put it, punishing people has become 'a big business': a multinational industry involving not only security firms, but also catering companies, construction firms, suppliers of prison furniture and clothing, and many others with a commercial interest in incarceration (see also Nathan 2003b). In such a context prison values concerning, for example, prisoners' safety, decency and rehabilitation, may be undermined by concerns of profitability and administrative efficiency.

This chapter examines the roles that accounting, in particular instruments of prison rating and performance measurement, can play in the organization and management of such value conflicts. The focus in this chapter is on the effects of prison privatization and private sector-based performance measurement on Her Majesty's Prison Service (hereafter HM Prison Service, or simply the Prison Service). Since 2008, HM Prison Service has been an executive agency[4] of the British Ministry of Justice. It is the government body responsible for the management of public sector prisons. Until 2008, before the creation of the Ministry of Justice, the Prison Service operated under the Home Office. HM Prison Service is part of the National Offender Management Service (NOMS), which today, is also an executive agency of the Ministry of Justice. NOMS was established in 2004 to bring together the commissioning and provision of offender services in prison (HM Prison Service) and in the community (Probation Trusts).[5] Neither NOMS nor the Prison Service take part in the daily management of private prison establishments. However, NOMS is responsible for the enforcement of private prison contracts (NAO 2012), and all private prisons have a 'controller' linking them to NOMS.[6] Controllers are appointed by the government to monitor private prison contracts on site, and to oversee the 'fair and lawful treatment of prisoners'.

Coinciding with and stimulated by the first prison privatizations, since the early 1990s the government, the Prison Service in cooperation with the Home Office, and later NOMS in cooperation with the Ministry of Justice, have been developing prison performance measures and ratings, not only to oversee contract fulfilment in private prisons, but also to transform public sector prisons into economically-minded, calculating organizations. As will be shown in more detail below, the measures were developed in an attempt to enhance private and public prison accountability, to compare public and private prison performance, to stimulate inter-organizational competitiveness, and to increase the economy and efficiency of public prison establishments. The following sections trace the development of these performance measures from 1992 to 2010, investigate their intertwinement with prison privatization, and examine their effect on prison value (re-)configurations in the Prison Service.

According to Espeland and Stevens, one virtue of quantification is that 'it offers standardized ways of constructing proxies for uncertain and elusive qualities' (1998: 316). Another virtue is that it is 'useful for representing value' (ibid.), as it condenses and reduces the amount of information people have to process and simplifies decision-making processes. In a similar vein, Miller (1992: 61) has emphasized the 'transformative capacity' of quantified performance indicators, arguing that 'the neutrality and social authority accorded to the single figure is one that is set above the fray, apart from disputes and political interests, and endowed with a legitimacy that seems difficult to contest or dispute' (ibid.: 68–69).

In the case studied here, formalized performance measurement systems were, on the one hand, aimed at bringing the economy of prison management to the fore, seeking to focus prison governors' attention on issues of cost management and efficient process management. On the other hand, as will be shown below, the performance measurement systems came to be

enrolled in attempts aimed at prison value balancing, by including along-
side measures of cost and efficiency, measures of decency, dignity and
rehabilitation (see for example Liebling 2004). As Espeland and Stevens
(1998) highlighted, accounting, performance measurement, and quantification more generally, can offer 'a rigorous method for democratizing
decisions and sharing power', particularly in situations 'characterized by
disparate values, diverse forms of knowledge, and the wish to incorporate
people's preferences' (ibid.: 330). This chapter queries the extent to which
accounting can be called upon to play the role of a 'mediating instrument'
(Miller and O'Leary 2007) where conflicting values are at stake. It raises
the question of the extent to which accounting can be appealed to as a
link connecting 'a multitude of actors and domains' (ibid.: 701), including
disparate values and rationalities, such as those of security, decency and
economy.

The next section describes and analyses the specifics of the market for
prison services in England and Wales, examining the organization of both
public and private prison service provision. The section after that takes
a closer look at the different values and risks at stake, and examines the
roles that accounting instruments of rating and performance measurement
can (or cannot) play in the organization of value conflicts. This section
examines how different prison values and objectives – administrative
efficiency, cost management, security, safety, decency, rehabilitation and
equality – were translated by the Prison Service, NOMS, the Home Office
and the Ministry of Justice into calculable organizational performance
measures. These performance measures, and the values they represented,
did not come to exist on an equal plane. They were hierarchized. At the
level of public and private sector prison organizations, worries about
organizational reputation management came to the fore, driven first and
foremost by concerns about managerial process, cost and security. The
observed hierarchization of prison values was, however, also accompanied
by attempts aimed at value (re-)balancing, for example, in the form of the
development of measures that seek to capture subjective experiences of
prison life (see Liebling 2004). Because of their ambivalent nature and the
criticisms they attract, performance measurement and prison ratings came
to oscillate between value hierarchization and value balancing. They functioned as an important catalyst of problematization and a platform for
debate about prison values and reform. The performance measures came
to be perceived as a 'mediating instrument' – a platform for value reconfiguration that should help interlink and mediate between disparate values
and objectives, such as security, decency and economy. To be sure, any
practical realization of such aspirations is far from straightforward and, to
quote Miller and Rose (1990), may very well be fated to be a congenitally

failing operation. The chapter concludes with a discussion of implications of these findings for our understanding of the relationship between market organization, quantification and value configuration.

Methods

The analysis is based on the study of media and parliamentary data, government reports, reports by the HM Prison Service, the National Offender Management Service (NOMS), the Home Office, Ministry of Justice, National Audit Office (NAO) and HM Inspectorate of Prisons, research published by academics and practitioners, and reports published by interest groups seeking to improve prison conditions, such as the Prison Reform Trust (PRT)[7] and the Howard League for Penal Reform. The chapter focuses on the case of prison privatization in England and Wales, as this was the first place in Europe where, following the example of the US, fully privatized prisons were opened. Furthermore, England and Wales is where ideas about market-oriented New Public Management (NPM) (Hood 1991, 1995) first surfaced, spreading from there to other countries in Europe.

THE MARKET FOR PRISON SERVICES

In many spheres of activity where the task is to provide services cost-effectively in response to customer demand the private sector is better equipped to do this. The disciplines of the market place ensure that, to be successful, private sector companies control their costs and provide products at a price and quality, which attract customers in a competitive environment. Innovative solutions to problems are often found in response to the new challenges which healthy competition constantly sets for private sector managers. (Home Office 1988: 7)

Since the 1980s, public services in the UK have undergone a series of far-reaching reforms. Instead of state coordination, market competition came to be seen as an effective lever for driving efficiency and innovation (Hood 1991; Miller and Rose 1990; Pollitt 1993). The reforms, codified as 'New Public Management' by scholars (see for example Hood 1991), were aimed at introducing private sector styles of management practice into the public sector. They were based on a conception of accountability that, as Hood (1995: 94) formulates it, reflected high trust in the market and private business methods, and low trust in public servants and professionals (see also Humphrey et al. 1993). New Public Management ideas also took hold in the Prison Service (Bennett et al. 2008; Bryans 2007; Coyle 2005; Coyle et al. 2003; Liebling 2004; Liebling et al. 2011), providing fertile ground for plans of prison privatization.

Against the background of the neoliberal reform agendas of the Conservative government of that time, the rise of New Public Management, and a prison system perceived to be in a state of crisis due to overcrowding, exploding costs and a series of serious incidents that occurred in various public prison establishments in the late 1980s and April 1990 (King and McDermott 1989, Resodihardjo 2009, Woolf 1991),[8] prison privatization was promoted as a way to facilitate organizational change and reform (HAC 1987; Home Office 1988, 1991; King and McDermott 1995). It was believed that selective privatizations and the threat of 'market testing'[9] public prisons, where the Prison Service had to bid against private prison providers for the running of its own prison establishments, would stimulate the development of a 'business culture' (Black 1993: 27) and yield 'cross-fertilization benefits' (Harding 2001). As Home Secretary Kenneth Clarke argued in a newspaper editorial:

> [Privatization and market testing] will . . . cause the prison service to examine its own performance in the light of competitive pressure and encourage the spread of those reforms across public sector prisons much more quickly than would otherwise have been the case. (Quoted in Pozen 2003: 266–267)

In August 1992, HM Prison Manchester (Strangeways) became the first public prison to be market tested (PRT 1994: 26–33). Here, HM Prison Service tendered successfully against commercial companies and managed to retain the management of Strangeways in public hands. In the years that followed, however, further prisons were put out to tender (that is market tests), and the management of some of these landed in private hands.

Originally, proposals for prison privatization and market testing were articulated and advanced by actors outside government, in particular neoliberal think tanks such as the Adam Smith Institute (Young 1987) and global security corporations like the Corrections Corporation of America (CCA), Wackenhut (now part of G4S) and Group 4 (now G4S), who had been lobbying for the contracting out of prisons and prison-building programmes in the UK since the 1980s (James et al. 1997; Nathan 2003a).

The lobbying for private prisons and market-oriented accounting reforms coincided with an 'institutional crisis' in the Prison Service (Resodihardjo 2009) and a decline of the rehabilitative ideal within prisons. As Pozen (2003: 263) writes, by 1990, England alone was imprisoning more people than any other Western European country. In the early 1980s, a third of the offenders in custody were sharing with one or two others cells designed for only one person and, in June 1989, Wandsworth prison in London had only eight cells with access to sanitation at night versus 1149 without access (ibid.). In view of these issues, and the lobbying efforts of the security industry, neoliberal think tanks and the general preference of the Thatcher government for free enterprise, market-oriented reforms were put forward as a solution to the problems facing the Prison Service, despite fierce opposition from the entire British penal lobby and the Labour Party. From 1992 onwards, the Prison Service began to undergo reorganization in terms of a 'mixed economy', with a mix of public and private prison service providers (King and McDermott 1995). As Pozen (2003) observes, by the late 1990s the debate had shifted from whether the government should allow private prisons to how it could best manage them, including the assessment of the efficacy and effects of privatization schemes.

Similarly to most of the markets discussed in this volume, the market for prison services in England and Wales is highly regulated and characterized by state intervention. Indeed, the market we are dealing with is not characterized by free trade and exchange. The goods traded are not private goods: they are public services aimed at the delivery of public security, punishment and rehabilitation at a reasonable cost. Private prisons act on behalf of the government. They are supervised by the state and accountable to parliament. Private prison providers have to obey the same rules and regulations as public prison establishments. The state is the sole 'buyer' of prison services, acting in the interest of a third party – the public. Prison services do not represent a good that is consumed. Prisoners do not have 'a choice' and, also, prison establishments cannot choose which prisoners they want to house. Prison governors and officers have to manage and balance a range of different, often conflicting values and objectives (Bennett et al. 2008; Bryans 2007; Liebling 2004): values of decency, safety and rehabilitation may clash with values of public security and punishment, and objectives concerning the economic management of the prison. Privatization and New Public Management can make such value conflicts more pronounced, by shifting attention away from individual rehabilitation to objectives of cost management, administrative efficiency, and the economic value of prisoners as a workforce and source of profitability.

As Liebling (2004: 71) highlights, with privatization a 'new rationality of governance' (Miller and Rose 1990, 2008) was introduced into the Prison Service, where auditing and accounting practices originating from 'the world of finance' were applied to the non-financial practices and systems of the Prison Service. The introduction of such private sector business methods led to a 'managerialization' of prisons and a reconfiguration of prison values and objectives (Bryans 2007; Coyle 2005, 2008; Liebling 2004), where, as Coyle (2005: 49) puts it, increased emphasis came to be placed 'on process, on how things are done, rather than on outcome, that is, what is being achieved' (see also Liebling 2004). Concerns about financial accountability came to the fore. Close attention was placed on budgets, target-setting, strategic plans and cost management (Lewis 1997; Nellis 2006), and prison values were reconfigured accordingly. As Bryans (2007: 64) writes, prison governors were required to adopt a more managerial ethos, and prisons were to be managed in a more passionless and bureaucratic manner. On the other hand, this 'accountingization' (Kurunmäki et al. 2003; Power and Laughlin 1992) of the Prison Service not only lead to a reduction of the focus of prison administration but also to issues of economic management. Private sector accounting techniques were also enrolled in attempts to deal with value conflict, and were called upon to revive rehabilitative ideals.

QUANTIFYING AND STANDARDIZING PRISON VALUES

As Resodihardjo (2009: 153) points out, from the very moment prisons were introduced,[10] prison services around the world have experienced changes in their priorities, aims and administration. Rehabilitation came into and went out of fashion, systems of isolating prisoners were intro-duced and abandoned, and changes were made to prison administrations, for example by turning prison services into government agencies or the introduction of public-private partnerships and privatization. Throughout history, prison governors and prison officers have been confronted with the management of conflicting values (see for example Bryans 2007; Liebling et al. 2011; see also Figure 2.1).

One core task of prison officers consists in the provision of safe custody, order and discipline. On the other hand, they form relationships with pris-oners and, in accordance with penal reform ideals, are supposed to provide care (Liebling et al. 2011). Prison governors are responsible for the overall security of prisons (Bryans 2007). They need to ensure that no escapes or riots occur, that everything is 'under control'. Subsequent to several penal reform movements, they have also become responsible for the creation and maintenance of a decent, rehabilitation-enabling environment for prisoners (Bryans 2007). And, particularly since the rise of New Public Management in the early 1990s, they are increasingly concerned with the efficient management of resources and the lowering of costs (ibid.; see also Coyle 2008). Prison governors and prison officers have always had to deal with conflicting values, however, the composition and prioritization of these has changed over time. The opening of private prisons and the

Decency	vs	Economy
Prisoner safety	vs	Security
Rehabilitation	vs	Punishment
Individual transformation	vs	Administrative efficiency
Moral responsibility	vs	Control

Figure 2.1   Conflicting values in the prison service

introduction of market testing have led to changes in the value configurations and working practices of prison officers and governors (Bennett et al. 2008; Bryans 2007; Coyle et al. 2003; Liebling et al. 2011; Taylor and Cooper 2008). Figure 2.1 summarizes conflicting values identified in the material examined (own compilation).

Since the 1980s, the Prison Service of England and Wales has focussed increasingly on the achievement of 'greater economy, efficiency, and effectiveness in the use of resources' (McDermott and King 1989: 163). In this context, not only cost issues were problematized, but also the conditions of prisons and the need to modernize were articulated (HAC 1987). As highlighted earlier, in the years prior to the first private prison opening in England and Wales in 1992, the Prison Service had experienced a severe 'institutional crisis' (Resodihardjo 2009), further aggravated by severe riots in 1990.[11] Following the riots, the media portrayed the entire Prison Service as malfunctioning and unable to maintain control (ibid.: 112). In response to the crisis, MPs installed an inquiry headed by Lord Justice Woolf.

In the report that was published following the inquiry, in 1991, Woolf argued that a re-prioritization of Prison Service goals was needed, shifting public and politicians' attention from, as Resodihardjo (2009: 112) puts it, 'an almost complete focus on security to a more balanced view'. In particular, the Woolf Report recommended a balancing of three values: justice, control, and security (Woolf 1991). Following the Woolf Report, the Home Office published a White Paper, entitled 'Custody, Care and Justice' (Home Office 1991), which re-emphasized the need for value balance. In addition to the importance of having 'effective physical security measures'[12] in place, the White Paper emphasized that prison staff 'have a responsibility not only for the custody but also for the *care* of prisoners', which 'must be demonstrated through providing programmes and conditions for prisoners which treat them with humanity, dignity and respect' (ibid.: 9). The White Paper, *inter alia*, recommended greater openness with prisoners and preparation of 'a code of standards for conditions and activities in prisons which will be used to set improvement targets in the annual contracts made between prison Governors and their Area Managers' (Home Office 1991: 15).

The code of standards was to help to create an environment 'in which constructive relations between prisoners and staff can be established' (Home Office 1991: 14). It was envisaged that the standards should consist of clear targets, so that 'the provisions in any particular establishment could be judged' and the management of the Prison Service be enhanced (ibid.: 61–62; see also Lygo 1991). A series of standards already existed in relation to the frequency of visits, for example. However, most of the values articulated in the Prison Service's Prison Rules were not codified, and the existing standards did not focus directly on the service to be provided *for* prisoners (Home Office 1991: 61).[13] Before quantified performance measures were introduced, prison values and objectives had been articulated in Circular Instructions, which had been criticized for being 'uncoordinated and uncosted' and 'lacking a mechanism for ensuring the initiatives they contain are implemented' (Lygo 1991; PRT 1992).

The first set of standardized key performance indicators (KPIs) and targets was introduced into the Prison Service in 1992–93 (see also Liebling 2004: 56–70). The introduction of the KPIs and targets was not only initiated by the recommendations of the Woolf Report and the 1991 Home Office White Paper (Home Office 1991; Woolf 1991). It was also the result of the organizational restructuring of the Prison Service in April 1993 into an executive ('Next Steps') agency, that is a government agency that would act independently from day-to-day ministerial oversight (Lygo 1991), the foundation of private prison establishments whose performance needed to be regulated and accounted for, and objectives aimed at increasing the competitiveness of private and public sector prison establishments through regularly published prison ratings and quantified comparisons. The Prison Service's new structure was set out in a Framework Document, in which goals were specified with the help of quantified KPIs and targets. Following the restructuring, the Prison Service issued a Corporate Plan for 1994–97, setting out a statement of purpose, a vision, five values, and eight strategic priorities. It also identified eight KPIs which should measure, quantitatively, the achievement of six primary goals (Coyle 2005: 48; Lewis 1997; see also Figure 2.2). Derek Lewis, the Prison Service's first

KPI 1 – Escapes from establishments or escorts

KPI 2 – Number of assaults on staff, prisoners and others

KPI 3 – Proportion of prisoners held in units of accommodation intended for fewer numbers

KPI 4 – Number of prisoners with 24 hour access to sanitation

KPI 5 – Number of hours which, on average, prisoners spend in purposeful activity

KPI 6 – Proportion of prisoners held in prisons where prisoners are unlocked on weekdays for a total of at least 12 hours

KPI 7 – Proportion of prisoners held in prisons where prisoners have the opportunity to exceed the minimum visiting entitlement

KPI 8 – The average cost per prisoner place

Source: Prison Reform Trust (1996).

Figure 2.2   KPIs in HM Prison Service, 1994–1995

chief executive following the restructuring, was recruited from the private sector and played a major role in the introduction of the KPIs.

The noted KPIs were applied to all public prisons, and the performance of private prisons was evaluated on the basis of similar, contractual performance measures. The introduction of quantified measures was closely connected to the general rise of New Public Management in public services and pressures to publicly *demonstrate* private and public prison performance (see for example House of Commons 2003; NAO 2003). Private prison contracts were drawn up based on detailed performance specifications in an attempt to enhance their legitimacy and aid 'commensuration' (Espeland and Stevens 1998) between different prison establishments (see also Mennicken 2013). Standardized KPIs and targets were introduced to endow prison privatizations with public accountability and to establish a 'common language' (Power 2004: 774) for making judgements about the success or failure of private versus public prison entities. But what prison values should be included in the measurement of prison performance? How should one prioritize between different KPIs and targets? And to what extent could different (public and private) prisons be treated as comparable entities, if they differ significantly in terms of size, prison population, age and regional location? These questions arose among those who developed the KPIs (for example Lewis 1997), those who used the KPIs to evaluate prison performance (for example House of Commons 2003; NAO 2003; PRT 1996), and the prison officers and governors who were to use the KPIs in their daily practice (for example Bryans 2007; Liebling et al. 2011).

We know from the numerous performance measurement studies in the critical accounting literature (see, for example, Bowerman et al. 2001; Cooper and Taylor 2005; Humphrey 1994; Lapsley and Mitchell 1996; Miller 1992; Modell 2009; Pollitt 1986) that even seemingly straightforward accounting measures, like measures of cost, are far from unproblematic. Performance measurement – even if diversely set up – can lead to a 'narrowing of accountability' (Kurunmäki 1999), for example, by promoting a focus on managing the numbers rather than wider processes, issues and social relations. As many previous performance measurement studies have shown, performance measures often yield only very limited insight into 'what is going on' in the entity they seek to measure and represent. This was also the case, at least to some extent, with HM Prison Service (see for example Hough et al. 2006; Liebling 2004; Mennicken 2013).

With respect to the initial eight KPIs applied in the Prison Service in 1994–95, a report from the Prison Reform Trust, a state-independent prison interest group,[14] observed that:

> There are difficulties in identifying the most appropriate KPIs for an organisation as complicated as the Prison Service. First, people may not agree as to the most important goals. Second, measuring performance in a quantitative way gives no indication of quality. Third, goals which cover general areas of work can be measured using a number of different KPIs. For example, helping prisoners to return to the community is not achieved solely by providing more than the minimum visiting entitlements; it is also achieved by enabling prisoners to gain educational qualifications, or by helping them find accommodation after release. Fourth, the data may not be accurate or objective. Finally, even if there is agreement as to the KPIs, the target performance may be set too high or too low. (PRT 1996: 3)

The report further highlighted limitations of certain measures, such as the measure of 'purposeful activity', which embraced many different activities, such as time spent in education, working, playing sports, attending group work or cleaning public facilities, and did not provide any information about the differential impact that these different activities were likely to have on individual prisoners (ibid.: 6).

Following these and other criticisms, the KPIs were reviewed and extended in the following years. In the late 1990s, new indicators accounting for drug abuse, the seriousness of assaults and the number of completed offender behaviour programmes were added. Yet, the different

KPIs did not come to exist on an equal plane. Initially introduced in an attempt to balance the different, potentially conflicting prison values of 'custody, care and justice' (Home Office 1991), the KPIs soon came to be hierarchized. In the years after 1995 in particular, following the escapes of nine high security prisoners in 1994–95 from Whitemoor and Parkhurst (both public sector prisons), we observe a departure from the Woolf agenda, and a shift in Prison Service priorities from 'value balancing' to an enhanced focus on security, at the expense of rehabilitation (Liebling 2004; PRT 1996; Resodihardjo 2009). The KPIs were implicated in this process of value reconfiguration. Calls for the reform of the KPIs were made, and the KPIs came to be envisioned as an instrument by which to facilitate this change.

Following the noted escapes, an independent inquiry into the Prison Service's security was set up, headed by General Sir John Learmont (Home Office 1995). In his report, Learmont 'considered there was too much emphasis on care issues, which are measured by five KPIs, in comparison to custody and control, which are measured by one KPI each' (PRT 1996: 8). He argued for closer monitoring and audit arrangements, and recommended a number of changes to the current list of KPIs, placing greater emphasis on issues of security, discipline and control. *Inter alia*, the report recommended that the Prison Service develop additional KPIs in the areas of physical security, staff morale, inmate behaviour (disciplinary cases and suicides), drugs and recidivism (Home Office 1995: 170). The report further recommended that the escapes indicator 'should be supplemented by indicators that show progress towards preventing escapes'; that assault figures should 'show percentage changes separately for assaults on staff, inmates and others'; and that 'greater care should be taken to monitor the way "purposeful activity" data is captured'.

The report reinforced the importance of formalized, quantified performance management. It gave also a further boost to proponents of prison privatization, as it questioned whether the escapes from Parkhurst and Whitemoor prison would ever have arisen if the Prison Service had had the same monitoring and audit arrangements as were compulsory, at that time, for the private sector (Home Office 1995: 106).

In the years that followed, KPIs proliferated throughout the Prison Service. They came to be used as a basis for identifying 'low' and 'high' performers along cost and other performance dimensions (focusing in particular on the values of security, safety, administrative effectiveness and economy), where the lowest public and private sector performers were 'market-tested' (Liebling 2004: 67), that is put up for competition with each other. In 2003, the government introduced a 'Benchmarking Programme', requiring both public and private prisons to undergo formalized performance tests on a regular basis. Since 2003, all prisons are rated on a performance scale of 1–4, where establishments that excel and deliver 'exceptionally high performance' are given a 4, and 'poor performers' are given a 1.[15]

Particularly between 1992 (when the first private prison was opened) and 1999, the accounting instruments of performance measurement put issues of efficient and effective organizational management, instead of the individual prisoner, to the fore. As former prison governor Bryans writes on the effects of the KPIs, governors were becoming 'increasingly concerned with process issues, "box-ticking", efficiency and economy', and ran the danger of losing sight of 'humanitarian, ethical and moral principles and concerns' (Bryans 2001: 9). Poor performance became regarded as the failure of operational management, which, in turn, reinforced a focus on issues of 'structures' and 'systems', at the expense of softer, more subtle 'processes' and 'commitment' (Bennett et al. 2008; Bryans 2007; Coyle 2007; Hough et al. 2006; Liebling 2004; Owers 2010).

A prison reform agenda was followed, which, with the help of quantified KPIs, reconfigured prison values around managerial ideals promoting, as Bryans put it, 'a focus on process without looking at quality' (Bryans 2001: 9).[16] This process of value reconfiguration and quantification was to a great extent driven by the government's commitment to market-oriented public policies, including the privatization of prisons, its belief in the superiority of private sector accounting and audit tools, and penal policies aimed at demonstrating that the government was being 'tough on crime' (Newburn 2007). As Liebling (2004: 26) observes:

> Privatization, and experiments with market testing, formed part of a pragmatic, 'control model' approach to the delivery of penal services. 'The delivery of penal services' was an instrumental notion with little relevance to the ethics of imprisonment. The type of quantification (performance measurement) and the regime aspirations arising out of these developments ... left crucial questions of moral responsibility and individual transformation untouched.

Despite these and other criticisms (see for example the writings of the PRT), however, private sector accounting tools of performance management were not abandoned. Instead, from 1999 onwards, several attempts were made to reform the performance measurement system 'from within', through the development of new performance measures aimed at 'value rebalancing'. In 2000, in an attempt to counteract impoverished versions of performance measurement, the Home Office commissioned Professor Alison Liebling, Director of the Prisons Research Centre at Cambridge University, to conduct a research project aimed at developing 'quantitative measures of qualitative dimensions of prison life' (Liebling 2004: xx, xxiii).

Liebling and her team developed new performance measures along two dimensions: relationships (respect, humanity, trust, staff–prisoner relationships and support) and regimes (fairness, order, safety, well-being, personal development, family contact and decency) (Liebling 2004). A detailed assessment of the success of this research project in reshaping and rebalancing prison value configurations is beyond the scope of this chapter. However, what can be said is that the Prison Service's KPIs contributed not only to value hierarchization and infusion of the Prison Service with market-oriented ideals of efficient, economic management. They also served as a platform for debate about prison values and reform, not least because of the public attention and criticism they attracted. Liebling and her team perceived the KPIs as a 'mediating instrument' (Miller and O'Leary 2007), a mechanism that could be reformed from within and utilized to link up and mediate between conflicting concerns and prison values, such as those of security, economy, and decency. They used quantification as a way to bring prison values relating to questions of rehabilitation and care back in (see in particular Liebling 2004).

In other words, accounting instruments of performance measurement are more than faulty reflectors of what is going on. As Miller puts it, accounting measures, including prison KPIs, can 'alter the power relations that they shape and are embedded within'; they can influence 'the capacities of agents, organizations and the connections among them'; and they can 'enable new ways of acting upon and influencing the actions of individuals' (Miller 2001: 379; see also Cheliotis 2006). To be sure, the effects of systems of quantification on value configurations are highly ambivalent. Performance measurement instruments, such as the prison KPIs studied here, can easily lead to a narrowing of accountability and an increase in value hierarchization, for example by leading to a prioritization of issues of security and procedural correctness over values of rehabilitation and individual prisoners' dignity. But equally, we should not be too quick to dismiss the potential of performance measures to animate and focus the debate, even though this might only be a secondary, unintended effect.

CONCLUSION

In the Prison Service of England and Wales, privatization and private sector-oriented managerial reforms have led to the adoption and spread of business instruments of calculation and quantification. Prisons have become managerialized, and prison managers and prison officers preoccupied with the documentation of calculable outputs. Although the entire prison system has not been privatized, the fundamental change that has come about with the introduction of selective privatizations is, as Coyle (2005: 54) argues, the concept of prison as a 'marketplace' and a business that will inevitably expand.

As in other public services (see for example Pollitt 1993), increased emphasis has come to be placed on financial accountability, managerial process, cost control and performance management. Private sector accounting instruments, such as KPIs, have facilitated this shift in emphasis. Accounting instruments, such as prison ratings, benchmarking and performance measurement, have helped to redefine prisons as competitive units concerned with administrative efficiency, security and procedural correctness. As a result of the introduction of the KPIs, prison values were reconfigured. Less attention came to be placed on individual prisoners' needs, issues of care and decency. The measures made prison governors 'focus on process without looking at quality' (see Bryans 2001: 9). On the other hand, attempts were made to use the KPIs as a vehicle to achieve a rebalancing of values and to bring concerns about 'quality' and prisoners' decency back onto the agenda. Because of their ambivalent nature and the criticisms they attract, accounting instruments of prison rating and performance measurement can, as this chapter illustrates, function also as an important catalyst of problematization.

Despite the prison KPIs studied here being flawed and, at least at present, unsuitable as an effective, stand-alone instrument for assuring value balancing due to obvious limitations (a proneness to failure, misrepresentation and value hierarchization), they nevertheless provoke reflection and debate about market organization. As Espeland and Stevens (1998) highlight, quantification need not only come to be seen as a threat, but also as 'a hopeful beginning', particularly in situations characterized by disparate values and diverse forms of knowledge. Such desires and hopes aimed at inclusion and value balancing are not easy to realize. But even if unrealized, they contribute to the further rise and expansion of accounting calculation and quantification, making the accounting instruments immune to their practical limitations and failings.

NOTES

1. Sections of this chapter are based on Mennicken (2013). Helpful comments on earlier drafts were received from colleagues at LSE, both in the Department of Accounting and at the Centre for Analysis of Risk and Regulation, the Stockholm Center for Organizational Research, and the editors of this volume. The author gratefully

acknowledges the financial support received from the Centre for Analysis of Risk and Regulation at LSE.

2. See http://www.justice.gov.uk/about/noms, accessed 12 September 2012.
3. See http://www.justice.gov.uk/contacts/prison-finder/contracted-out-prisons, accessed 12 September 2012.
4. Executive agencies were introduced in the late 1980s as part of the government's 'Next Steps' reforms. In 1988, a working party of the UK Conservative Government issued the Next Steps Report, which, as James (2001) writes, claimed that several features of the traditional system of public administration were inhibiting performance. Asserting that the civil service was too big to be managed as a single entity, the Report argued for decentralization and the creation of (governmental) agencies with 'clearly defined aims and associated units of budget'. The agencies were supposed to 'focus managers' attention on getting the job done efficiently and effectively, reducing costs where this did not compromise effectiveness' (Next Steps Report 1988, cited in James 2001: 26). According to James the idea of 'agencies' was heavily influenced by an Anglo-American big business model of multi-divisional organization in which specialist units are given freedom to manage within a framework of focused accountability for the performance of each unit.
5. See http://www.justice.gov.uk/downloads/about/noms/noms-org-chart.pdf, p. 2, accessed 16 September 2012.
6. See http://www.justice.gov.uk/about/hmps/contracted-out, accessed 16 November 2012.
7. The Prison Reform Trust (PRT) is a charity founded in 1981 to contribute towards the creation of 'a just, humane and effective penal system' (see http://www.prison reformtrust.org.uk/WhoWeAre/History, accessed 19 November 2012). Since its foundation, the PRT has observed developments in both public and private prisons.
8. In 1987–88, the average prison population was 49,300. Average operational cost per prisoner was £14,300 ('Report on the work of the Prison Service', Home Office 1988 Cm516). Regarding the issue of overcrowding, the report states: 'The pressure of the population . . . reached an intensity not experienced before. There was a nightmare-like sense, felt more sharply than ever before at the top of the Service and, we know, shared by regions and establishments, of always running and never catching up' (ibid.: 1).
9. Market testing permitted the private sector to compete directly with the public sector for the management of prisons that were considered to be 'failing', that is not meeting performance targets, for example with respect to cost management or security standards (evidenced for example by prisoner escapes or riots). Market tests were introduced to the Prison Service in the early 1990s. Later, they were replaced by performance tests, whereby, as Bryans (2007: 73) writes, 'poorly performing prisons are publicly identified and given six months in which to improve their performance'. A failure to improve means that the prison faces closure or being contracted out to the private sector, with no opportunity for in-house bidding (ibid.). In 2010 the government revived market tests, and in 2011 NOMS announced that nine prisons would be subjected to a market test. Further market tests are to follow. These tests are no longer driven by prison performance, but represent an attempt to enhance inter-organizational competitiveness in the provision of prison services more generally. See http://www.pcs.org.uk/en/prison_service_group/operation--penal-policy/prison-market-testing-update.cfm, accessed 19 November 2012.
10. It is difficult to date the birth of the modern prison exactly (Foucault 1977: 231). Two important examples of early modern penal detention are the San Michele Hospice in Rome, founded in 1704, and the Maison de Force in Ghent, opened in 1775.
11. The riots started in Strangeways Prison (Manchester) in April, and spread thereafter to more than 20 prisons throughout the country. As Resodihardjo (2009: 93) writes, for Great Britain, these were 'the most serious series of riots ever experienced. . . . When the quiet returned, three people had died, 133 inmates and 282 prison staff had been injured and there [sic] the cost of the damage ran into millions of pounds'.

12. Examples of the new security measures to be introduced included: the issue of a new security manual; the conduct of security audits (at least annually); the review of the security of prison roofs; the installation of x-ray machines in all prisons holding Category A prisoners; and an extension of the use of electric locks (Home Office 1991: 21).

13. McDermott and King (1989: 118–119) highlight the absence of standards and targets at the time. They write:

> According to Function 17 listed in Circular Instruction 55 of 1984, prison department establishments are expected 'to provide, with a view to occupying prisoners as fully as possible throughout the whole week, a balanced and integrated regime, which may include work, education, physical education, access to libraries and individual and collective leisure facilities'. . . . it would hardly be surprising, given the reduction in time spent out of cells, if there were not some curtailment of regime activities. Whether what remains constitutes a 'balanced and integrated regime' which occupies 'prisoners as fully as possible' is, in the absence of standards, a matter of judgement.

14. See http://www.prisonreformtrust.org.uk/WhoWeAre/History, accessed 19 November 2012.

15. See for examplehttp://www.justice.gov.uk/downloads/statistics/hmps/prisons-annual-performance-ratings2010-11.pdf, accessed 28 February 2012.

16. Bryans goes on to say that:

> Managerialism looks to quantitative measures rather than qualitative ones, often because quantity is easier to measure than quality. For example, 'time out of cell' was a key performance indicator, and governors were encouraged to increase time out of cell. However, for many prisoners increased time out of cell with nothing productive to do other than be on 'association' increased monotony, the possibility of bullying, potential violence and institutionalisation.

REFERENCES

Bennett, Jamie, Crewe, Ben and Wahidin, Azrini (eds) (2008). *Understanding Prison Staff.* Cullompton: Willan Publishing.

Black, John (1993). The prison service and executive agency status – HM Prisons plc? *International Journal of Public Sector Management* 6(6): 27–41.

Bowerman, M., Ball, A. and Graham, F. (2001). Benchmarking as a tool for the modernisation of local government. *Financial Accountability and Management* 17(4): 321–329.

Bryans, Shane (2001). The managerialisation of prisons: Efficiency without a purpose? *Prison Service Journal* 134: 8–10.

Bryans, Shane (2007). *Prison Governors: Managing prisons in a time of change.* Cullompton: Willan Publishing.

Cheliotis, Leonidas K. (2006). Penal managerialism from within: Implications for theory and research. *International Journal of Law and Psychiatry* 29: 397–404.

Cooper, Christine and Taylor, Phil (2005). Independently verified reductionism: Prison privatization in Scotland. *Human Relations* 58(4): 497–522.

Coyle, Andrew (2005). *Understanding Prisons: Key issues in policy and practice.* Maidenhead: Open University Press.

Coyle, Andrew (2007). Policy and operational implications of prison privatisation.

In *Scottish Consortium on Crime and Criminal Justice. Colloquium on the implications of prison privatisation for penal policy in Scotland.* King's College London, International Centre for Prison Studies.

Coyle, Andrew (2008). Change management in prisons. In Bennett, Jamie, Crewe, Ben and Wahidin, Azrini (eds), *Understanding Prison Staff.* Cullompton: Willan Publishing, pp. 231–246.

Coyle, Andrew, Campbell, Allison and Neufeld, Rodney (eds) (2003). *Capitalist Punishment: Prison privatization and human rights.* London: Zed Books.

Espeland, Wendy N. and Stevens, Mitchell L. (1998). Commensuration as a social process. *Annual Review of Sociology* 24: 313–343.

Foucault, Michel (1977). *Discipline and Punish: The birth of the prison.* London: Penguin.

Gaes, Gerald G., Camp, Scott D., Nelson, Julianne B. and Saylor, William G. (2004). *Measuring Prison Performance: Government privatization and accountability.* Walnut Creek: Altamira Press.

Harding, Richard W. (1997). *Private Prisons and Public Accountability.* Buckingham: Open University Press.

Harding, Richard W. (2001). Private prisons. In Tonry, M. and Petersilia, J. (eds), *Crime and Justice: An annual review of research, Vol. 28.* Chicago: University of Chicago Press.

HAC (1987). *Contract Provision of Prisons. Fourth Report from the Home Affairs Committee, Session 1986–87.* London: HMSO.

Home Office (1988). *Private Sector Involvement in the Remand System.* London: HMSO.

Home Office (1991). *Custody, Care and Justice: The way ahead for the prison service in England and Wales.* London: HMSO.

Home Office (1995). *Review of Prison Service Security in England and Wales and the escape from Parkhurst Prison on Tuesday 3rd January 1995 by Sir John Learmont.* London: HMSO.

Home Office (2000). *Modernising the Management of the Prison Service: An independent report by the targeted performance initiative working group. The Laming Report.* London: Home Office.

Hood, Christopher (1991). A public management for all seasons? *Public Administration* 69(1): 3–19.

Hood, Christopher (1995). The 'new public management' in the 1980s: Variations on a theme. *Accounting, Organizations and Society* 20(2/3): 93–109.

Hough, Mike, Allen, Rob and Padel, Una (eds) (2006). *Reshaping Probation and Prisons: The new offender management framework.* Bristol: Policy Press.

House of Commons (2003). *Committee of Public Accounts. Forty-ninth Report of Session 2002–03: The Operational Performance of PFI Prisons.* London: House of Commons.

Humphrey, Christopher (1994). Reflecting on attempts to develop a financial management information system for the probation service in England and Wales: Some observations on the relationship between the claims of accounting and its practice. *Accounting, Organizations and Society* 19(2): 147–178.

Humphrey, Christopher, Miller, Peter and Scapens, Robert W. (1993). Accountability and accountable management in the UK public sector. *Accounting, Auditing and Accountability Journal* 6(3): 7–29.

James, Adrian L., Bottomley, A. Keith, Liebling, Alison and Clare, Emma (1997). *Privatizing Prisons: Rhetoric and reality.* London: Sage.

James, Oliver (2001). Evaluating executive agencies in UK government, *Public Policy and Administration* 16(3): 24–52.

King, Roy D. and McDermott, Kathleen (1989). British prisons 1970–1987: The ever-deepening crisis. *British Journal of Criminology* 29(2): 107–128.

King, Roy D. and McDermott, Kathleen (1995). *The State of Our Prisons*. Oxford: Clarendon Press.

Kurunmäki, Liisa (1999). Making an accounting entity: The case of the hospital in Finnish health care reforms. *European Accounting Review* 8(2): 219–237.

Kurunmäki, Liisa and Miller, Peter (2011). Regulatory hybrids: Partnerships and modernising government. *Management Accounting Research* 22(4): 220–241.

Kurunmäki, Liisa, Lapsley, Irvine and Melia, K. (2003). Accountingization vs. legitimation: A comparative study of the use of accounting information in intensive care. *Management Accounting Research* 14(2): 112–139.

Lapsley, Irvine and Mitchell, Falconer (1996). *Accounting and Performance Measurement: Issues in the private and public sectors.* London: Paul Chapman Publishing.

Lewis, Derek (1997). *Hidden Agendas: Politics, law and disorder*. London: Hamish Hamilton.

Liebling, Alison (2004). *Prisons and Their Moral Performance: A study of values, quality, and prison life.* Oxford: Oxford University Press.

Liebling, Alison, Price, David and Shefer, Guy (2011). *The Prison Officer*. Milton Park: Willan Publishing.

Logan, Charles H. (1990). *Private Prisons: Cons and pros*. Oxford: Oxford University Press.

Lygo, Admiral Sir Raymond (1991). *Management of the Prison Service*. London: Home Office.

McDermott, Kathleen and King, Anthony D. (1989). A fresh start: The enhancement of prison regimes. *Howard Journal of Criminal Justice* 28(3): 161–176.

Mennicken, Andrea (2013). 'Too big to fail and too big to succeed': Accounting and privatisation in the Prison Service of England and Wales. *Financial Accountability and Management* 29(2): 206–226.

Miller, Peter (1992). Accounting and objectivity: The invention of calculating selves and calculable spaces. *Annals of Scholarship* 9(1/2): 61–86.

Miller, Peter (2001). Governing by numbers: Why calculative practices matter. *Social Research* 68(2): 379–396.

Miller, Peter and O'Leary, Ted (2007). Mediating instruments and making markets: Capital budgeting, science and the economy. *Accounting, Organizations and Society* 32(7–8): 701–734.

Miller, Peter and Rose, Nikolas (1990). Governing economic life. *Economy and Society* 19(1): 1–31.

Miller, Peter and Rose, Nikolas (2008). *Governing the Present: Administering economic, social and personal life.* Cambridge: Polity Press.

Modell, Sven (2009). Institutional research on performance measurement and management in the public sector accounting literature: A review and assessment. *Financial Accountability and Management* 25(3): 277–303.

Moyle, Paul (2000). *Profiting from Punishment: Private prisons in Australia: Reform or regression?* Annandale: Pluto Press.

Nathan, Stephen (2003a). Prison privatization in the United Kingdom. In Coyle, Andrew, Campbell, Allison and Neufeld, Rodney (eds), *Capitalist Punishment: Prison privatization and human rights*. London: Zed Books, pp. 162–178.

Nathan, Stephen (2003b). Private prisons: Emerging and transformative economies. In Coyle, Andrew, Campbell, Allison and Neufeld, Rodney (eds), *Capitalist Punishment: Prison privatization and human rights*. London: Zed Books, pp. 189–201.

NAO (National Audit Office) (2003). *Report by the Comptroller and Auditor General: The operational performance of PFI prisons*. London: HMSO.

NAO (2012). *Report by the Comptroller and Auditor General: Restructuring of the National Offender Management Service*. London: HMSO.

Nellis, Mike (2006). NOMS, contestability and the process of technocorrectional innovation. In Hough, Mike, Allen, Rob and Padel, Una (eds). *Reshaping Probation and Prisons: The new offender management framework*. Bristol: Policy Press, pp. 49–68.

Newburn, Tim (2007). 'Tough on crime': Penal policy in England and Wales. *Crime and Justice* 36(1): 425–470.

Owers, Anne (2010). *Valedictory Lecture, Westminster Central Hall, 13 July 2010*. London: HMSO.

Pollitt, Christopher (1986). Beyond the managerial model: The case for broadening performance assessment in government and the public services. *Financial Accountability and Management* 2(3): 155–170.

Pollitt, Christopher (1993). *Managerialism and the Public Services*. Oxford: Blackwell.

Power, Michael (2004). Counting, control and calculation: Reflections on measuring and management. *Human Relations* 57(6): 765–783.

Power, Michael and Laughlin, Richard (1992). Critical theory and accounting. In Alveson, N. and Willmott, H. (eds), *Critical Management Studies*. London: Sage.

Pozen, David E. (2003). Managing a correctional marketplace: Prison privatization in the United States and the United Kingdom. *Journal of Law and Politics* 19: 253–282.

PRT (Prison Reform Trust) (1992). *Comments on the Report by Admiral Sir Raymond Lygo 'Management of the Prison Service'*. London: PRT.

PRT (1994). *Privatisation and Market Testing in the Prison Service*. London: PRT.

PRT (1996). *The Prisons League Table: Performance against key performance indicators*. London: PRT.

PRT (2005). Private punishment: Who profits? In *PRT Briefing*. London: PRT.

Resodihardjo, Sandra L. (2009). *Crisis and Change in the British and Dutch Prison Services*. Farnham: Ashgate.

Taylor, Phil and Cooper, Christine (2008). 'It was absolute hell': Inside the private prison. *Capital and Class* 32(3): 3–30.

Woolf, Lord Justice (1991). *Prison Disturbances April 1990: Report of an Inquiry by the Right Hon. Lord Justice Woolf (Parts I and II) and His Honour Judge Stephen Tumin (Part II)*. London: HMSO.

Young, Peter (1987). *The Prison Cell: The start of a better approach to prison management*. London: Adam Smith Institute.

3. Customer satisfaction over patient security? Value hierarchization in pharmaceutical retail

Jenny Cisneros Örnberg

INTRODUCTION

Pharmaceutical retail is an area with a generally high degree of state control in the form of regulated pricing, regulation of the marketplace via rules regarding opening hours, number and/or location of pharmacies, ownership arrangements and demands on professional qualifications. For example, within the EU alone, there are several different organizational models when it comes to pharmaceutical retailing, based on values such as safety, health, professionalism, availability and efficiency.

In 2009, after 38 years of public monopoly on pharmaceutical retail, the Swedish government decided to reorganize the market. Almost overnight, both the market for prescription drugs and over the counter (OTC) medicines were exposed to competition. Although the realization of the demonopolization could be perceived by the general public as a hasty political decision, I demonstrate in this chapter how the regulation of pharmaceuticals has been debated in the political sphere and has long been a hard issue to solve in Sweden. The political disagreement on the topic has been based in part on different views of what values should take priority when it comes to pharmaceutical retail.

As early as in the 16th century, the pharmacy market was subject to regulations and control. All pharmacies in Sweden at that time were privately owned, but in order to operate a pharmacy one had to be granted a special privilege by the king, requiring that certain conditions and skills be met. Centuries later, around 1920, an extensive reform was undertaken, leading to the economic collectivization of the pharmacy industry. Income regulations were introduced for pharmacists, meaning that pharmacists gradually went from being self-employed businessmen to becoming public employees (Gennser 1998). In both 1946 and 1963, state-commissioned inquiries into the organization of pharmaceutical retail were initiated by the social democratic governments in power. The still-private system was at that time controlled by the Swedish Pharmaceutical Society (Apotekarsocieteten), an organization consisting of pharmacists, and organized around a privilege system where each permit-holder was a local monopolist. The system was perceived as obsolete and inefficient, with low professional standards. Values such as security and a generally negative attitude towards profiting from sick people were put forward. Furthermore, economic problems raised values such as efficiency in the debate (Läkemedelsvärlden 2002). Among the members of the pharmaceutical academy, it was essentially only the holders of pharmacy privileges that defended the system (Swedish Pharmaceutical Association n.d.). From a political standpoint, there was hardly any debate, and all of the political parties voted in favour of monopolization. In September 1969, the government and the Swedish Pharmaceutical Society came to an agreement that entailed nationalization of the supply of pharmaceuticals in Sweden. As of 1 January 1971, the state took over the purchasing and distribution of pharmaceuticals by forming a state-owned enterprise for this purpose, Apoteket AB (Apoteket, for short).

From 1971 to 2009, Apoteket was the sole retailer of both prescription and OTCs in Sweden. According to the agreement with the Swedish state, Apoteket was to provide nationwide coverage for the supply of medical products in Sweden, as well as providing alternative distribution channels, such as pharmacy agents and later also electronic distribution, to ensure a satisfactory distribution system. The agreement required Apoteket to supply all drugs covered under national health benefits, and to ensure that stocks and delivery capacity were sufficient to meet the demands of the public and the health care system. The company was also required to apply uniform pricing with respect to what consumers paid for each medical product, and provide independent advice and information to the consumers (Carlsson 2002). It is also these characteristics that are emphasized in the arguments for the monopoly system, both during the monopoly years and in the later demonopolization debate.

Governments have traditionally often monopolized commodities or services, for instance, gambling, prescription drugs, tobacco and alcohol (see Chapter 2 in this volume), supported by values such as health and public order (Room 1993). An historical argument for having monopolies has been to provide revenue for the government but, as Room argues, 'From the point of view of state revenue, it is the wholesale level which it is crucial to monopolize. [. . .] But from the point of view of public health and order interests, the wholesale level is almost irrelevant: it is the retail level that is crucial' (1993: 183). Another common argument for monopolizing is to regulate the market and eliminate private profits (Room 1993; Holder

1993) on the basis of security and health values. The values of availability and equality have also been raised, since monopolies offer the same products for the same price all over the country, something that a competitive market does not usually do (Cisneros Örnberg and Ólafsdóttir 2008). The expressed purpose of the pharmacy monopolization in Sweden was articulated in terms of values such as efficiency (control of rising prices on pharmaceuticals and personnel costs), health (pharmaceuticals is a special commodity that should be regulated) and patient security (product neutrality and lack of private profit). The monopoly has also been defended with the argument that access to pharmaceuticals is a part of the welfare system and should be based on need. The state also wanted to ensure that the public received correct information, independent of manufacturers' interests, and to guarantee the proper distribution of pharmaceuticals in Sweden (Meyrowitsch 2005; Apoteket Omstrukturering AB 2009). Other explanations for the monopolization have been prevailing left-wing views and skepticism toward private profits in the wake of the thalidomide scandal[1] (Läkemedelsvärlden 2002).

However, public sector activities in many parts of the world have increasingly been called into question in recent decades. Where regulations were previously seen as the obvious solution, open competition is now of greater interest. In Sweden, a wave of deregulation and opening up the public sector to competition gained momentum in the 1990s when the electricity, airline, postal services, telecommunications and railway markets were opened to competition, along with education, health care, elderly care, dental care, and motor vehicle inspections, with reference to the expressed value of greater efficiency (Karlsson 2005; Munkhammar 2007; see also Chapter 2 by Mennicken and Chapter 5 by Tamm Hallström and Gustafsson in this volume).

The purpose of and what public functions a state should offer have varied over the years and according to political ideology (Rothstein 2002). What we have seen in the last two decades is that 'the principle of choice' has been given an increasingly important role in the development of public service (Clarke et al. 2007). This chapter analyses how values have shifted, and how they have affected organizational outcomes regarding the pharmaceutical market in Sweden. The chapter illustrates in particular how different market actors have contributed to a reconfiguration of values to facilitate the demonopolization of the Swedish pharmaceutical retail market in 2009. How this reconfiguration came about, and what arguments, interests and underlying values can explain the outcome will be looked at. Compared to other commodities, such as alcohol and gambling, that have remained contested for centuries due to continuous efforts to sustain and renew value conflicts (see Chapter 2 in this volume), this chapter will show how discussion of the Swedish pharmacy market has increasingly, regardless of ideological standpoint, been focused on values such as profit, availability, efficiency and customer service. Although the differences in values over time and between different actors in this case are shown to be rooted mainly in ideas of what public functions the state should offer, a general hierarchization process has occurred whereby certain values have been given priority, which in turn have given certain organizational solutions precedence.

METHODS

To analyse how values are configured to facilitate an organizational change such as the demonopolization of pharmaceutical retail in Sweden, I have examined the values at stake before and during the reform, including a focus on how certain values disappear or, during some periods, are considered less important than in previous times. Using questions such as when and why values appear or disappear from the discourse and practices, and how and by whom values are framed, I illustrate how different market organizers put forward certain values that support certain organizational solutions. Much public discourse is ideologically shaped, drawing on well-established social orientations, attitudes and other group beliefs, so-called 'framing'. 'Writers and speakers commonly frame public issues by mentioning certain relevant topics and subtopics while ignoring others. In so doing, they are in effect setting the context so as to invoke a certain context model' (Huckin 2002: 355). This means that when some market organizers are given or take a larger space in the debate certain values are given preference.

In the case of the demonopolization of the Swedish pharmaceutical retail market, values do not disappear during the period analysed. Instead, some values receive an obvious, greater focus in the political and public debate. The analysis is based on a study of both primary and secondary sources. Since the discussion of what values should be given priority, that is a value conflict, with respect to pharmaceutical retail has mainly been expressed at a political level, political documents constitute the basis of the analysis. Government reports, government bills and parliamentary debates have been analysed, in addition to annual reports and syntheses of public authorities such as the National Institute of Public Health (Folkhälsoinstitutet), the Dental and Pharmaceutical Benefits Agency (TLV), and organizations such as the earlier noted Swedish Pharmaceutical Association (Sveriges Farmacevtförbund). Furthermore, an overview of comments submitted (Government Offices of Sweden 2008) from some

100 bodies to which the proposed change in the pharmaceutical area was referred for consideration clearly showed the important stakeholders and their opinions on the matter. This material is complemented by previous research and news articles. The media sources include several debate articles, most from Sweden's largest daily newspaper, *Dagens Nyheter.*

I begin below by presenting the empirical case of pharmaceutical retail in Sweden and how a reconfiguration of values has facilitated a liberalization of the area. First, I analyse the shift from monopoly to the demonopolized market, focusing on important market organizers and their values that influenced the development. This is followed by an account of the organizational model that resulted from the reconfiguration of the pharmaceutical retail market. The chapter concludes that a process of value hierarchization has occurred in this area, resulting in a prioritization of the values associated with open competition and a free market, such as profit, availability, efficiency and customer service, over values such as security, control and health. A final reflection is also made about the possible tension that may follow and lead to further value reconfigurations.

FROM MONOPOLY TO DEMONOPOLIZATION OF THE MARKET

Pharmaceuticals have always been a contested commodity. However, the market solutions to this contestation have varied between countries and over time (Malmstig 2004). Some commodities are more contested than others, but the contestation is always an outcome of negotiation and a power struggle between a wide range of market organizers, such as the state, firms, interest groups and individuals (cf. Chapter 1). When configurations change through active positioning, they open the way to new forms of organization. As expected, in this case, the Swedish state played an active part both in the reconfiguration and in the market organization of the pharmacies, possessing power both as the regulator and, for almost four decades, as the owner of the monopoly on pharmaceutical retail. Just as in the cases of the Swedish gambling and alcohol monopolies, the state has taken an active part in the configuration of value conflicts. During the main period analysed, however, this has occurred not as a means to protect the status quo of the market organization, but with the intention to demonopolize.

As mentioned above, the prevailing values in Sweden from the 1970s to the end of the 1990s were availability, efficiency, patient security, health and the lack of private profit; values that were achieved by using a monopoly as an organizational solution. Since the values of efficiency and

availability are present in the debate before, during and after the demonopolization in 2009, it is mainly the views on private profit and manufacturers' interests that have changed. Closely connected to the value of a
lack of private profit is the argument that the lack of private profit motives
generates product neutrality, security and control that an open market
cannot offer. Patient security is thereby connected to the availability of
drugs, but also to secure control and the competence of staff.

In the 1990s, both the right- and the left-wing political blocs appointed
commissions to investigate the pharmacy monopoly, suggesting that the
retail of prescription drugs should be opened to privately owned pharmacies (LFU 92 1994; SOU 1998:28, see also Gennser 1998). It was thought
that complete abolition of the monopoly would increase possibilities for
the rationalization and effectivization of pharmaceutical supply, a belief
supported by organizations such as the National Social Insurance Board,
National Audit Office and Commercial Employees' Union. It was also
supported by the Swedish Competition Authority, which had argued for
a deregulation of retail of OTCs already in the mid-1980s. A deregulation
of OTCs was a part of the changes proposed in a report by conservative Member of Parliament Margit Gennser (LFU 92 1994), but not by
Lars Jeding in a report commissioned by the social democratic government six years later (SOU 1998:28). Jeding suggested instead that OTCs
should only be sold by pharmacies. He also argued for free price-setting
and generic drug substitution. Most of the parties concerned supported
Jeding's proposals but, at the political level, the reactions were more
mixed. The minister for health and social affairs, Margot Wallström,
indicated her support for the demonopolization of OTCs, but was more
skeptical towards a total demonopolization of prescription drugs and
free pricing. Regarding generic substitution, both the Swedish Medical
Association and the trade association for research-based pharmaceutical
industry (LIF) strongly opposed the suggestion. Both reports cited lower
prices, increased availability of pharmaceuticals and an adjustment to
customer demands as the main reasons for policy change. The lack of
support from the conservatives for Jeding's report has been explained as
being due to 'the right message from the wrong messenger', but also to a
lack of strong public opinion against the monopoly at the time (Swedish
Pharmaceutical Association n.d.:8).

Salaries and Enterprising Spirit

The Swedish Pharmaceutical Association had been an active advocate
for the monopoly when it was introduced in 1971. However, the Jeding
report in 1998 became the point of departure for a lobby campaign for

the demonopolization of the pharmacy market with a view to speaking up for the pharmacist profession. The explanation for the change in views was that, during the 1990s, pharmacists had experienced staff cuts, a low-wage trend and limited advancement opportunities in the state-owned enterprise, Apoteket. Apoteket customers were described as having long distances to travel to the pharmacies and being exposed to inconvenient opening hours and long queues. The Pharmaceutical Association also argued that a pharmacy market characterized by multiple actors would lead to enhanced professional development, a spirit of enterprise, new ways to improve the use of pharmaceuticals, better availability for patients and consumers, and better advancement opportunities for the individual pharmacist (Swedish Pharmaceutical Association n.d.). As will be shown, these are values that recur in later political statements from the Ministry of Health and Social Affairs.

Compatibility with EU Law

However, the real contestation of the pharmacy monopoly started at the beginning of the new century, led by Bringwell, a leading alternative medicine company in the Nordic countries. This marked the start of a more public debate about the values surrounding the pharmacy market. Different frames became clearer, where some market organizers made use of EU legislation to promote their values of competition, efficiency and customer service. At this stage, the social democratic government supported the values of health, safety, control and equal availability for all.

The general manager of Bringwell International, Krister Hanner, began to sell OTCs (Nicorette patches and chewing gum) in a health food store, in violation of Swedish law, which stipulated the retail sale of this type of product be restricted to Apoteket. The sale of these goods was preceded by provocative newspaper ads comparing the Swedish prime minister of the time with Kim Jong Il and Fidel Castro. The Swedish authorities brought criminal proceedings against Hanner and the public prosecutor pointed out that the Nicorette products in question were classified as medical products by the Swedish Medical Products Agency (MPA), and therefore fell under the state monopoly. Hanner, on the other hand, claimed that the Swedish pharmacy monopoly was in breach of Articles 28 EC (free movement of goods), 31 EC (commercial state monopolies) and 43 EC (right of establishment), and he could therefore not be penalized for the alleged offences. The Stockholm District Court requested a preliminary ruling from the Court of Justice of the EU (CJEU) (Allroth et al. 2005).

Since the Swedish monopoly on pharmacies had not been adjusted at all in accordance with previous EU legal requirements, the court limited itself by stating that the Swedish system for the retail sale of pharmaceuticals lacked a system that would entitle producers whose products were not selected to be informed of the reasons for selection decisions. Neither did the Swedish system provide an opportunity to contest such decisions before an independent supervisory authority. The ruling should be interpreted such that were a product plan to be established, and a system that guaranteed independence and an objective selection of products with requirements on motivation and legal review by an independent supervisory body, the Swedish monopoly should be consistent with EU law (Allroth et al. 2005; Hettne 2009). As a result, the Swedish District Court cleared Hanner in July 2005 and later that year the regulations were adjusted to comply with the ruling. Hanner's acquittal also led to a new law that took effect on 1 March 2008 (SFS 2007:1455), regulating the retail sale of nicotine medicines. The new act allows actors other than Apoteket to sell nicotine products, provided that those activities are reported to the municipality in which trade is conducted. The expressed purpose of the deregulation was to increase the availability of nicotine products to facilitate smoke cessation. Hanner thus succeeded in changing the 'value label' for nicotine products, from a potentially dangerous product to a self-care product that should be available to everyone. The Hanner case also served to amplify a framing that distinguishes between prescription drugs that still need to be controlled by the profession (that is pharmacists) and drugs that are seen as harmless and can be handled by ordinary commerce.

Although the Hanner case had no direct, formal implications for the Swedish pharmacy monopoly, EU membership opened a window of opportunity for market organizers to contest the present organization of the market with the support of EU law. The legal and economic support Hanner received from the federation for Swedish grocers (Svensk Dagligvaruhandel) illustrated with clarity the interest among large grocery chains to develop the so-called 'self-care' market. Factors relating to the value of availability, such as opening hours, number of shops, product range and low prices, were again put forward as important.

A New Conservative Government

In 2006, a shift in government led to a more serious political debate about the demonopolization of the pharmacy market and a clarification of what values were considered important. Representatives from the state-owned Apoteket argued that a deregulated pharmacy market would lead to inferior quality, less focus on information and advice, and fewer resources for security and control. The argument was also that sales campaigns with questionable health arguments, lower environmental ambitions, a smaller assortment, undermined product neutrality, and unsound alliances between pharmacies and pharmaceutical producers, could be expected (Carlsson 2002).

Nevertheless, in December 2006, Minister of Health and Social Affairs Göran Hägglund gave economist Lars Reje the assignment of evaluating the possibility of a re-regulation, not deregulation, of the pharmacy market in Sweden in order to achieve greater efficiency, better access for consumers, lower prices, and a safe and effective use of drugs. Reje had a background at the Confederation of Swedish Enterprise and had officially expressed confidence that exposing previous, state-owned monopolies to competition would result in increased efficiency, increased supply and availability, and better service (Confederation of Swedish Enterprise 2004), a view Hägglund shared. Hägglund's predecessor, social democrat Ylva Johansson, on the other hand, was critical towards the idea, arguing that there was already some level of misuse and overuse of pharmaceuticals, and that a demonopolization would diminish the state's ability to control (Lagercrantz and Bergeå 2007).

Reje's inquiry led to five reports (SOU 2007:53; SOU 2008:4; SOU 2008:28; SOU 2008:33; SOU 2008:46). The main report (SOU 2008:4) again proposed that the monopoly on both prescription and OTC drugs should be abolished. It also proposed that it should be possible to sell certain OTC drugs in places other than pharmacies and with no requirement for pharmaceutical training.

Lobbying, Scandals and New Collaborations

The process toward a demonopolization of the pharmacy market attracted immense interest from several influential market actors. Apoteket, which in 2002 had been critical of organizational change and defended its position, did an about-face and suddenly began to express values such as that a monopoly restrained positive development of the availability of pharmacies and pharmaceuticals, the product assortment and customer service (Carlsson and Fernvall 2008). Many pharmacists held out hope of opening their own business, in Europe the big pharmacy chains waited eagerly for the start signal, and at the national level other commercial interests also wanted a piece of the pie. The future of Apoteket has been argued to be one of the biggest lobby issues in Sweden. The pharmaceutical market was described as 'a steady stream of consultants and a pharmacy lobby where everyone knows everyone' (Sundling 2009). Large amounts of money were collected by PR firms and lobbyists, including Lars Jeding, who jumped back and forth between his mandate as government investigator of the pharmacy market, lobbyist for Apoteket, and later also consultant to

Apoteket's competitor Kronans Droghandel. Later yet, he also served as supervisor of the demonopolization, reporting to the minister of health and social affairs, Göran Hägglund (Sundling 2009).

In 2007, Apoteket received a lot of criticism over a planned cooperation with the American company Medco Health Solutions. According to information leaked to the media, together with Medco, Apoteket planned to develop an electronic system for prescription monitoring. The Pharmaceutical Association was highly critical of Apoteket's actions and claimed that this was not merely a technical solution but a much more extensive collaboration between Medco and Apoteket, where the latter was attempting to gain a head start in anticipation of the demonopolization (Kvist Wadman and Stenberg 2008). Apoteket argued, on the other hand, with the support of the government, that the new system was a safety programme that would contribute substantially to diminishing unnecessary drug-related side effects and deaths, as well as helping to decrease medical costs and leading to increased quality of care for patients, especially the elderly (News Medical 2010).

The so-called Medco scandal meant that there were a number of market organizers with somewhat conflicting interests that suddenly joined forces in a common cause. The Pharmaceutical Association took the initiative to form an 'alliance for competition' (Allians för konkurrens), consisting of, among others, Kronans Droghandel, Tamro, Svensk Dagligvaruhandel, Lif and Svensk Egenvård. The strategy was to call on ministers, write debate articles and use other initiatives to start a discussion, in order to stop Apoteket's plans to strengthen its position (Swedish Pharmaceutical Association n.d.). The alliance put forward values such as open competition, at the same time as the scandal caused Apoteket's reputation as safe, secure and equitable to suffer a blow. The state-owned Apoteket became, at least for a limited time, associated with profit-seeking and nepotism, which meant a loss of prestige for the company, seriously damaging its influence over the demonopolization process.

Values at Stake

In January 2008, Hägglund supported the conclusions made in the inquiry led by Reje and declared, almost a year before the final bill, that the government's goal was to reform the pharmacy market:

> Patients in Sweden should be able to buy their pharmaceuticals in an easy and safe manner. The government's goal is to increase availability and improve service for patients and customers at the pharmacies around the country. Buying your medicines will be easier. By giving more [companies] the opportunity to operate pharmacies, we will free the enterprising spirit and power

of initiative that are locked up today. It is about both giving pharmacists the opportunity to own their own businesses and realize their own ideas, and about chain stores being able to offer new services and concepts. (Hägglund 2008)

Patient and customer rights are put forward with values such as availability and service. However, the individual consumer's right to lower prices was secondary here to the advantages of self-employment, supported by values such as professionalism, efficiency and service. When the main report by Reje (SOU 2008:4) was sent out for comment, it was sent to just over 100 bodies, of which some 90 responded. In addition to this, about 20 NGOs and others also submitted their considerations (Government Offices of Sweden 2008). Of the municipalities and county councils that replied, the vast majority under right-wing rule were in favour of demonopolization, whereas the municipalities and county councils with left-wing rule tended to be more negative. The foremost advocates, apart from right-wing governed municipalities and county councils, were market organizers that had an economic interest or were in other ways convinced that an open market with free competition has advantages at both the individual and societal level, including the Competition Authority, Apoteket, Kronans Droghandel, the National Board of Trade, the Swedish Federation of Trade, Confederation of Swedish Enterprise, Federation of Business Owners and the Association for Generic Pharmaceuticals in Sweden.

Among the critical voices, the views heard included that the present system was working well and/or there was a sceptical attitude towards the argument that demonopolization would lead to increased availability and lower prices. Several actors also feared that a deregulated market ran the risk of developing an oligopoly of large foreign cooperations with short-sighted profit interests. The report suggested uniform prices for the entire country on drugs covered by national health benefits, but retail competition for OTC drugs. This was a suggestion that was opposed in only two instances, indicating a broad consensus on the value of equality in pricing for all citizens in Swedish society when it comes to prescription drugs. Pharmaceuticals for self-medication, on the other hand, were considered in most instances to be like any other commodity on the market. Furthermore, the report made the judgment that demonopolization would lead to an increased number of pharmacies in the country, although new establishment would be higher in cities than in rural areas (Government Offices of Sweden 2008). One could therefore argue that there is a general support among most market organizers for the value of increased availability of pharmaceuticals.

The National Pensioners' Organisation was among one of the few interest groups that openly argued that re-regulation should be characterized by a decreased use of pharmaceuticals rather than by the ability to make a profit. However, even actors who were generally positive to demonopolization emphasized that the inquiry was too focused on pharmaceuticals as a commodity (Swedish Medical Association). Independent of their point of departure, several organizations argued that it is a complicated area that has not been sufficiently investigated (Parliamentary Ombudsman, the Uppsala County Administrative Court, the Institute of Public Health, the National Pensioners' Organisation). Furthermore, most actors objected to the proposal that the infrastructure and IT system was to be maintained by a state-owned company rather than a public authority or included in the activities of the county councils (Government Offices of Sweden 2008). This could be interpreted as a suspicion that the suggested organizational model put profit values in the forefront rather than values such as availability and customer service.

In retrospect, one can argue that the negative comments to the report (SOU 2008:4) had little impact on the final proposition that paved the way for a demonopolization of the retail sale of pharmaceuticals. This shows the influence the government has as a market organizer in this case. It also shows that, even though there are different views about the proper way to organize the pharmaceutical retail market, there are certain values that get more attention in the debate, and that there is increasing consensus about what values are important.

Upon review of the inquiries conducted, the political debate and the stakeholders' arguments, irrespective of their views on demonopolization, the analysis shows that it is the customer that is in focus. Sometimes the customer may be referred to as a 'patient' but he/she is nevertheless always said to be in need of increased availability and lower prices on pharmaceuticals and OTCs. With few exceptions, values such as patient security and health are absent or secondary in the debate. There is, on the other hand, a general focus on resources, costs, products and taxpayers' money, by both proponents and opponents of the demonopolization. For example, the social democratic spokesperson for medical service issues, Ylva Johansson, argues that one has to question whether the government has placed ideological reasons before responsible handling of common resources (Johansson 2009b, 2009c).

Very few bring up the issue of the potential harm caused by incorrect usage and, if they do, it is usually in connection with either the 18-year age limit for purchasing drugs, or the proper training of personnel presented as a solution. Neither is there discussion of the potential problem for citizens and society at large, of an increased marketization of a highly profitable area with health consequences. Values such as health and security are thereby given less attention. One exception may be the pharmacy workers' union (Farmaciförbundet), which expressed fear that a demonopolization of the retail sale of OTC medicines could lead to over-consumption, side effects and poisoning. Another is the official statement from the 'red–green' opposition (made up left-of-centre and environmental parties) in 2009 that they would rescind the deregulation should they return to government in 2010, arguing that pharmaceuticals are part of the health care system and not a commodity (Johansson 2009a). However, these statements are drowned out in the discussion on cost-effectiveness, profit margins and increased pharmaceutical costs. Most differences in opinion are therefore expressed in an economic frame, where different ways of calculating cost are set against one another. There is a noticeable political divide, however, in that the 'red–green' parties focus more on the costs for society, whereas the right-wing alliance tends to focus more on the individual's right to availability and low prices.

ORGANIZING THE PHARMACEUTICAL RETAIL MARKET

So far I have shown that the prevailing values in the pharmaceutical retail market in Sweden from the 1970s to the end of the 1990s focused on patient security, health and the lack of private profit achieved through using a monopoly as an organizational solution. Over time, several market organizers have invested efforts in reconfiguring these values. The following paragraphs give an account of the outcome of that reconfiguration and an analysis of the type of organization Sweden ended up with after the demonopolization.

In February 2009, the government presented a bill proposing a re-regulation of the earlier state-owned pharmacy monopoly based on the argument that it would lead to increased availability, better prices and better service (Prop. 2008/09:145). In April of the same year, parliament passed the bill, meaning that as of July 2009 private pharmacies were allowed in the Swedish market. Furthermore, starting in November 2009, specific OTC medicinal products were allowed to be sold outside pharmacies (SFS 2009:730). At the same time, 466 of the 933 formerly state-owned pharmacies were sold for a total of almost 6 billion SEK to four large actors: Apoteket Hjärtat, Kronans Droghandel Retail AB, Medstop Holding and Vårdapoteket i Norden AB (Apoteket Omstrukturering AB 2009; KPMG 2012).

In 2012, there were 26 actors in the market, of which the state-owned company, Apoteket AB, is still the largest, with a market share equal to the expressed permitted limit of 35 percent (KPMG 2012). Although the Swedish pharmacy market is now demonopolized, it is still highly regulated. The monitoring of compliance with the laws and control of the system is, as before, mainly performed by two authorities: the Swedish Medical Products Agency (MPA) and the Dental and Pharmaceutical Benefits Agency (TLV). The new law on sales of medicinal products (SFS 2009:366) gives anyone the right to own a pharmacy, with the exception of those with a vested interest, such as producers or prescribers of medicinal products (for example. doctors, dentists and veterinarians). Every pharmacy must have a permit from the MPA. The permit guarantees compliance with the requirements regulating ownership and pharmaceutical competence, and requirements regarding premises, staffing, and so on. The MPA also maintains the supervision over all of the pharmacies in Sweden (for a more detailed account of the MPA and TLV, see for example Cisneros Örnberg 2012).

Furthermore, after the demonopolization, a new state-owned enterprise was introduced, Apotekens Service AB, responsible for the overall infrastructure and service systems that used to be administrated by Apoteket. The systems have been transferred to the new company in order to make them available to private as well as state-owned pharmacies. Apotekens Service is also responsible for the review and authorization of IT systems used by the pharmacies for dispense of prescriptions. More than 80 percent of all prescriptions are electronic today, and Apotekens Service therefore has a key position when it comes to patient security. The values of patient security are thereby still present as an argument for state control of certain parts of the market, even though it is not as salient a feature in the debate as other values.

When it comes to retail sales of over the counter drugs, interested actors must report such business to and follow the rules and regulations set out by the MPA. It is the MPA that decides which OTC medicines may be sold outside pharmacies, and there is an age limit of 18 years for the purchase of all OTCs. Municipalities have the main responsibility for the supervision of this segment of the market, but have no right to impose or set requirements (Örstadius 2010). At the beginning of 2012, about half of all OTC medicines were approved to be sold outside pharmacies (approximately 450 substances), at about 5,700 points of sale. This approval is based on criteria established by parliament and on the assessment of the medicinal product's appropriateness for self-medication, whether it has serious side effects, and with appropriate consideration of patient safety and the protection of public health. The OTC sales outside pharmacies are dominated by analgesics, nicotine replacement products and nasal sprays (Apotekens Service 2011). It could be argued that the demonopolization of OTCs has resulted in a diminished importance of the value of security, since supervision and follow-up are now less prior-itized measures.

CONCLUSIONS: FROM PATIENT SECURITY TO CUSTOMER SATISFACTION

When it comes to the pharmacy monopoly, the advocates of demonopo-lization strongly emphasized that changing the pharmacy market was not about deregulation but re-regulation, where the expressed difference between the two concepts is that 'deregulation' entails removing regula-tions, and 're-regulation' implies less changes and that the pharmacy market – even post-monopoly – requires central functions and regula-tions. On the other hand, the stated rationale for deregulation is often that fewer and simpler regulations will lead to more competition, and therefore higher productivity, greater efficiency and lower prices (see for example Chapter 5 by Tamm Hallström and Gustafsson, in this volume), the same values put forward in this debate. I would therefore argue that, in the case of the pharmacy market looked at here, the reluctance to use the word 'deregulation' (rather than 're-regulation') is based in part on a political wish to diminish a value pluralism that would otherwise be more apparent.

Both when the monopoly was introduced in the 1970s and when it was abolished 39 years later, there seems to have been political motives behind the reorganizations, and a belief that these would lead to higher efficiency (Wikberg 2010). After the demonopolization in 2009, the advocates, both from government and different market organizers, consider the reform successful based on the objectives of more actors in the market and better availability through an increased number of pharmacies and longer opening hours. Other values, such as security and health, have received a more remote position in the debate. However, these values are still present in the form of an organizational structure that remains under state control. Nevertheless, an ongoing redistribution of responsibility can be observed, from the public sector to private companies. Markets are put forward as a viable, more efficient and effective way of organizing pharmaceutical retail. Privatization processes and freedom of choice are taken for granted and their implications are seldom discussed in detail.

During the monopoly period, Apoteket was steered by its public mandate to offer the whole population a high availability of Apoteket products and services. Apoteket's aim and legitimacy has since changed as a result of the demonopolization. In a market exposed to competition, Apoteket is forced to reflect more about profit and the needs of the spe-cific business, rather than professional competence and patient security.

Apoteket 'users' are thereby transformed from citizens to customers (Arén et al. 2011; Clarke et al. 2007; Nestius 2011).

It is also clear that the market has been organized by those other than the people affected by the decisions. The consumers/citizens have not been visible in the demonopolization process, and it is not until very recently that their discontentment has started to crystallize, for example, in the media. In the Stockholm metropolitan area in particular, the service level has failed to live up to the sharp increase in the number of pharmacies. Several market organizers believe that the problem is due to the 'generic' model, introduced in 2002, meaning that thousands of medications are replaced every month to keep the state's pharmaceutical costs down (Wallér et al. 2012). Others believe that the increasing number of pharmacies, with a fairly constant number of prescriptions in society, serves merely to spread out the drugs to more pharmacies, where few manage to keep all prescription medicines in stock.

Also, post-demonopolization evaluations have focused mainly on whether the articulated goals of price, availability and service have been met. The Swedish Consumer Agency has reported that the population's confidence in pharmacies has fallen because citizens feel that they receive worse advice, assistance and information from the pharmacy staff. According to the government's own investigation, it has become more difficult to obtain prescription medicines within a reasonable period of time. According to state regulations, all pharmacies including privately owned ones are obliged to remain open until March 2013. Thereafter, each pharmacy owner may do as he/she pleases, which poses a threat to many pharmacies in sparsely populated areas, which will likely have to close due to lack of profitability. Media reports have revealed that some privately owned pharmacies are using advanced tax shelter schemes, then arguing a lack of profitability and requesting increased subsidies from the state. The solution from political quarters has been to appoint an investigative committee which, above all, will make proposals regarding information to customers and increased supervision. Critics believe that it is notable that, to date, no studies have looked at whether the release of a wide range of products for sale outside pharmacies has increased the consumption of these products, or if adverse reactions and toxicities are becoming more common (Havsöga and Åkesson 2012). This criticism indicates that a period of increased conflict, when it comes to the values related to the organization the pharmaceutical retail market, could be expected.

In conclusion, this chapter shows that the value configuration in the case of pharmaceutical retail in Sweden played an important part in the reorganization of the market. However, it is possible that a new value configuration will develop if the assumed outcomes for the customer

– lower prices, and greater availability and service – are not met. A future of increased value pluralism may also be expected if state expenditures increase at the same time as private pharmacies are making profit, or if the privatization leads to increased consumption or inappropriate use of pharmaceuticals.

NOTE

1. Thalidomide is a sedative introduced in the late 1950s, and also used to treat morning sickness. In Sweden it was launched as Neurosedyn, sold as an OTC drug, around 1960 and withdrawn at the end of 1961, after being found to cause birth defects. The thalidomide scandal was of central importance since it led to increased pharmaceutical control.

REFERENCES

Allroth, E., Hettne, J. and Meyrowitsch, A. (2005). *EU och svenska monopol – teori, verklighet och framtid*, Sieps 2005: 6.
Apotekens Service (2011). Försäljningen av receptfria läkemedel utanför apotek har stabiliserats. Available at: http://www.apotekensservice.se/Nyheter-och-Press/arkiv/Forsaljningen-av-receptfria-lakemedel-utanfor-apotek-har-stabilise rats/ (accessed 3 April 2012).
Apoteket Omstrukturering AB (2009). Apotekskluster säljs för 5,9 miljarder kronor, Press release, 9 September. Available at: http://www.mynewsdesk.com/se/pressroom/apoteketomstruktureringab/pressrelease/view/apotekskluster-sael js-foer-5-9-miljarder-kronor-339012 (accessed 25 September 2012).
Arén, M., Grapengiesser, A., Janse, R., Kronvall, A. and Nyman, A. (2011). Omregleringen av apoteksbranschen – en studie som undersöker de organisatoriska förändringarna och dess effekter i Apoteket AB. Stockholm School of Economics.
Carlsson, S. (2002). Hundra miljoner sparas. Debate article, *Dagens Nyheter*, 14 November.
Carlsson, S. and Fernvall, E. (2008). Bra för våra kunder att monopolet upphör. Debate article, *Dagens Nyheter*, 15 March. Available at: http://www.dn.se/debatt/bra-for-vara-kunder-att-monopolet-upphor (accessed 25 September 2012).
Cisneros Örnberg, J. (2012). The demonopolization of pharmaceuticals in Sweden: Policy, actors and arguments. In Hellman, M., Roos G. and von Wright J. (eds) *A Welfare Policy Patchwork. Negotiating the Public Good in Times of Transition*. Helsinki: NVC.
Cisneros Örnberg, J. and Ólafsdóttir, H. (2008). How to sell alcohol? Nordic alcohol monopolies in a changing epoch. *Nordic Studies on Alcohol and Drugs*, 25: 129–153.
Clarke, J., Newman, J., Smith, N., Vidler, E. and Westmarland, L. (2007). *Creating Citizen-consumers. Changing publics and changing public services*. London: Sage.
Confederation of Swedish Enterprise (Svenskt näringsliv) (2004). Avreglering i

motvind? Perspektiv på regelutredningens uppdrag. Available at http://www.
svensktnaringsliv.se/multimedia/archive/00000/Avreglering_i_motvind__422a.
pdf (accessed 25 September 2012).
Gennser, M. (1998). *Den rätta medicinen. Apoteksmonopolet vid vägs ände.*
Stockholm: Timbro.
Government Offices of Sweden (2008). Remissammanställning över betänkandet
Omreglering av apoteksmarkanaden (SOU 2008:4). Promemoria S2008/184/HS,
Ministry of Health and Social Affairs.
Hägglund, G. (2008). Apoteket ska brytas upp för en sund konkurrens. Debate
article, *Dagens Nyheter*, 5 January. Available at: http://www.dn.se/debatt/
apoteket-ska-brytas-upp-for-en-sund-konkurrens   (accessed   25   September
2012).
Havsöga, B. and Åkesson, A. (2012). Följ upp folkhälsa och patientsäkerhet när
läkemedel säljs utanför apoteken. Debate article, *Dagens Apotek*, 17 February.
Available   at: http://www.dagensapotek.se/debatt/folj-upp-folkhalsa-och-pat
ientsakerhet-nar-lakemedel-saljs-utanfor-apoteken/   (accessed   25   September
2012).
Hettne, J. (2009). Transforming monopolies – EU-adjustment or social changes?
In Gustavsson, S., Oxelheim, L. and Pehrson, L. (eds), *How Unified is the
European Union? European integration between visions and popular legitimacy.*
Berlin: Springer.
Holder, H.D. (1993). The state monopoly as a public health approach to consump-
tion and alcohol problems: A review of research evidence. *Contemporary Drug
Problems*, 20(2): 293–322.
Huckin, T. (2002). Textual silence and the discourse of homelessness. *Discourse
Society*, 13: 347–372.
Johansson, Y. (2009a). Vi tänker riva upp en apoteksreform. *Svenska Dagbladet*, 19
February. Available at: http://www.svd.se/opinion/brannpunkt/vi-tanker-riva-
upp-en-apoteksreform_2489997.svd (accessed 25 September 2012).
Johansson, Y. (2009b). Det måste bli ett slut på apotekscirkusen. *Newsmill*,
25 September. Available at: http://www.newsmill.se/node/11666 (accessed 25
September 2012).
Johansson, Y. (2009c). Ylva Johansson om utförsäljningen av Apoteket AB:
Statens kostnader kommer att öka, 10 November. Available at http://www.s-
info.se/region/show_news.asp?id=120&news=13811   (accessed   25   September
2012).
Karlsson, M. (2005). *Avreglering, konkurrensutsättning och ekonomisk effektivitet
– offentligt eller privat? En översikt av svensk empirisk forskning.* Department
of Economics, Uppsala University. Available at: http://www.kkv.se/upload/
filer/forskare-studenter/projekt/2004/proj117-2004.pdf (accessed 25 September
2012).
KPMG (2012). Projekt Avicenna. Unpublished report to the Ministry of Health
and Social Affairs, Stockholm.
Kvist Wadman, L. and Stenberg. I. (2008). Avtal mellan Apoteket och Medco
klart. *LäkemedelsVärlden*, 31 March. Available at: http://www.lakemedels
varlden.se/zino.aspx?articleID=11398 (accessed 25 September 2012).
Lagercrantz, S. and Bergeå, N. (2007). Ministern vill pressa priserna.
LäkemedelsVärlden, 27 January. Available at: http://www.lakemedelsvarlden.
se/zino.aspx?articleID=4953 (accessed 25 September 2012).
LFU   92   (1994).   Omsorg   och   konkurrens: slutbetänkande   av

Läkemedelsförsörjningsutredningen. *Swedish Government Official Reports*, Stockholm: Fritzes.
Läkemedelsvärlden (2002). Vänstervinden blåste bort de fria apoteken, 21 May. Available at: http://www.lakemedelsvarlden.se/nyheter/v%C3%A4nstervinden-bl%C3%A5ste-bort-de-fria-apoteken-1236 (accessed 25 September 2012).
Malmstig, E. (2004). *Mera stat och mera profession? En exkursion med farmaceutprofessionen – från privata företagare till statstjänstemän i Apoteksbolaget.* Score Rapportserie 2004:2. Stockholm: SCORE.
Meyrowitsch, A. (2005). *Apoteket AB –The Legitimacy of the Swedish Retail Monopoly on Pharmaceuticals in the European Union.* Master's thesis, Faculty of Law. Lund University.
Munkhammar, J. (2007). *Försäljning av statliga bolag under tre decennier*, Stockholm: Timbro.
Nestius, M. (2011). Konkurrensen ger sug efter bra säljare och inte farmaceuter. *Dagens Apotek*, 17 February. Available at: http://www.dagensapotek.se/blo gg/ledarbloggen/konkurrensen-ger-sug-efter-bra-saljare-och-inte-farmaceuter/ (accessed 25 September 2012).
News Medical (2010). Apoteket and Medco Health Solutions develop centralized prescription safety program, 7 January. Available at: http://www. news-medical.net/news/20100107/Apoteket-and-Medco-Health-Solutions-devel op-centralized-prescription-safety-program.aspx (accessed 25 September 2012).
Örstadius, K. (2010). Medicin säljs utan controller. *Dagens Nyheter*, 10 May. Available at: http://www.dn.se/nyheter/sverige/medicin-saljs-utan-kontroller/ (accessed 25 September 2012).
Prop. 2008/09:145, Omreglering av apoteksmarknaden. Government Bill, 20 February 2009, Ministry of Health and Social Affairs. Available at: http://www. regeringen.se/sb/d/108/a/120969 (accessed 25 September 2012).
Room, R. (1993). The evolution of alcohol monopolies and their relevance for public health. *Contemporary Drug Problems*, 20(2): 169–187.
Rothstein, B. (2002). *Vad bör staten göra? Om välfärdsstatens moraliska och politiska logik.* Stockholm: SNS förlag.
SFS (2007:1455). *Lag om detaljhandel med nikotinläkemedel.* Stockholm: Code of Statutes.
SFS (2009:366). *Lag om handel med läkemedel.* Stockholm: Code of Statutes.
SFS (2009:730). *Lag om handel med vissa receptfria läkemedel.* Stockholm: Code of Statutes.
SOU (1998:28). *Läkemedel i vård och handel: om en säker, flexibel och samordnad läkemedelsförsörjning: betänkande av Läkemedelsdistributionsutredningen.* Stockholm: Fritzes offentliga publikationer.
SOU (2007:53). *Sjukhusens läkemedelsförsörjning: delbetänkande av Apoteksmarknadsutredningen.* Stockholm: Fritze.
SOU (2008:4). *Omreglering av apoteksmarknaden: huvudbetänkande av Apoteksmarknadsutredningen.* Stockholm: Fritze.
SOU (2008:28). *Apoteksdatalagen: delbetänkande av Apoteksmarknadsutredningen.* Stockholm: Fritze.
SOU (2008:33). *Detaljhandel med vissa receptfria läkemedel: delbetänkande av Apoteksmarknadsutredningen.* Stockholm: Fritze.
SOU (2008:46). *Handel med läkemedel för djur: slutbetänkande av apoteksmarknadsutredningen.* Stockholm: Fritze.
Sundling, J. (2009). Miljonrullning i apoteksstridens spar. *Resumé*, 29 April.

Available at: http://www.resume.se/nyheter/pr/2009/04/29/miljonrullning-i-apoteksst/ (accessed 25 September 2012).
Swedish Pharmaceutical Association (*Sveriges Farmacevtförbund*) (n.d.). Historien om hur monopolet blev historia. Available at http://www.farmacevtforbundet.se/forbundet/satyckerforbundet/Documents/farmacevtforbundet_40%20sid.pdf (accessed 25 September 2012).
Wallér, J., Björk, T., Jansson, C., Wedin, M. and Ribeiro, S. (2012). Ständiga byten av medicin bade dyrbart och riskfyllt. *Dagens Nyheter*, 25 September. Available at: http://www.dn.se/debatt/standiga-byten-av-medicin-bade-dyrbart-och-riskfyllt (accessed 25 September 2012).
Wikberg, E. (2010). Omorganisering av apoteksmarknaden. Score Report Series 2010:6, Stockholm Centre for Organizational Research (Score).

4. Trust in transparency: value dynamics and the reorganization of the Baltic financial markets

Sebastian Botzem and Matilda Dahl

INTRODUCTION

Values influence the organization of markets. Not only do they guide the exchange of physical or financial products and services, they also structure the interaction between individuals and organizations engaged in these markets. As this edited volume shows, however, values do not come in the singular; rather, markets are places where multiple values are at stake, and the relation between values and markets is manifold and not always easily recognized. Extreme events, such as crises, however, accentuate the value dimension of markets.

The financial crisis of 2008 – where public discourse highlighted the individual misbehavior of managers, excessive bonuses and the immoral behavior of greedy bankers – can serve as an example of how crises are interpreted through the lens of values. Such attempts to moralize market actors and activities point to the relevance of studying value configurations in financial markets. Furthermore, they underline the fragility of financial markets on display in exceptional circumstances such as crises.

Since the early 1990s, the Baltic financial markets have undergone a remarkable modernization as economies in transition. In doing so, they opted for a radical version of neoliberal free market policies and were severely affected by the financial crisis. In this chapter, we take a closer look at values and value configurations in financial markets in times of crisis. These markets are populated by large, powerful and internationally active organizations such as banks and stock exchanges. Banks and stock exchanges shape markets not only by offering or purchasing services, but also by establishing social relationships and organizing activities. The chapter aims to analyze and compare the post-2008 crisis responses of stock exchanges and banks in the Baltic states, in terms of a reconfiguration of fundamental values – a shift to a system-based trust in transparency. Interestingly, in both banks and exchanges, transparency emerged as a core underlying value drawn upon to legitimize reforms. In the exchange industry, trust in transparency came into play as an ex-post justification of markets and their efficiency; while, in banking, trust in transparency instead brought on reforms aimed at redefining business practices and introducing new risk management systems. We explain the differences in the usage of transparency in exchanges and banks, respectively, and through this analysis discuss the reconfiguration of values in financial markets in times of crisis.

The empirical data consists of interviews with bankers employed at Swedish banks in the Baltic states (2008–2009), interviews with experts in Swedish regulatory agencies, and documentation issued by international bodies such as the Bank for International Settlement (Basel Committee), the OECD and the IMF. Changes in the exchange industry were analyzed by way of annual reports, documents and secondary literature. We also consulted various corporate information available and used additional primary documents as sources of information.

TRANSPARENCY: AN ABSTRACT FOUNDATION OF MARKETS

According to classic economic theory, transparency is a basic condition for well-functioning financial markets. Its absence is often seen as problematic, as this is assumed to cause a lack of trust and subsequently undermine individual transactions as well as the operation of markets as such. In the words of the organization that has put transparency on the global political agenda (Transparency International): 'Trust in financial markets vanished when the lack of transparency became apparent; it is only through transparency that investor confidence and public trust can be won back'.

A rather loose understanding and characterization of transparency has helped the worldwide expansion of the concept. Often transparency is operationalized quite technically in abstract standards or numerical objectivity, such as data for market surveillance in the exchange industry or capital adequacy requirements in banking. Accounting standards in particular have been found to promote transparency and give investors concrete figures, thereby enabling the application of market logics (Jang 2006; Power 2010). In this context, transparency is seen as a remedy for disfunctional financial markets.

Garsten and Lindh de Montoya (2008) analyze transparency as a narrative and conclude that it has the capacity of a 'travelling keyword' that often travels with other compelling terms, in a 'not so innocent manner' (ibid: 283). In this chapter, we argue that, in financial markets, transparency travels together with trust. The popularity transparency enjoys with financial market actors has to do with its capacity to 'black-box' social phenomena. This is frequently done by referring to and relying on mathematical models and calculations, as in the case of risk management. 'Trust in numbers', as Porter (1997) famously called it, is often equated with transparency. Although numbers may hide more than they reveal, the many efforts by financial actors such as banks and exchanges to promote standards, ratings and calculations are often argued for in terms of transparency.

For stock exchanges, the relevance of transparency is discussed in economics literature and among exchange operators' managers in a fairly straightforward fashion: a transparent market is generally considered to be a liquid market, in which low transaction costs occur because of well-informed intermediaries engaging in a competitive environment. In contrast, in the case of banking, we show that transparency is invoked to reinforce the application of risk management. It becomes a tool for organizational reform and a guideline for redirecting business practices. These business practices are in turn crucial in markets where banks and exchanges operate, especially when the markets are new and small, and the organizations important in creating these markets, as was the case in the Baltic states when they became independent. We now turn to the Baltic states, which can be seen as liberalizing experiments of the organizing of financial markets and the value dynamics inherent to these processes.

FINANCIALIZATION, STOCK EXCHANGES AND BANKS IN THE BALTIC STATES

Financialization and Transformation in the Baltic States

Soon after their independence, the Baltic states were financialized, leading to a rapid growth of financial markets and their organizations. The most growth was seen in the financial sectors of Latvia and Estonia, where modernization and privatization policies were implemented, inspired by liberal market economies such as Great Britain. While national differences with regard to institutional complementarities prevail (cf. Hall and Soskice 2001), financial markets are considered to be particularly internationalized: 'All financial systems in advanced capitalist economies have changed substantially over the last two decades, though bank-based systems are typically viewed as having undergone more radical change, many see them as converging in a market-based system' (Deeg 2010: 315).

In the Baltics this trend is particularly obvious and banks played an important role in providing private consumers with household credit. In cooperation with international development organizations, stock exchanges were assigned a macro-economic task of supplying an infrastructure for the privatization of state-owned assets. Strengthening capital markets followed a market-based development model. Being 'rapid liberalizers' (IMF 2005: 9), ambitious policies were implemented and the establishment of a sound banking sector was sought (Mygind 1997: 18ff.). Market-based pension reforms in the three countries were also initiated, in part through fostering the creation of institutional investors needed to efficiently operate capital markets (BOFIT 2002: 22). In short, the Baltic states 'excelled in market radicalism [. . .] Fiscal and monetary institutions, small budgets, currency boards, and independent central banks acquired dominance in mediating the relationships between the international and the Baltic political economies' (Bohle and Greskovits 2007: 462).

During the financial crisis of 2008–2010, the Baltic states experienced a drastic economic slump showing their high degree of dependence on international capital. 'Financialization', defined as an increasing importance of profit generation through financial channels instead of trade and commodity production (Krippner 2005: 174), is one of the phenomena observed in the Baltics in which the rise of a shareholder value ideology and an appreciation of market-oriented means of coordination are particularly pronounced (cf. Epstein 2005; Froud et al. 2006). Before the crisis, financial activities fostered credit-based growth, short-termism and higher levels of risk-taking, driving the marketization of Baltic states (cf. Djelic 2006) and aligning them with mainstream economic thinking diffused by, among others, intellectual advocacy networks such as the Mont Pelerin Society, who actively engage in framing public debates, often via think tanks (cf. Plehwe 2010). Market liberals have hailed the three countries as success stories when looking for best-in-class performers for their ideological arguments (for example Erixon 2010). They recovered surprisingly fast from the crisis and were again applauded by economists. The financial markets were left surprisingly intact; it was the public sector that underwent reform and cut spending in order for the countries to recover from the economic downturn caused by the reliance on foreign credit (Åslund 2010).

Indeed, the Baltics provide interesting insights for the discussion on how market organizers attempt to reconfigure values. Going from the Soviet Union to the European Union in barely more than two decades is a remarkable modernization trajectory, bringing the Baltics in line with dominant liberal world-cultural principles that 'license the nation-state not only as a managing central authority but also as an identity-supplying nation' (Meyer et al. 1997: 160) in which financial market structures feature among the 'basic tenets of nationhood' (ibid.). In fact, the Baltic states can be characterized as being particularly neoliberal, advocating commodification of many societal spheres and promoting market- and price-based coordination. As such, the Baltics were forerunners in flat tax policies and introducing currency boards, pegging their currencies to foreign currency. In the Baltics, substantial foreign direct investment (FDI), including foreign control of banks and exchanges, led to the 'reincarnation of economic liberalism as neoliberalism' that was pursued 'in a rather radical and uncompromising fashion' (Bohle and Greskovits 2007: 445).

Banks and exchanges not only make up the core of national financial markets, they also provide links to international capital. In fact, when they become subsidiaries of foreign financial service providers, as happened with most relevant banks and exchanges in the Baltics throughout the 2000s, these market organizers shape values both as entities that provide capital, and as agents of internationally active corporations, where they serve equity investors, individual corporations and the economy as a whole. The transformation of financial markets exhibits two dynamics in which organizations play a key role. First, the role of these organizations is changing and, as providers of capital and services, they contribute to and drive changes oriented towards financialized capitalism. Second, in the course of opening the region to foreign capital, as they are acquired by international corporations, banks and exchanges in the Baltics are becoming the objects of socio-economic transformations.

Trust in Foreign-Owned Markets: Stock Exchanges in the Baltics

The newly founded stock markets in the Baltics quickly became a relevant infrastructure that enabled and facilitated the economic transformation of these countries. Exchanges were important for the privatization of state-owned businesses, fostering private retirement schemes and facilitating FDI because they allowed for the inflow of foreign capital and became the nucleus of national capital markets. As in other economies in transition, the stock exchanges in the Baltic states became a 'core technology of financial globalization' (Weber et al. 2009: 1319). In the Baltics, national stock exchanges were founded in the early 1990s and commenced trading in 1993 (Lithuania), 1995 (Latvia) and 1996 (Estonia) (BOFIT 2000: 6). By 2004, all of the Baltic stock exchanges had been bought up by foreign investors, eventually all ending up under the umbrella of OMX

Nordic Exchanges, a Stockholm-based international exchange operator. Formally, the Baltic exchanges remained separate entities with regard to legal requirements, but were effectively owned by one organization that operated the three markets.

All three exchanges were founded following the enactment of national legal provisions to establish exchanges, securities depositories and supervisory agencies. However, it soon became apparent that the markets were not big enough to stand alone, and different modes of organizational cooperation were experimented with to increase capital flows and to bring about well-functioning markets. Eventually, a series of takeovers led to all three exchanges being operated by the same financial service provider: NASDAQ OMX.

Sometime before ending up in the hands of foreign owners, the Baltic exchanges had unilaterally introduced international accounting standards as part of the listing requirements for large firms to demonstrate its orientation towards foreign investors. 'In the Baltic countries, the Stock Exchanges have taken the lead in introducing international standards and practices, both in terms of regulation and enforcement' (OECD 2000: 134). In Lithuania, for instance, international engagement was important to instill trust in the financial markets: 'One more reason for this relative lack of development [of financial markets] is that there are still many Lithuanians who do not trust the local financial sector and keep their savings in cash. Stable, foreign-owned banks will presumably take care of this problem in coming years' (BOFIT 2002: 15).

As we will show in the following section, in comparison to banks, exchanges have coped quite successfully with the financial crisis by relying on internationally accepted standards. They have not only managed to steer clear of the distortion suffered by much of the financial industry, but have been able to draw on neoclassical versions of market transparency to bring about high liquidity and deeply integrated markets, allowing for minimal transaction costs. In practice, this meant integrating all markets into one electronically operated Baltic market, essentially creating a single market aiming for economies of scale in running the exchanges. The goal was to make Baltic shares attractive to investors by increasing liquidity, which serves to offer more competitive prices.

Despite powerful images of hectic activity on trading floors, today's exchanges are fundamentally shaped by electronic trading, for which speed of transactions is a central characteristic. Many market participants, such as large investors, base their investment decisions on frequently changing price signals, and usually follow the assumption that prices in some way adequately reflect the value of a share. This puts an emphasis on the transparency of price-setting processes, as prices are assumed to be 'real' only if markets are not experiencing distortion or excessive information asymmetries. Conceptions of price-setting in finance rely heavily on neoclassical assumptions of the functioning of markets.

Today, digitalization and internationalization characterize securities trading and have led to the partial disembedding of trading, as trades are increasingly exercised via computers and take place 24 hours around the globe. This means that trust is shifted from people to machines. 'Algo-trading', where programmed computers trade exclusively with other computers based on sophisticated algorithms, is one of the fastest growing market segments, and derivatives trading has also contributed to changes in the trading business (MacKenzie and Millo 2003). These changes are leading in part to personal relationships being replaced by formalistic, computer-based decision-making procedures based on econometric modelling. At the same time, in order to exercise the function entrusted to them as trading infrastructure (Lee 2010), stock markets remain highly regulated with regard to listing requirements and trading activities that have been harmonized between the Nordic and Baltic exchanges belonging to NASDAQ OMX, to ensure the international flow of capital.

The European level of decision-making is also affecting the organization of Baltic securities markets. The European Commission has proposed revising the Markets in Financial Instruments Directive (MiFID). These proposals consist of different regulatory provisions and aim to make financial markets 'more efficient, resilient and transparent', and to strengthen the protection of investors. The new framework also seeks to increase the supervisory powers of regulators. This is in line with the regulative responses to the financial crisis on the banking side as well (European Commission 2012).

These factors notwithstanding, exchanges have experienced a remarkable degree of organizational change over the last years. In the Baltics they have become part of a globally operating profit-driven financial service provider, and today belong to NASDAQ OMX. Initially, however, they were organized as mutuals, essentially cooperatives run by banks and brokers. At that time, profit-making was not the central goal of these organizations; their focus was on establishing and running a regulated market to serve the local economy. Members of an exchange were predominantly entrusted with a high degree of self-regulation, but also had to be able to absorb potential losses or cover the losses of others. This led to a close-knit social environment in which personal trust was important.

In the Baltics, demutualization of the exchanges took place between 1998 and 2002. A consequence of this was the fragmentation of formal organizations and a shift of resources and power from local market actors to a global stock exchange operator. It was not only the owners of Baltic exchanges that were foreign, however. Interestingly, the largest customers trading on these exchanges were Swedish banks (or their Baltic subsidiaries). In 2010, Swedbank and SEB made up roughly 60 percent of the total value of trade on the three Baltic exchanges.

In sum, Baltic exchanges went from being local monopolies collectively run by a small community, to subsidiaries of large international exchange operators. Since the privatization of much of the productive industry has been carried out, the Baltic exchanges have declined in overall importance but continue to provide a link between globalized financial markets and local actors. By doing so, they evoke and stabilize a particular set of values, which can be linked to a notion of near-perfect neoclassical markets characterized by high liquidity, low transaction costs and clear price signals. The value of transparency is tightly coupled to efficiency, and together they constitute a major ingredient in bringing such an understanding of markets to life. Drawing on this particular notion of a market as a mode of distributing capital helped to distance exchanges from the otherwise crisis-ridden financial markets, and continues to make them icons of neo-liberalism. 'As exchanges became more and more markets for promises, it became essential for them to create an environment where trust prevailed both between those directly participating in the trading process and the buyers and sellers for whom they acted' (Michie 2010: 8). Because of the increase in international capital flows and electronic trading, efficiency and transparency are considered core values if one wants to establish trust in securities markets. Providing price information that is interpreted as meaningful by financial market actors is associated with liquid markets. Stock exchanges illustrate a case of a tight link between efficiency, liquidity and transparency – a link that was not broken by the financial crisis.

Organizing for Transparency: The Bankers' View on the Crisis

A second example that highlights how transparency is becoming a core value for financial markets is the banking sector and its subsequent regulation. In this section, we describe the changing roles of banks, and how business and regulation are perceived by bankers. This provides us with an inside view on the crisis and a sense of the values guiding bankers' behaviour and the structure of the organizations they work in. This perspective is important in order to understand value configurations, both in the market as a whole and within its organizations, and, in particular, how and why transparency is growing in importance and who makes it happen.

Authorities supervise banks to make sure they handle risks in an adequate manner. If banks take large risks for their own winnings at the expense of their customers, this has severe consequences for owners, customers and third parties – and a bank crisis is a threat to the economy as a whole. Although banks are often privately-owned companies, they do provide a public good. That is why there has always been a public interest in supervising and regulating banks to ensure the economy's provision with capital, as well as an interest for banks to be perceived as trustworthy.

Regulations directed towards banks are aimed at addressing one of the central problems of the banking industry, namely, the aim for private profits while providing a public good. Generally, profits are private, but in case of severe economic distortion losses are often socialized, as was seen in many countries during the financial crisis. As states are hesitant to let big banks fail, bail-outs are often preferred over letting larger financial organizations go bankrupt.

At the organizational level, the perspective is somewhat different. In fact, some of the actors interpret the relationship of profit-making and regulation as a game. According to one old banker (former employee of a big Swedish bank), regulators always come up with new rules while banks strive for innovative ways to cope with them, in other words, to avoid or bypass them. A former board member of one of the big Swedish banks similarly explains that the board only talked about risks and regulations in times of crises; generally, the focus is on profit-making, which often means increasing market shares in existing markets or expanding to new markets.

There is broad consensus that the growth of the financial sector and the credit expansion of banks were an important factor in triggering the crisis. Consequently, regulators responded with new capital adequacy rules, requiring banks to keep more capital as a buffer. These new rules can be interpreted as a result of distrust in banks' risk management of the past 20 years. Before deregulation of financial markets in the 1980s, banks had to be very restrictive with credit and avoided high-risk investments. But deregulation led to a reshaping of financial markets, enabling banks to grow and expand.

The agreement between a banker and his/her customer is seldom transparent; it often falls under business confidentiality. The operations of a bank, however – how it takes on risk at an aggregate level – is of societal interest. There is also an inherent conflict between being a bank and being transparent – banking and secrecy have a long tradition. Standards directed at banks, such as the Basel I, II and III capital adequacy rules, are attempts to control the banking sector and to create more transparency. Governing through standards rests on a belief in rationality and in the capability of organizations to be measured in calculated models (Ponte et al. 2012). Swedish banks were heavily engaged in the development of the Baltic markets, not least through FDI in the financial sector. This was often presented as a way to enable the modernization of the countries, and the banks 'educated' customers (and thus also created customers) on how to take on household debt, for instance.

This education contributed to building up a new credit market, but has also led to a housing bubble. In the words of one board member of a Swedish bank: 'It was all about gaining market shares. If we didn't take them, they [other banks] would'. As noted by the same interviewee, one of the problems in the Baltics was that 'old-fashioned banking' was not the focus. Referring to the expansion of the banks' business in the Baltic states, he went on to explain that: 'Rule number one in banking is to know your customer. And that rule was obviously forgotten at some point'. 'Knowing your customer' reflects a trust in people, whereas, once banks start relying on standards, trust can be seen as shifted to systems.

In line with a general trend in society and in the financial sector, banks rely increasingly on standardized models for calculating risk. This also applies to Swedish banks' expansion abroad. The degree of knowledge banks had about the specificities of the countries, however, was relatively low. Rather, they relied on information provided by investment banks and other international agencies. International consultancy firms encouraged cross-border expansion of the banks, which traditionally maintained a national orientation and had little international experience. As a board member of one of the Swedish banks explained (with a sigh), there were always these consultants who came to the board with ideas on how the bank could grow. One tempting path was to enter markets in which there were no major competitors yet, but where the number of potential customers was relatively high, such as in the Baltic states.

To make sense of the crisis, and of the dramatic losses experienced by Swedish banks, bankers highlighted the intra-organizational differences that were traced back to internationalization of the banks. Swedish bankers also made sense of the crisis in terms of a lack of supervision. Peer review was mentioned as one example. The Swedish managers said they realized that their Baltic colleagues did not hold peer review meetings as was common in the Swedish branches. In this context, peer-review meetings were held between bankers who presented their respective deals to each other. This provided a second opinion on whether credit should be granted. This practice was seen as part of the 'Swedish banking culture' at this particular bank, and was perceived as difficult to transfer to another national context. The lack of such a peer-review culture in the new markets was seen as one explanation for why too much credit had been granted. Peer review can be seen as a technique similar to monitoring and reporting, which helps to enhance transparency. Bankers saw peer review as a tool whereby decisions (about credit, for example) become visible to a wider array of people than the single banker. This can be interpreted as a way to work for enhanced transparency and less secrecy.

In addition to not identifying the limits of transferability of risk-rating models, practitioners also failed to recognize the organizational dimension of adequately accounting for risk: 'This [the crisis] has nothing to do with risk; it is all about organization', said one banker. This can be seen as a way to construct the crisis as something exogenous. It is also a way of saying that there is nothing wrong with the systems (for example the risk-rating systems), but that the problem lies elsewhere, in the organization. The trust in systems thus seems to prevail, whereas blame is shifted to internal organizational matters and to a competitive market environment. As another interviewee reflecting upon the crisis explains: 'Then one could claim that we should have moved more slowly in the Baltic states. But I don't agree. Because going slower wouldn't have changed anything; because then Bank A, and especially Bank B, would have granted the exact same credit, and driven the housing bubble just as much [as we did]'.

As a political response to the financial crisis of 2008, a new international regulatory standard has been developed, the Basel III. Basel I and II were regulatory recommendations initialized by the Basel Committee on Banking Supervision, and Basel III is an extension and expansion of the former rules developed as a response to the financial crisis. Basel III is described as 'a comprehensive set of reform measures' aimed at strengthening 'the regulation, supervision and risk management of the banking sector'. The aim of the measures is presented as composed of three parts. The first is to improve the banking sector's ability to absorb shocks arising from financial and economic stress. The second is to improve risk management and governance, and the third is to strengthen banks' transparency and disclosures (Bank for International Settlements 2012).

MARKET ORGANIZATION AND VALUE CONFIGURATION

So far, the chapter has given us a general picture of recent developments in financial markets in a specific context: that of the Baltic states. The overall aim of the chapter has been to illustrate and explain the growing trust in transparency in financial markets. These developments are reflected in, as well as driven by, organizations active in markets such as banks and exchanges. Along the way in our quest to understand the growing trust in transparency, various value configurations in these markets have been revealed. They explain the general developments and in particular the convergence around a general trust in transparency. The time has now come to unpack, highlight and analyse the value configurations that we believe to be central to understanding the development depicted in the empirical story told above. In the following sections, we will develop and explain different processes of value configuration.

Neoliberal Market Reforms: An Overshadowing Value System

Today, the vast majority of states are considered market economies. Globalization, the collapse of the Soviet system, and the increasing mobility of people, goods and ideas are often put forward as central components of the processes of marketization. Regional integration, such as in Europe, has also spurred market-oriented reforms, in particular seeking membership to the EU. It is thus not surprising that the Baltic states were eager to shake off their legacies of the past and integrate with a modern Europe through becoming market economies.

What is remarkable in hindsight, however, is the strong belief in what could be called the 'neoliberal value system' that became the norm of these market economies. The Baltics were particularly eager to opt for market-based coordination to replace pre-existing modes of state-led coordination quickly and thoroughly. We suggest that the development of marketization and the focus on macro-economic stability can be best understood as a successful reconfiguration of values. This reconfiguration was enabled and driven by core organizational actors that put much emphasis on transparency. The rise of transparency is characterized by a shift in trust from people to machines, and by redirecting resources and power from locally embedded actors to globally active firms.

The developments in the financial markets in the Baltic states from the early 1990s up until the crisis of 2008 are due to a major paradigm shift: the transition from planned economy to market economy. This transformation has been depicted as the greatest social experiment in modern times. A key byproduct of this major transformation was the introduction of an overshadowing value system: namely, that of a market economy. This is not something that happens in the abstract; rather, the shadow is enacted and constructed by organizational practices. The entrance of foreign actors, such as banks and stock exchanges, strongly contributes to a value reconfiguration from a planned to a market economy.

As the new states emerged, they quickly focused on institutional change. One of the early steps in this endeavour, taken already in the early 1990s, was the creation of stock exchanges. Exchanges facilitated the introduction of international standards common to market economies. Furthermore, they enabled the privatization of state assets and contributed to marketization of other spheres, such as pensions. Another crucial element in creating the value system of a market economy was the acquisition of foreign capital. Here, foreign banks came to play a crucial role, together with European Union structural funds. With capital, rules and organizations in place, the newly created states began to operate as market economies and could thus start their path towards becoming accepted as members of the European Union. These developments led to the new values overshadowing the pre-existing ones.

Our point here is that, in order to understand the rapid transformation of these new countries in a very specific direction, we posit that the market economy be interpreted as a strong and coherent value system that is enacted largely by the activities of new actors, such as foreign investors and international organizations – although in conjunction with local actors. While the ideas guiding this value system may be abstract, its actual coming into being is largely dependent on organizational activities at the market level. The creation of stock exchanges and the foreign direct investment of banks into what they see as 'new markets' are core to the processes of creating a value system attached to a market economy. The above description of an overshadowing value system can be seen as the background against which different value configurations play out during and after the financial crisis of 2008.

Value Conflicts Highlighted by Crisis

The 2008 financial crisis led to a clash of values that challenged the newly established market-based order. Core ingredients of the former success model, such as private credit, home mortgages, deregulated labour markets and dependence on foreign corporations, were suddenly identified as the causes of a financial bubble that discredited the pre-crisis macro-economic growth model. The clash was most apparent in the case of banking, since the banks were the hardest hit by crisis or, perhaps more correctly, the most active in causing the crisis. The financial crisis led to a collision of values – between profit maximization and being responsible market actors that avoided too much risk. The way to resolve this clash has been a rather technical focus on risk management procedures and stricter capital adequacy standards meant to alter banks' business models and foster reorganization.

The massive influx of foreign private capital in the region was often described as both a prerequisite for and a token of the success of the Baltic states in developing their economies. The underlying reason for commercial banks to enter or conquer these markets was to secure their own growth, and to increase profits and gain market shares in new markets. Often these three aspects are depicted as going hand in hand: growth, profits and market shares. As the interviewees attest to, a bank's main goal – except in times of crisis – is to make profits and gain market shares. A fundamental and classic idea in finance, around which modern portfolio theory is built, is that in order to increase profits one needs to take on higher risk. Or, put the other way around – higher risk-taking is rewarded by greater profits. Profit and risk are thus closely tied. In order to make profit, banks need to take on risk.

Swedish banks considered the Baltic states as 'new markets' to be conquered, and the game of the day was to take as big a 'share' as possible. The values evoked here draw on a basic notion of markets, namely, that of competition. A competition, to be clear, for market shares that led to a neglect of organizational risk management. Rather than seeing themselves as constructors opening up new markets, banks merely saw themselves as competitors in established markets. Swedish banks neglected a sound, long-term strategy in the pursuit of quick and easy success. Quotes such as 'if we hadn't driven the bubble, others would have' illustrate this type of logic. When the bubble bursts, and the crisis becomes a fact, another set of values surfaces – values that emphasize stability, security and risk avoidance (see Table 4.1). These values challenge the over-optimistic growth model and in some respects openly contradict neoliberal value configurations accentuating profit generation, gaining market shares and short-term growth.

Table 4.1   Values in focus before and after financial crisis

Values in focus before crisis	Values in focus after crisis
Growth	Stability
Risk	Risk avoidance
Profit	Security

The severity of the crisis led to an immediate and critical discussion in which the banks themselves engaged as their rescue depended on public finances. The crisis served as a wake-up call that changed the rhetoric of many actors, but the preferred solution to the clash of different values involved rather incremental adjustment. Regulatory tools such as international standards and, in particular, standards for risk-management remain the focus, which in turn leads to the creation of transparency based on calculation of risk. An illustrative example of this is the new Basel III framework, which calls for much more elaborate risk management and more stringent disclosure requirements.

When we look at the responses to the crisis at the organizational level, however, the picture gets more complicated. Bankers discuss other types of value clashes and refer to cultural differences as an explanation for their failure in the Baltic countries. To justify their actions and shift blame, they invoke the image of differences in national and organizational cultures that lead to misunderstandings and miscommunication being ultimately to blame. These differences were cited as important factors in explaining the inability of the banks to foresee and prevent the bubble. Interestingly, this interpretation can be related to the suggestions of regulators regarding to improve post-crisis procedures, namely, to enhance transparency and tighten internal control within the organizations. Whereas regulators focused on the transparency vis-à-vis other actors and the ability of banks to reassure the public that risks will be managed in a better way in the future (for example through higher capital bases), bankers would focus on centralizing the organization and working for a more homogeneous internal culture. The two interpretations of transparency aim at overcoming a very differently diagnosed clash of values.

Escaping, Linking and Balancing as Strategies to Resolve Value Conflicts

So far, we have seen that freedom, modernity and independent statehood – crucial to the emergent national identities in the Baltics – were configured together with values of transparency, efficiency and privatization. The project of becoming a modern democratic state was thus tightly linked to a neoliberal agenda and values that accompany it. These value sets were linked together into new configurations by a broad coalition of actors ranging from the EU to national governments, international investors, and local and foreign banks, as well as consumers and pensioners in the Baltics. This new configuration seemed to benefit a vast majority and therefore became very hard to resist or question. The conditionality of EU membership naturally also played a role: to become members, countries need to be democratic and prove that they adhere to the logic of functioning markets.

An even more important explanatory factor of this specific configuration is the early and strong presence of what is sweepingly called 'market forces' upon the independence of these states. Modernity became coupled with market capitalism through organizations that created, and then also profited from, the financial markets in the Baltic states. It was through the presence and practice of financial organizations such as the banks and stock exchanges analysed in this chapter that it was possible to link values of efficiency, liberalism and private ownership – to each other and to values of democracy and being European. Indeed, modernity was linked through a whole set of neoliberal values by the practices of organizations that were able to embody and combine various value sets.

Through the work of stock exchanges, the values of efficiency, low transaction costs and rational price orientation were tightly coupled. Each value is constructed as highly dependent upon the other. Furthermore, stock exchanges were treated as prime indicators of functioning markets and served as a building block of modern statehood. This meant that organizing financial flows became the core of a political project: building an independent state. Interestingly, the crisis did not cause turmoil in the tightly coupled value sets on which stock exchanges rely. By being constructed as arenas rather than actors, that is, marketplaces rather than market actors, the stock exchanges escaped the accusations levelled at the banks. While banks actively engage in fuelling the bubble by handing out credit, stock exchanges are a seemingly neutral infrastructure that facilitates capital flows. In truth, they turn a good profit via various financial services, ranging from listing and trading, to data management. The technological systems on which exchanges rely are essential not only in creating an image of efficiency and transparency, but also in focussing on being an arena rather than an actor, which leads to a vast underrating of their impact on processes of economic and institutional change.

The foreign direct investments in the banking sector used to be put forward as stellar examples of the successful integration of the new economic region around the Baltic Sea. When the crisis hit, however, the role of the banks was put under scrutiny and their role in driving the credit bubble was compared to a similar event in Sweden in the early 1990s. Banks were identified as responsible for the bubble, and greedy bankers depicted as the core of the problem. The banks' response was to balance conflicting values such as growth and stability by means of risk management and transparency. In fact, they turned to transparency and increasingly drew on it as an overarching value that appears to signal change but is consistent with both a neoliberal ideational framework and with what were presented as solutions to the crisis. Exchanges managed to escape value conflicts by successfully referring to abstract neoliberal values, linking price mechanisms and efficiency to its operations, and maintaining the image of being an arena or part of the infrastructure. Rather than highlighting their own actorhood, they depicted themselves as a marketplace that needs to be transparent for other actors to be able to work properly. Banks, on the other hand, were unable to escape, but rather were forced to find a way to balance conflicting values, which they tried to do by combining risk management and transparency.

Conclusion

The transformation of the Baltic states can be interpreted as a value reconfiguration at multiple levels. First, the primary reform is that of abandoning the planned economy and creating a market economy. This initial process can be termed 'overshadowing', where the old system was covered on the surface and did not simply disappear. A second important process is that of reconfiguring values in sets. The successful interlinking of the values of efficiency and transparency, and profit-making and risk, are examples. In these processes, organizational activities such as reintroducing risk management in banks are particularly relevant. More generally, values are brought together and become enacted, thereby becoming part of a taken-for-granted social reality. Finally, processes of clashing values and resolving the clashes can also be identified at the organizational level. These clashes might even reinforce different value configurations, but can also be used as a way to explain and make sense of a crisis situation. The rise of transparency is particularly relevant in this context. As a value, transparency's high degree of abstraction allows it to become more than a 'travelling keyword'. It is interlinked with other values and used as a solution to various types of value clashes. Its attraction lies in the ambiguity inherent to transparency, a seemingly neutral and objective value that is difficult to argue against. This makes it possible for various actors to use transparency to legitimize their actions in very different struggles over value configurations.

REFERENCES

Åslund, Anders (2010). *The Last Shall Be the First: The East European financial crisis*. Peterson Institute for International Economics.

Bank for International Settlements (2012). International regulatory framework for banks, retrieved 17 January 2013 from http://www.bis.org/bcbs/basel3.htm?ql=1.

BOFIT (2000). Baltic Securities Markets. Bank of Finland Institute for Economies in Transition, Working Paper No. 5. Prepared by Iikka Korhonen, Toivo Kuus and Villu Zirnask. Helsinki.

BOFIT (2002). Banking and Finance in the Baltic Countries. Bank of Finland Institute for Economies in Transition, Working Paper No. 11. Prepared by Tuuli Koivu. Helsinki.

Bohle, Dorothee and Béla Greskovits (2007). Neoliberalism, embedded neoliberalism, and neocorporatism: Paths towards transnational capitalism in Central-Eastern Europe. *West European Politics*, 30 (3), 443–466.

Deeg, Richard (2010). Institutional change in financial systems. In Morgan, Glenn et al. (eds), *Oxford Handbook of Comparative Institutional Analysis*. Oxford: Oxford University Press.

Djelic, Marie-Laure (2006). Marketization: From intellectual agenda to global policy-making. In Marie-Laure Djelic and Kerstin Sahlin-Andersson (eds), *Transnational Governance*. Cambridge: Cambridge University Press, pp. 53–73.

Epstein, Gerald A. (2005). *Financialization and the World Economy*. Cheltenham, UK and Northampton, MA, USA: Edward Elgar.

Erixon, Fredrik (2010). Baltic Economic Reforms: Crisis Review of Baltic Economic Policy. ECIPE Working Paper 04/2010. Brussels.

European Commission (2012). New rules for more efficient, resilient and transparent financial markets in Europe. Available at: http://europa.eu/rapid/press-release_IP-11-1219_en.htm?locale=en, accessed 7 January 2012.

Froud, Julie, Johal Sukhdev, Adam Leaver and Karel Williams (2006). *Financialization and Strategy: Narrative and numbers*. London: Routledge.

Garsten, Christina and Monica Lindh de Montoya (2008). *Transparency in a New Global Order*. Cheltenham, UK and Northampton, MA, USA: Edward Elgar.

Hall, Peter A. and David Soskice (2001). *Varieties of Capitalism. The institutional foundations of comparative advantage*. Oxford: Oxford University Press.

IMF (2005). Capital Account Liberalization, Capital Flow Patterns, and Policy Responses in the EU's New Member States. IMF Working Paper WP/05/213. Prepared by Zsófia Árvai. Washington, DC: IMF.

Jang, Yong Suk (2006). Transparent accounting as a world societal rule. In Gili S. Drori, John W. Meyer and Hokyu Hwang (eds), *Globalization and Organization: World society and organizational change*. Oxford: Oxford University Press, pp. 167-195.

Krippner, Greta R. (2005). The financialization of the American economy. *Socio-Economic Review*, 3 (2), 173–208.

Lee, Ruben (2010). *The Governance of Financial Market Infrastructure. Report.* Oxford: Oxford Finance Group.

MacKenzie, David and Yuval Millo (2003). An equation and its worlds: Bricolage, exemplars, disunity and performativity in financial economics. *Social Studies of Science*, 33 (6), 831–868.

Meyer, John W., John Boli, George M. Thomas and Francisco O. Ramirez (1997). World Society and the Nation-State. *The American Journal of Sociology*, 103 (1), 144–181.

Michie, Ranald (2010). Exchanges in historical and global context. In Larry Harris (ed.), *Regulated Exchanges. Dynamic Agents of Economic Growth*. Oxford: Oxford University Press, pp. 3–69.

Mygind, Niels (1997). Different paths of transition in the Baltics. In Borge Dahl and Rei Shiratori (eds), *Law, Economics and Business in the Melting Pot: The case of regional development and cooperation in the Baltic States*. Tokai University European Center/CBS, pp. 1–39.

OECD (2000). *Economic Survey 1999–2000. The Baltic States: a Regional Assessment*. Paris: OECD.

Plehwe, Dieter (2010). The making of a comprehensive transnational discourse community. In Marie-Laure Djelic and Sigrid Quack (eds), *Transnational Communities: Shaping global economic governance*. Cambridge: Cambridge University Press, pp. 305–326.

Ponte, Stefano, Peter Gibbon and Jakob Vestergaard (2012). *Governing Through Standards: Origins, drivers and limitations*. Basingstoke: Palgrave Macmillan.

Porter, Theodore M. (1997). *Trust in Numbers: The pursuit of objectivity in science and public life*. Princeton: Princeton University Press.

Power, Michael (2010). Fair value accounting, financial economics and the transformation of reliability. *Accounting and Business Research, International Accounting Policy Forum*, 40 (3), 197–210.

Weber, Klaus, Gerald Davis and Michael Lounsbury (2009). Policy as myth and ceremony? The global spread of stock exchanges, 1980–2005. *Academy of Management Journal*, 52 (6), 1319–1347.

5. Value-neutralizing in verification markets: organizing for independence through accreditation

Kristina Tamm Hallström and Ingrid Gustafsson

PROLIFERATING VERIFICATION MARKETS

> Throughout the ongoing bargaining process, we [the Swedish Building Workers' Union] will promote the requirement of introducing occupational health and safety certification of all workplaces. . . . We demand occupational health and safety certification as an important part of the efforts to create a better working environment, something we all gain from and which saves lives. More consideration in the workplace is needed. (*Dagens Nyheter*, 7 November 2011, p. 6)

The above citation is taken from a newspaper article in which two union representatives propose occupational health and safety certification as a formal requirement for construction companies, as an entry barrier to the Swedish construction market. The problem behind the proposed measures, according to the authors, is insufficient consideration by construction firms of safety and work environment values in their business activities. Although this statement seems local in context, it is illustrative of the current global trend of ensuring certain values, such as safety and the work environment, through the act of commercial verification. In this chapter, we examine these expanding markets for verification.

As noted by Power (1997; see also Lindeberg 2007), during the past decades, there has been a reworking of inspection institutions, entailing a shift from inspection as a governmental function to a greater emphasis on systems of self-inspection, often by way of standards and certification routines (Bernstein and Cashore 2007; Bartley 2010, 2011). In line with this trend we see a change in the institutional forms of verification bodies – from state inspection organizations tasked with guaranteeing values such as occupational health and product safety, to commercial verification companies auditing these same values (cf. Mennicken 2010). This evolution is symptomatic of the general trend for governments to take a precautionary approach – to liberalize, to deregulate, to privatize markets, to delegate numerous responsibilities to the private sector, and to otherwise use market approaches, structures and incentives to meet their regulatory goals (see Aman 1999, referred to in Haufler 2001, pp. 1, 21). In short, the deregulation of former state inspection services has created new markets for verification services. As the quote in the introduction illustrates, verification organized in accordance with market logic, with private firms selling verification services, seems to have become taken for granted as the rational solution to societal problems linked to, for example, occupational health and workplace safety. Support comes from state agencies, consumer organizations, trade unions and companies seeking verification, as well as the verification companies themselves – all of whom are in favour of the basic organization of verification as a commercial practice.

Elevators, motor vehicles, food, technical devices and bicycle helmets are other examples of goods and equipment targeted by commercial verification due to safety issues. The implications of unsafe products are massive. An unsafe product may cause harm to individual consumers, such as an injury due to a faulty helmet, leading to societal problems in terms of health and medical care. The idea that products themselves, or the process through which they are produced, need to be verified by an external party as a measure to protect the value of safety, has grown strong. This type of verification is often referred to as 'third party certification', that is third party in relation to the verified objects (first party) and the buyer of such objects (second party).

The markets we are interested in are those dealing with 'verification services', which is the term used in the chapter to refer to inspection and certification jointly. Verification is an act of control – an audit – conducted by an external party, using a standard as the point of reference. The result of a successful verification audit is an approval that the product or organization subject to verification meets the criteria of the applicable standard. Standards used for verification can promote not only safety, as illustrated in the introductory example, but also a variety of values, such as quality, fair trade and sustainability. The values promoted through standards are typically not financial values connected to profit maximization, but are values cherished specifically by others. Trade unions, environmental organizations, human rights organizations and intergovernmental organizations are examples of organizations that take a great interest in promoting and supervising businesses' attention to values other than economic ones.

We may thus conclude that verification is a complex service that cannot be provided with just profitability in mind, not if the verifiers want to be seen as trustworthy value verifiers. In the case of misconduct during the provision of verification services – for example, if a company is approved despite non-compliance with the requirements of a standard and the company later causes harm due to its failure to consider the values promoted by the standard – the verification auditor responsible may receive serious criticism. This in turn means that we could expect markets for verification to be value-laden.

We are intrigued by the fact that the two verification markets examined and discussed in this chapter seem to function and grow fairly smoothly, without much discussion or critical debate about the values embodied in verification standards or by the way these values are set out to be guaranteed. However, there is one value specifically emphasized in these markets and that is the procedural value of independence, meaning a focus on what the verifiers do rather than what values the verification act seeks to protect. Critical auditing research has taken an interest in how auditors face the delicate challenge of maintaining professional conduct, including expectations of independent and objective auditing, at the same time as being commercially dependent on the customer (Sikka and Willmott 1995; Jeppeson 1998; Pentland 2000; Power 2003; Sikka 2009). One negative consequence of too close a relationship between auditor and auditee may be the tendency to accord rather than reject verification (Power 1997). Hence, there is a balance between commercial interests and the necessity to appear trustworthy. Scandals regarding the misconduct of auditors, who do not maintain the necessary professional independence and expertise, indeed surface in the media on a regular basis (Wallerstedt 2009). Despite such scandals, however, the overall idea of commercial auditing and verification as something valuable is sustained.

One explanation could be the high degree of professionalization observed in the field of financial auditing and the disciplinary measures undertaken by the auditing profession as a response to such scandals (Sikka and Willmott 1995; Sikka 2009). It is argued that the fact that the providers of these services are professionals neutralizes the business relationship and the balance between commercial dependence and the independence of the act of auditing (Sikka 2009). In the terminology of this volume, we would say that the professionalization of auditors has considerable impact on the value configuration at hand in verification markets, and more specifically that a downplay or neutralization of commercial values takes place through the emphasis on the value of independence, that is, through the emphasis on the procedural aspects of the auditor's work.

In this chapter we take a closer look at two verification markets, where we find similar patterns regarding the importance of, and emphasis on, the value of independence. These markets also share similarities in terms of their rapid proliferation despite regular occurrences of verification scandals, such as greenwashing scandals due to the failure of verification suppliers to detect misconduct in the companies being verified (Elad 2001; Bartley 2011). We are, however, puzzled by the low level of professionalization of auditors in these markets, which is the main promoter of the value of independence in more traditional auditing markets. Thus, our overall question reads: *How can we explain the configuration of commercial and independence values at hand in verification markets?*

To provide an answer to this question, we need to examine more thoroughly the organization of the two verification markets analysed in this chapter and the actors involved in promoting the value of independence. In the final section, we draw conclusions about the organization of independence in verification markets.

METHODOLOGY

The two markets examined are the Swedish market for motor vehicle inspection (Case 1), which was deregulated in 2010 after decades of controversy and political debate, and the Swedish market for management system certification (Case 2), a market that has grown considerably since the 1990s in many countries. An advantage of the first case is the good access to empirical material: the controversies and recent deregulation of this market mean that it has been thoroughly debated, in public investigations and in the media. The second case, a mature market, brings the advantage of a long history, enabling us to follow the market over time. The differing backgrounds of these markets, one formerly state-driven and the other originally private, as well as differences regarding the underlying values targeted by various verification standards, also means that we can expect variations with respect to the organizing strategies of self-regulation and state involvement. The aim of analysing the two markets in one study is not necessarily to explain such differences, neither is it comparative, but rather to use the material from the two studies to identify value-configuring activities that may help to explain the specific organization of these proliferating markets.

The case study of the motor vehicle inspection market is based on documents relating to formal legislation such as the government bill (Proposition 2009/10:32) that constitutes the main political decision regarding this market, and legislative documents on inspector certification criteria issued by the Swedish Transport Agency (Transportstyrelsen), a public authority. In 2011, three interviews were conducted with representatives from the two inspection companies in the market at that time: Svensk Bilprovning (interview with the communications manager) and Carspect (interviews with the CEO and the technical manager). The questions posed concerned work related to the accreditation process such as: what the companies believed to be important to emphasize in their work, and the potential risks in marketization of a former state-run inspection service. Data for the study was also gathered from websites, including: Transportstyrelsen, Swedac, Carspect and Svensk Bilprovning. A media search for articles concerning the deregulation/market creation was also conducted to augment the material with different opinions on the topic.

The analysis of the second case builds on a study of the management system certification market in Sweden and four client organizations that comply with the ISO 9001 standard for quality assurance, ISO 14001 for environmental management, and/or two forest management standards issued by the Forest Stewardship Council (FSC) and the Programme for the Endorsement of Forest Certification (PEFC). A total of 16 interviews were conducted. Nine interviews were with auditors performing management system certification, one with two officials working at FSC Sweden, and the remainder with representatives of client organizations. Four days of participant observation were also conducted to observe certification auditing processes at client premises. In addition, document studies, of standards, critical reports posted on websites, and formal complaints regarding non-compliance, for example, were carried out. Finally, it should be mentioned that both case studies are part of a larger research project on the organization and legitimacy of labelling, certification and accreditation.

In the subsequent section, we discuss the similarities and differences observed in the two cases in terms of strategies used by the market actors themselves and the level of state involvement, in regards to the organization of the value of independence in the two markets.

ORGANIZING VERIFICATION MARKETS IN PRACTICE

Case 1. The Motor Vehicle Inspection Market

Inspection of motor vehicles is compulsory in Sweden. Since 1965, motor vehicle inspection has been a public policy tool to ensure road safety. A high number of traffic accidents, caused by unsafe cars, resulted in a decision by government to create a uniform, compulsory inspection of vehicles, with the intention of reducing the number of road accidents and increasing people's traffic safety awareness (Svensk Bilprovning interview, 12 May 2011, www.bilprovningen.se accessed 13 May 2011). In other words, road safety is the overall value at stake in terms of what is verified and guaranteed in this specific market. Until July 2010, inspections were carried out by Svensk Bilprovning (SB), a state-run monopoly. SB was the last of seven state-run testing sites to be deregulated during the period 1990–2010. The debate about this deregulation had been simmering for almost two decades, fuelled over the years by various proposals, investigations and consultancy reports, though never really reaching top billing in the news media. The arguments for privatization have cited potential efficiency gains and better service quality, based on the idea that the creation of a market (by privatizing) would lead to a growth in the number of inspection bodies and competition, which in turn would lead to better service, longer opening hours and shorter wait times for inspection. The arguments against deregulation have concerned the commercialization of the act of inspection – putting profit first and safety second.

The new, commercially driven inspection sites that have opened following privatization emphasize a more customer-oriented service, as hoped for in the political proposals. For example, inspection sites are conveniently situated in city centres, rather than in industrial areas outside of town. In one case the site is in a shopping mall, providing coffee, newspapers and magazines. Moreover, the inspection service has become more 'interactive': the customer can view the entire process through a window from a lounge and, according to the CEO of one of the new inspection companies, the consumer is the focus of attention and the company's internal mantra (Carspect interview, 12 May 2011). This CEO emphasizes the need to simplify the inspection process in order to communicate with customers in a better way, and to show that the vehicle inspection is a service-minded business, not a state inspection:

> [The former inspection sites during the monopoly era] were not customer-friendly; there was nowhere to go as a customer ... When we build our inspections sites, we build them as we would like them. There should be a nice atmosphere in the customer lounge; you should be able to choose whether or not you would like to be present during the inspection procedure or whether you would like to sit down and have a nice cup of coffee and read a magazine; there should be big windows out to the inspection hall; there should be pictures showing who we are, what we want, and what we want to give to you as a customer. We have had some very nice feedback from customers saying: 'It doesn't look at all like an inspection site!' (Carspect interview, 12 May 2011)

The former monopoly actor SB has adapted to the new commercial conditions as well. With 52 percent (as of 2011) of the shares owned by the

Swedish state and the rest by NGOs (www.bilprovningen.se, accessed 14 January 2011), the company still dominates the market of local inspection sites. Moreover, the company possesses competent human resources, making it hard for new actors to enter the market (as highlighted in the media, for example *Dagens Nyheter*, 18 September 2010). But rather than marketing themselves as a service-minded alternative, SB needs to emphasize that they are, in fact, not a public authority, contrary to what most people believe:

> We try to emphasize that we are just another company in this market [referring to people demanding an immediate appointment for inspection, thinking that SB is a public authority with certain obligations]. But to be honest, we no longer have that obligation; it is a deregulated market. Of course, we try to accommodate them anyway, since it is in our blood. We try to live up to our former civic mission, but that's not actually our responsibility anymore. (Svensk Bilprovning interview, 12 May 2011)

The company is also launching a new service called Car Diagnosis, where a more in-depth inspection is provided. It is part of the shaping of a new image, 'the company who knows cars', an image of a company that does more than just inspection, also providing additional services to car owners and car buyers (Svensk Bilprovning interview, 12 May 2011). The company develops a more aggressive strategy towards customers and potential customers through identification of additional, non-inspection services.

A car inspection that focuses on the consumer – an urban, service-minded provider next door to your local grocery store – is fundamentally different from the vehicle inspection in an industrial area on the outskirts of town. However, an inspection carried out in a secluded industrial area with no coffee, newspaper or extra consultancy services has one advantage: it appears trustworthy, stable and credible, 'putting safety first' and hence not primarily driven by commercial interests. As the public debate about a deregulated inspection service with commercial companies in a market proceeded, the concern of assuring the independence of inspection companies grew. In other words, when the value of road safety was put at stake by commercialization of the verification act, the procedural value of independence of the verification actors was stressed in the debate and the reform documents. The dilemma of how a commercially run inspection services could guarantee impartial, independent and trustworthy testing activities became apparent. There were concerns about substandard inspections caused by the dominating financial interests of the inspection firms, which in turn might harm the credibility of the market reform as such. This concern was explicitly expressed by one interviewee:

[On balancing the commercial aspects of inspection]: These are things that may threaten the business of the entire market . . . that is why impartiality is so important. We have affirmed it many times; it is a precondition for this business working . . . The whole idea of traffic safety is lost if there is any hint of us saying: 'Come to us. This is where you pass your car the easiest'. The entire point of doing vehicle inspections is lost; the point of ensuring security and a traffic-safe car. It is a precondition for the entire market that this [impartiality] works; otherwise the market is dead'. (Svensk Bilprovning interview, 12 May 2011)

The deregulation of vehicle inspections puts the credibility of the inspection system at risk: an inspection function that enjoys the credibility of a state authority is being replaced by a system based on market logic. One measure taken to preserve the idea of an independent yet commercial inspection is to prohibit the provision of certain services, such as the fabrication, import, repairs, rentals or trading of vehicles or vehicle parts (Proposition 2009/10:32). Neither should the inspection body have any commercial or financial relations with companies that carry out such services. A third measure undertaken when deregulating the vehicle inspection sector, was to keep state supervision but organized somewhat differently:

It is essential that the quality and trust of vehicle inspectors is guaranteed in a deregulated market . . . since the demands on vehicle inspection must be high with respect to quality and trust, and since inspection is an exercise of public authority. Businesses must be supervised by the state. (Proposition 2009/10:32)

In interviews with the two inspection companies, one specific measure used to establish credibility and trust is emphasized: it is through the accreditation conducted by the Swedish Board for Accreditation and Conformity Assessment (Swedac), a government authority. Through accreditation, market actors prove their ability to balance operating a commercial and service-minded business with providing an independent inspection. Hence, accreditation is a mode of ensuring the procedural value of independent verifications, thereby guaranteeing safe and secure cars as an 'outcome' of such independent verification acts. Regulation of the independence of inspection bodies relies heavily on the international accreditation standard, ISO 17020. ISO 17020 covers three levels of independence: A, B and C, where type A contains the highest requirements for impartial inspection. The proposed legislative wording concerning independence in the government bill (Proposition 2009/10:32) corresponds to level A in the ISO 17020.

Accreditation is compulsory for inspection firms, just as regular inspection of vehicles is compulsory for vehicle owners. Both companies that were interviewed stated that the accreditation process is rigorous. The CEO of the new firm, Carspect, says that there is no need for additional measurements or controls beyond the regulations of the accreditation standard, as the accreditation itself is thorough enough. SB, on the other hand, has developed its own audit system to internally supervise and monitor their inspectors as an added measure to ensure independence. The interviewee from SB lists a number of things included in this internal supervision, such as internal samples, a crisis management group and managers constantly keeping their eyes open (Svensk Bilprovning interview, 12 May 2011). Both companies refer to a zero tolerance regarding bribes, as this could hurt the independence of inspectors (there are, however, a couple of police reports on this matter each year).

From being organized as only one inspection actor (the former monopoly SB), the new market faces a system of accreditation that involves a threefold order of verification. Firstly, every company entering the market needs accreditation that, in practice, is similar to a management system type of control that we discuss in Case 2, that is control of the company's routines and organizational resources. Secondly, if there are several units in the company, the parent organization as well as all of the company's local inspection sites must be accredited. Thirdly, an additional verification is required, since every individual inspection technician must be certified by an accredited certifier (as stipulated in the legislation from Transportstyrelsen, TSFS 2010:90). During the monopoly era, SB had in-house training for their technicians. Following deregulation, however, an inspection firm is not permitted to train and certify its own employees, as this is considered a threat to the independence of both the inspectors and the inspection company. Consequently, SB had to sell its school for inspectors and the school is now accredited to certify inspectors.

To sum up, we see a value (road safety) formerly protected through state inspection. The value of road safety was considered to be put at stake through the commercialization following a market reform. With the value of road safety 'threatened', it becomes important to ensure the procedural value of independence, which is done through mandatory state supervision – the accreditation process. The guaranteeing of independence through accreditation makes deregulation more of a 're-regulation', as the organization of the inspection market is now denser and more complex than prior to the reform. Here, accreditation thus neutralizes the commercialization of vehicle inspections.

Our second case, that of the management system certification market, now follows and illustrates a market with a different background.

Management system certification has been practiced as a commercial activity for several decades, and many of the firms active in the field have a long history. However, as will be shown below, the two markets also share several characteristics, regarding both the threat of lacking legitimacy that companies face in their role as a commercial business acting as a third, independent party, and how they attempt to handle the threat of failing trust.

Case 2. The Management System Certification Market

As noted in the introduction, the use of management system standards has been steadily growing as a regulatory mechanism since the 1990s, and the number of values addressed in such standards is also increasing. ISO 9001 (quality assurance), ISO 14001 (environmental management), OHSAS 18001 (occupational health and safety), FSC (sustainable forestry), SA 8000 (sustainable work conditions), ISO 26000 (social responsibility) and ISO 27000 (information security) are all examples of management system certification standards used (with the respective values they address in parentheses).

A management system builds on the establishment of a carefully thought-through structure for an organization, including appropriate departments, positions, processes and routines for the organization's daily activities. Various values may thus be emphasized in the management system, but the management standard itself does not usually state fixed goals, or levels (like performance levels measuring quality, sick leave, and so on), or the procedures and routines used to engage in the values emphasized in the standard. Rather, the idea is that an organization should determine and document its own goals with respect to certain values and the organizational methods to reach those goals, and clarify how to achieve continuous improvement of its daily activities. The standard provides a number of indicators that guide the organization (and the auditor verifying compliance) in establishing and documenting a management system that includes all relevant parts. ISO's management system standards typically follow this logic. The Forest Stewardship Council (FSC) standard for sustainable forestry differs somewhat, as it also includes a number of absolute levels and requirements regarding the content of forest management (including the obligation to set aside a certain percentage of the forest to be protected, for example). Still, a fundamental idea of all management system standards is that organizations should establish appropriate structures and routines, thereby demonstrating that they are giving the applicable values proper consideration.

In 2011, the market for firms providing certification audits of management system standards consisted of about ten companies in Sweden, some of which were large multinationals active in several countries accredited to certify a broad array of standards and that possessed certification expertise for several types of businesses. There are also a few smaller companies whose business activities are limited to the national, or even local level, and to a smaller number of standards and businesses. The typical legal organizational form for certification firms is the publicly listed company. However, this was not the typical form 100 years or more ago when some of these companies were founded, in particular those in the maritime sector. One example is Lloyd's Register, founded in 1760 as an independent organization with no institutional or private shareholders seeking profits, which strengthens its independent status (cf. Brunsson 1991). Founded in 1864, Det Norske Veritas (DNV) is another example of an independent foundation that started in the maritime sector with classification of vessels, but over the years has broadened its scope to include other industries. Today, the certification services offered in Sweden for management systems are provided through one of DNV's profit-making subsidiaries, the listed company DNV Certification AB, but the status (of the DNV parent organization) as a foundation carries a positive connotation in customer relations:

> The fact that we are a foundation means that we have no shareholders taking money out of the organization every year, but the money stays with the organization for research and development. R&D is quite important to us, not in the Swedish part of our activities but elsewhere. . . We have emphasized that we are a foundation, as it supports our independence. We live off of our independence. (Interview with auditor from DNV, March 2010)

Yet another type of organizational background is found in the listed company Intertek Certification AB, founded in 1993. A few years later, Intertek bought the company Semko, previously a state-owned inspection agency (Svenska Elektriska Materielkontrollanstalten), known to the public for its 'S' safety label (S-märkning). Semko was privatized in the late 1990s during the inspection site deregulation trend in Sweden described earlier, and was later integrated into the Intertek Group. Intertek Certification AB changed its name to Intertek Semko Certification AB and thus added the name Semko, probably because it enjoyed a high symbolic value, as one interviewee explains:

> Semko was the trademark known to the Swedish public really [compared to Intertek]. Semko was something Swedish, standing for security, safety, the S-label. (Interview with former auditor of Intertek Semko Certification AB, March 2010)

Unlike the market for motor vehicle inspection, there is no general requirement for firms conducting management system certification to be accredited for the certification standards used. However, most certification companies choose to become accredited and membership in the Swedish Association for Testing, Inspection and Certification (Swetic) is restricted to accredited firms only. Accreditation has thus become an informal requirement in the management system certification market – as a method to be seen as trustworthy and to obtain a good reputation:

> You could start a certification activity tomorrow and tell customers: I can audit your ISO 9001 management system and give you a nice certificate. But then there is no quality assurance of your work. And you're not allowed to join the national association for certification bodies, Swetic, if you're not accredited. Customers ask about this quite often – they want a firm that is accredited, in order to obtain a guarantee of the quality. Otherwise you could do the audit yourself really, or get your neighbour to do it. (Interview with auditor from an accredited certification firm, March 2010)

A similarity with the accreditation practice in the motor vehicle inspection market, is the accreditation conducted by the state-owned agency, Swedac, of firms in the management system certification market. The purpose of the ISO 17021 standard that Swedac uses to accredit firms that audit and certify management systems is formulated such that it states the value of independence (impartiality) as one of the central motives:

> Observance of [the] requirements [stated in this standard] is intended to ensure that certification bodies operate management system certification in a competent, consistent and impartial manner, thereby facilitating the recognition of such bodies and the acceptance of their certifications on a national and international basis. (ISO/IEC 17021:2011: vi)

In one segment of the management system certification market, it is in fact mandatory for certification firms to be accredited and this applies to firms conducting certification based on sustainability standards, such as the ones developed by the FSC and MSC (Marine Stewardship Council). Another difference between these firms and firms conducting ISO management system certification has to do with the body responsible for accreditation in the sustainability field: Accreditation Services International (ASI), which is an independent international accreditation body. ASI's vision is to be the first-choice independent accreditation body for firms operating natural resources, environment and social responsibility certification schemes, and ASI accreditation activities are based on four core values: professionalism, accountability, credibility, and effectiveness and efficiency. Through the use of concepts like professionalism, we see that the issue of independence is crucial here, as in other verification contexts. For example, in ASI's Quality Manual under the heading 'Conflicts of Interest', ASI clarifies that 'ASI takes conflict of interest seriously, and does not allow its personnel to perform professional activities where an actual or potential conflict of interest exists' (ASI 2009: 8). Unlike the dominant state-owned accreditation agency, Swedac, ASI is a for-profit limited liability company (GmbH) registered according to German law, which in turn is owned by the multi-stakeholder standard setter FSC, an authoritative standard setter in responsible forest management (Tamm Hallström and Boström 2010).

One organizational activity that we have observed in both accredited and non-accredited certification firms is the establishment of a certification committee, or, as stated in the accreditation standard used for firms conducting ISO management system certification, a 'committee for safeguarding impartiality' (ISO/IEC 17021:2011), thus an organizational aspect to assure independence. This is a group that includes external experts affiliated to the organization and representing various interests so that no single interest is predominant. The committee is described by certification firms as a way to manage risk and build trust, but the establishment of such a committee is also one of the formal requirements of the accreditation standard (ISO 17021:2011) used by Swedac. ISO 17021 also lists the tasks of such a committee, which include: assisting in the development of policies on impartiality, counteracting tendencies of commercial considerations that may affect the objectivity of certification activities, providing advice on matters that affect confidence in certification, and conducting annual reviews of certification activities (p. 7).

Moreover, the length of a contract between a specific certifier and a customer organization is of importance and a matter that is regulated in the accreditation standard: a certifier should not conduct certifications of the same customer practice for too long, as a long-standing business relationship may lead to social bonds and friendship between certifier and certified, which in turn may jeopardize the critical perspective – independence – of the certifier.

Yet another crucial dimension of certification is consulting and training, a similarity shared by the motor vehicle inspection market. According to ISO 17021, a certifier may not provide consulting services or training to the customer organization being certified, as such services may jeopardize independence. Thus, related management consulting and training services that certifiers could offer to client organizations before a certification could put independence and impartiality at risk. A certifier cannot assist a client organization in the creation and implementation of a management system, for example, and thereafter be neutral in the certification of its quality. At the same time, there are drivers pushing for consulting services: client organizations often want the certifier to provide advice in addition to just a plain conformity assessment, and consultancy services are good business for certification firms. In order to avoid scandals and mistrust (and loss of accreditation), some certification firms do not offer consultancy services at all, whereas others provide such services through a separate (decoupled) organization or unit and separate staff (cf. Meyer and Rowan 1977). Some of the certifiers interviewed for this study talk about a grey zone in which some kind of consultation, guidance, suggestions and training may take place without risking independence. When it comes to training, one solution is to provide training on general issues (for example *What is a management system? How can it be implemented?* and so on), but not on issues specific to an individual client. Another solution is to offer training to several clients at the same time (for example via a workshop or open course).

We now turn to our analysis of the organization of the two verification markets described to clarify mechanisms contributing to their legitimacy and proliferation, and in particular the promotion of independence as a crucial value.

ESTABLISHING LEGITIMACY IN VERIFICATION MARKETS

Markets in Quest of Authority – Accreditation as Meta-Auditing

As noted in the introduction, the tendency to deregulate former state-held obligations combined with the growing tendency to rely on international standards has created markets for verification services that did not exist to the current extent a decade ago. Thus, the deregulation of former state-run inspections is an answer to various institutional demands for more market and less state (although the reform also illustrates how attempts to deregulate can in practice lead to re-regulation).

Although the ideological conditions favour market-based solutions such as commercial verification, crucial values involved in verification activities have to an increasing extent been considered too fundamental for the market to handle alone, giving rise to a structure of meta-auditing. Based on our studies, we argue that the most prominent effort to organize these markets relate to accreditation, that is, certification of certifying companies and inspection of inspection companies (see Shapiro 1987). In Sweden, Swedac was assigned the task of accreditation. From an organizational standpoint, the strategy of creating an impartial, independent and autonomous meta-auditing body conducted by a separate public authority (in this case Swedac) combines the institution of the market and the institution of the hierarchical state.

In some markets (Case 1), accreditation is compulsory and thus functions as a market entry gatekeeper. In other markets (Case 2), accreditation is mostly voluntary and the strategies used to obtain credibility are left more to the market actors. The phenomenon of meta-auditing could also be regarded as a result of a 'quest for authority'. In the first case, the market is not considered sufficient to guarantee the values at stake, and mandatory accreditation represents a state presence in the market: a state authority. In the second case, accreditation is voluntary, or rather quasi-mandatory, and in most cases is conducted by the state (Swedac). However, in the field of sustainability, we see the NGO-owned ASI accreditation body performing this task, meaning that accreditation is backed by moral authority (cf. Hall and Biersteker 2002).

The purpose of an accreditation procedure is to guarantee the value of impartial and independent verification carried out by profit-making companies. In other words, accreditation is a strategy used to ensure credibility and trust in a fragile system of verification activities. As elaborated on below, accreditation neutralizes the tension between the independence of verification businesses and their commercial dependence on their clients. Moreover, the meta-auditing accreditation constitutes a form that ensures the hierarchical status of the government in a world characterized by network-like governance and governing at a distance. Whether conducted by the state or by NGOs, and whether mandatory or voluntary, we may conclude that there is a growing need for authority in the organizing to ensure credibility in these markets.

Value-Neutralization in Verification Markets

The standards used for the type of verification discussed in this chapter define what is appropriate behaviour for verification actors, both in terms of what they do when they verify and accordingly, how they perform their verifications. Accreditation as meta-governance is also defined and measured against these standards (for example ISO 17021). In this way, accreditation constitutes a hierarchical mode of organizing, which in turn contributes to the image of a 'non-market'. We may thus conclude that the commercial and potentially controversial values of verification markets are neutralized and overshadowed by the dense organization of these markets in terms of meta-auditing (accreditation), backed up by either a state or a moral authority linked to NGOs with symbolic power resources (Boström and Tamm Hallström 2010). We recognize the neutralizing value configuration from the field of financial auditing, in which commercial values are neutralized through emphasis on the value of independence based on expert authority stemming from a strong professionalization of auditors. However, as demonstrated in this chapter, the approach of organizing through meta-auditing to ensure independence, as well as the type of authority that the system of meta-auditing relies on, differs from the knowledge developed from studies of financial auditing, since in the current studies accreditation is not an attempt to professionalize individual auditors.

Plurality of Market Organizers

Just as there are many organizational efforts undertaken to construct credibility for verification markets – turning them into highly regulated and hierarchized – there are many market organizers actively involved in such efforts. In the first case, the state plays an important role as the accrediting actor and also as the rule issuer for other state supervision tasks, such as those conducted by Transportstyrelsen. In the second case, we see both the state and an NGO assuming the role of accreditation actors. We have also demonstrated how firms in these markets contribute to the specific organization of these markets through various self-organizing efforts, mostly in line with the content of the accreditation standards.

In addition to state actors, NGOs, companies and business associations, there are a number of other organizations in these sectors that contribute to the organization of verification markets. We know from studies of transnational governance that standard-setting work engages companies that follow standards as well as a large number of service providers who make a living selling consultancy services linked to certification standards (Tamm Hallström 2004). In the field of sustainability, we see an even wider range of stakeholders involved – consumer organizations, human rights organizations, and sometimes government organizations – as such standard-setting processes are often organized as multi-stakeholder arrangements (Tamm Hallström and Boström 2010). Although it is beyond the scope of this chapter to go into detail about how such actors contribute to the current neutralization of verification markets, we may conclude that there is a broad range of market organizers with varying interests in verification. Their involvement thereby contributes to reinforcing the idea of verification markets as something acceptable and necessary.

In future projects, it would be interesting to continue to compare verification markets and systems of meta-auditing – to further explore how they are organized and legitimized, what type of authority they rely on, and the type of market organizers involved in providing support for, or challenging these systems.

REFERENCES

ASI (2009). *Quality Manual ASI-QMS-20-100 Version 4.1*. Accreditation Services International GmbH.
Bartley, Tim (2010). Certification as a mode of social regulation. *Jerusalem Papers in Regulation and Governance*. Working Paper No. 8.
Bartley, Tim (2011). Transnational governance as the layering of rules: Intersections of public and private standards. *Theoretical Inquiries in Law* 12(2): 25–51.
Bernstein, Steven and Cashore, Benjamin (2007). Can non-state global governance be legitimate? An analytical framework. *Regulation and Governance* 1: 1–25.
Boström, Magnus and Tamm Hallström, Kristina (2010). NGO power in global social and environmental standard-setting. *Global Environmental Politics* 10(4): 36–59.
Brunsson, Nils (1991). Politisering och företagisering – om institutionell förankring och förvirring. In: Arvidsson, Göran and Lind, Rolf (eds), *Ledning av företag och förvaltning*. Stockholm: SNS Förlag. pp. 20–40.
Elad, Charles (2001). Auditing and governance in the forestry industry: Between protest and professionalism. *Critical Perspectives on Accounting* 12: 647–71.
Hall, Rodney Bruce and Biersteker, Thomas J. (eds) (2002). *The Emergence of Private Authority in Global Governance*. Cambridge: Cambridge University Press.
Haufler, Virginia (2001). *A Public Role for the Private Sector: Industry self-regulation in a global economy*. Carnegie Endowment for International Peace, Washington: Brookings Institution Press.
ISO/IEC 17021:2011. Conformity Assessment – Requirements for bodies providing audit and certification of management systems. International Organization for Standardization.
Jeppesen, Kim K (1998). Reinventing auditing, redefining consulting and independence. *The European Accounting Review* 7(3): 517–39.
Lindeberg, Tobias (2007). *Evaluative Technologies. Quality and the Multiplicity of Performance*. Copenhagen Business School. PhD Series 7-2007.
Mennicken, Andrea (2010). From inspection to auditing: Audit and markets as linked ecologies. *Accounting, Organization and Society*, 35: 334–59.
Meyer, John, and Rowan, Brian (1977). Institutionalized organizations: Formal structure as myth and ceremony, *American Journal of Sociology* 83(2): 340–63.
Pentland, Brian T (2000). Will auditors take over the world? Program, technique and the verification of everything. *Accounting, Organization and Society* 25(3): 307–12.
Power, Michael (1997). *The Audit Society: Rituals of verification*. Oxford, UK: Oxford University Press.
Power, Michael (2003). Auditing and the production of legitimacy. *Accounting, Organization and Society* 28(4): 379–94.
Proposition 2009/10:32 Fordonsbesiktning [Swedish government bill regarding motor vehicle inspections].

Shapiro, Susan (1987) The social control of impersonal trust. *American Journal of Sociology* 93(3): 623–58.

Sikka, Prem (2009). Financial crisis and the silence of the auditors. *Accounting, Organization and Society* 34(6–7): 868–73.

Sikka, Prem and Willmott, Hugh (1995). The power of 'independence': Defending and extending the jurisdication of accounting in the United Kingdom. *Accounting, Organization and Society* 20(6): 547–81.

Tamm Hallström, Kristina (2004). *Organizing International Standardization: ISO and the IASC in quest of authority.* Cheltenham, UK and Northampton, MA, USA: Edward Elgar.

Tamm Hallström, Kristina and Boström, Magnus (2010). *Transnational Multi-Stakeholder Standardization. Organizing fragile non-state authority.* Cheltenham, UK and Northampton, MA, USA: Edward Elgar. TSFS 2010:90. Transportstyrelsen. Swedish Transport Agency regulations and guidelines on training and skills for certification of inspection techniques. Swedish Transport Agency.

Wallerstedt, Eva (2009). *Revisorsbranschen i Sverige under hundra år.* Stockholm: SNS Förlag.

www.aftonbladet.se

www.bilprovningen.se

6. Harmony or hidden conflicts? Proactive self-regulation in the personal insurance market

Martin Gustavsson

COMPLICATED PRODUCTS IN A VALUE-LADEN MARKET

The market for private personal insurance is a complicated and value-laden marketplace. The customer pays for the product in advance, to possibly need it in the future, something neither party really wants to happen: the buyer hopes to remain healthy, and the seller hopes to avoid paying out claims. The customer's situation is complicated by the difficulty of assessing both the terms of the legal clauses that accompany the product and the seller's future financial ability to absorb its commitments. The seller's situation is complicated by the difficulty of assessing the risk – the customer's state of health – to be insured (Grip 1992, p. 124; cf. Ericson et al. 2003, pp. 186–188). The personal insurance market has historically also been characterized by periodically recurring value conflicts. According to early critics of life insurance at the beginning of the 1800s, and children's insurance at the end of the 1800s, it was not even morally defensible to establish monetary agreements relating to life and death (Zelizer 1979; Grip 1992, p. 127) or to set a value on 'priceless' children (Zelizer 1994). Today, the issue has almost the reverse character: insuring your children is not negatively charged but can rather be interpreted as the opposite – a morally responsible action that all parents should have the right to do. In this chapter, I show that the values that have stood at the centre of the disputes in the Swedish market have changed over time (see Table 6.1 for a summary).

That the market for private personal insurance is potentially mined with value conflicts and constantly complicated in this way has led to it being reorganized several times over the years. In the first half of the chapter, I show that these organizational changes can be related to numerous market organizers having, during various periods, highlighted and stressed the

Table 6.1   Central values at play in the Swedish personal insurance market, 1870–2011

	Central values	Period
1	Solidity, financial security, transparency	1870–1930
2	Greater democracy	1930–1980
3	Expanded market economy	1980–2000
4	Integrity, fairness, transparency	2000–

shifting values and fought various value battles, resulting in changes in how the market was organized. A high degree of private self-regulation has been an especially prominent feature. In the second half of the chapter, I move on to discuss how the self-organization that characterizes today's personal insurance market can explain that many of the values potentially at play do *not* spawn debate or radical organizational reform, but are instead subdued. The chapter thus illustrates the two directions of the book's main models, the 'loop' of the impact of value configurations on market organization and vice versa (see Chapter 1).

Method

The historical review of personal insurance in the first part of the chapter is carried out based on a study of previous research. By looking through a selection of relevant previous studies of the Swedish insurance market and state investigations in this area, I attempt in part to identify the values central to the debate on the personal insurance market in different periods, and in part to study what organizational measures were taken to deal with value conflicts in the field. The second part of the chapter is based on a study of disputes over the past 15 years, handled by two different review boards. Here, my focus is on children's insurance as it is an especially debated type of insurance where the lines of conflict between seller and buyer are particularly clear, facilitating analysis. With the aid of material from a digital news archive, in the second part of the chapter I also perform a quantitative study of articles on child insurance that appear during the Swedish press in the period 1982–2011, to investigate whether the self-organizing of companies influence which issues arise in the debate.

The self-regulatory bodies in the Swedish personal insurance market share many common characteristics with self-regulatory bodies in other countries. They emerged as an attempt to stave off political threats of increased regulation by the state, and to improve the companies' reputation among consumers and other stakeholders (cf. Haufler 2001, pp. 21,

26). They are, however, not a product of the growing globalization at the end of the 1900s (cf. Haufler 2003). I show that the historical roots of the self-regulatory apparatus companies use today go back a long way.

HOW SHIFTING VALUES AT PLAY CREATES ORGANIZATION

The basic argument in this first half of the chapter is thus that disputed values constantly have affected the organizing of the Swedish personal insurance market. I highlight key values in the debate during the period 1850–2011, the central actors that pursued these values and the legislated regulation that was carried out, and the self-regulation that took place as a result of these value battles.

Different Values Activated in Different Periods

For an insurance market to function, a mutual trust between a firm and its customers is essential (Larsson et al. 2005a, p. 17). Buyers must trust the company in order to risk the long-term investment of insurance. Sellers must trust the customer to even dare to offer personalized private insurance coverage. A lack of trust therefore represents a constant latent risk of conflict. However, different values have been stressed during different time periods (see Table 6.1). Around the turn of the century, 1900, the solidity of companies was an issue that threatened the confidence in the Swedish insurance industry. Unless companies were not seen as being financially able to meet their obligations to the insured at any given time, a legitimacy crisis threatened (Grip 1992, pp. 122, 152). At the turn of the millennium, 2000, customer integrity had emerged as an overarching and charged issue that required organizational solutions to avoid jeopardizing the trust between the firm and the customer.

At both of these times, transparency was a central value. At the beginning of the 1900s, however, it was customer transparency that was key, that is, the seller's right to have access to the customer's medical history. The way it works today in Sweden is that customers issue a power of attorney giving the firms access to the patient medical records kept by the public health care system. In contemporary markets, in the early 2000s, the emphasis is above all on the value of companies and their products being transparent (cf. Garsten and Montoya 2008), and that customers, conversely, should be able to keep sensitive information that could harm their integrity confidential (cf. for example, Ds 2005, p. 13). Like many other disputes, the conflict relating to integrity is connected to an underlying, highly charged issue: about what the balance between politics and economics should look like in society (compare the values of democracy and market economy in Table 6.1). Critics of the deregulated market were quick to point out that today's insurance companies have gone a step further into the private family sphere than the intervening state did in its time. The conditions written into insurance contracts are a form of private legislation that is equally binding as government legislation. But the firms regulate conditions in private spheres of life that governments have traditionally been expected to leave untouched by legislation. 'Indeed', conclude Tom Baker and Jonathan Simon (2002, p. 13), 'within a regime of liberal governance, insurance is one of the greatest sources of regulatory authority over private life'. The access of private firms to patient records in Sweden has even been described as a 'back door' to the individuals themselves (Gunnartz 2007, p. 112).

Different Sides of the Market: Conflict on One, Harmony on the Other?

Two different areas of the private personal insurance market are especially loaded in the sense that values constantly threaten to rise to the surface and create tension and conflict with other values circulating in the area:

- *Entrance to the market*: which customers' firms accept and have commercial exchanges with, and which they do reject.
- *Settlement of claims*: whether or not approved customers that file a claim receive compensation from the firms, or are compensated according to what they expected.

Regarding children's insurance, quite regularly over the past decade vociferous debates have appeared in the Swedish media about insurance firms' heavy-handed treatment of some prospective customers. For example, in the winter of 2001 *Dagens Nyheter*, Sweden's largest daily newspaper, wrote 'Henrik Andersson's 4-year-old son is strong-willed. So he can't take out child insurance.' The son's father was reportedly 'upset that a note in the child's records from the children's health centre could have such huge consequences'. According to the note in the patient record, the nurse had suggested that the father meet with a psychologist to get some support to deal with the son's (in and of themselves, normal) mood swings. The insurance company, however, interpreted the remark as if the son was in treatment and was not normal. In the eyes of Andersson and his wife, the fact that private firms were even given access to public hospital and health centre patient records, which are confidential, was absurd. 'Now we don't want to go and say anything to the children's health care centre.'

The Anderssons had missed the fine print on the application form that stated that signing the form meant giving the firm the right to request and access medical records (Weilenmann 2001a). 'It has to be made harder for firms to deny families child insurance protection,' read headlines in the daily newspapers ten years later in 2011 as well (Forslund and Haraldsson 2011).

This conflict holds a number of values. Firstly, the conflict has to do with integrity – the patient's integrity is threatened when private companies have access to patient records. Secondly, the conflict is about fairness – which, for example, is perceived as having been violated when 'strong-willed' children are denied insurance. Thirdly, the conflict is about transparency – which is perceived to not exist due to the delicate fine print of contracts. These three values – integrity, fairness and transparency – are considered to conflict with values that received more attention in the debate of earlier periods, but that nevertheless continue to be of central importance. It is a matter of the sellers' need for transparency with respect to information about the customer – they must have an adequate basis upon which to assess the conditions that should apply, if the risk is insurable at all. And it is a matter of the companies' solidity. Without transparent information about the customer the companies' solidity is at risk (their assessments can be inaccurate and premiums insufficient, which in the long term can give rise to a situation where the revenues from premiums do not cover the companies' settlement payments) and thereby jeopardizing another value aspect – the customer's financial security (cf. summary in Table 6.1).

While the debate about how insurance firms treat prospective customers, that is those who are denied entrance to the market, flares up in the media from time to time, what is virtually non-existent in the debate is how insurance firms treat some of their actual customers, that is those who are denied compensation. Why do value-related conflicts arise in one case, while harmony appears to prevail in the other? This question is also connected to which central values are activated in different parts of this market in different time periods. While the walls around the market today enliven the debate about fairness in that it can be seen as unfair that some people cannot take out additional private insurance coverage, the settlement of claims may activate less-loaded questions regarding contract law, about how the customer should receive compensation because he/she paid for the product. But this argument does not explain all of the asymmetry in the debate. The above-mentioned contemporary value-laden issue of integrity, which essentially has to do with how much information about insurance customers' medical history private companies should have access to, was namely just as topical with respect to purchasing new insurance policies as in claim settlements: in both cases, companies based their assessments on integrity-sensitive information from hospital records.

In this chapter, I argue that the presence of value-laden media debates about buying new child insurance policies, and the absence of a broader public debate on the insurance cases, can be explained by the organizing efforts of a number of market organizers.[1] While there is a large self-regulatory apparatus that handles the grievances of insurance companies' approved customers – private review bodies that handle insurance claims free of charge – there is a complete lack of private bodies that capture, stop and prevent the dissatisfaction of rejected customers, from escaping now and then as value-related conflicts into the mass media.[2]

Because the self-regulatory apparatus used today was constructed in earlier time periods, I take an historical approach and discuss which organizational strategies were used by business and government to manage value conflicts during different periods. I then revisit the insurance industry's contemporary attempts to handle disputes with consumers in and through self-regulatory bodies. In a concluding section, I discuss the effects that the organizing has on the – visible – level of conflict in the market and the central values constantly threatening to break the surface there.

Waves of Legislated Regulation and Self-Regulation, 1850–2011

Over the past 150 years, the Swedish insurance market has been characterized by an interplay between state-legislated regulation and private companies' self-regulation. Schematically speaking, we could say that the insurance industry practised self-regulation in anticipation of government legislation in the late 1800s and to avoid further government legislation in the mid-1900s and at the end of the 1900s.[3]

From the 1870s, the large private Swedish insurance firms were proactive in bringing about government legislation that regulated and controlled activities in the young market (cf. Fligstein 2001, p. 77). According to these nationwide firms' view, the public's confidence in the insurance system would be shaken if the industry, with the help of the state, did not self-regulate to rid itself of, among others, small and disreputable firms that lack liquidity. Here, we see solidity beginning to be highlighted by the large firms as a key legitimacy-creating value. In 1875, a trade organization was formed for the Swedish insurance industry, Svenska Försäkringsföreningen – a central market organizer – to drive – to drive the issue of government oversight and regulation in a more coherent manner the issue of government oversight and regulation in a more coherent manner (Grip 1992, pp. 122, 130–141). The state itself, however, took a wait-and-see approach. With legislation delayed, the organized insurance firms took their own measures to regulate the market, as seen in the self-regulation epoch of 1850–1902 in Table 6.2 (Larsson 1991, pp. 7, 14; Larsson et al. 2005a, pp. 17, 20–21, 52–53).

The first Swedish insurance legislation was adopted in 1903. One of the official main purposes of the act, which was essentially initiated and generated by the industry itself, was to achieve financial security and protection for the insured by stressing the value of solidity, a safeguard for managing the policyholders' capital so that any contracts entered could always be fulfilled. But the confidence-creating component of the legislation was also an important prerequisite for nationwide firms to recruit new customers. From this perspective, the legislation was rather motivated by a care for the companies than for the consumers (Grip 1992, pp. 124–125, 140, 150). During the epoch with gradually increasing state governance, 1903–1947, a law was also introduced in 1927 imposing upon policyholders a 'disclosure' requirement: an obligation to be transparent, to provide information about the risk when entering the contract, so that the firm would be able to assess what premium and other conditions should apply, if the risk is insurable at all (Larsson 1991, pp. 27-29; Larsson et al. 2005a, pp. 22, 51–53).

The interests of the state and firms began to drift apart in the beginning of the 1930s when a social democratic government took office. Increased government control over the capital market was an ideal aired in the debate. If the state took over the insurance firms, which possessed sizable capital resources, the allocation of resources to public-spirited projects would be facilitated. Greater democracy – not only a general political right to vote and influence over the state but also economic co-determination and influence over large companies – was a parallel value stressed by critics of the system. This threat of socialization led the insurances firms to join forces. In 1937, the entire threatened industry came together in a national federation of insurance companies, Sveriges Försäkringsbolags Riksförbund, yet another organization that would become a central market organizer. In 1942, the federation set up a board for accident- and medical insurance consumer disputes (Svenska Olycksfalls- och sjukförsäkringsnämnden, which is the focus of the analysis that follows in the next section), an early self-regulation initiative that was a step in the attempts to ward off the threat of socialization (Larsson 1991, pp. 6, 50–51; Larsson et al. 2005b, pp. 345–348; cf. Trosdahl 2007, p. 286). In the 1940s, however, political pressure grew when the Social Democratic Party Congress adopted a programme that required unconditional nationalization of the insurance system (known as the 'post-war labour program', *Arbetarrörelsens efterkrigsprogram 1944*, paragraph 18, p. 22). Business and industry and the bourgeoisie managed to mobilize a violent 'planned economy resistance movement' that put a stop to the

Table 6.2 Five epochs of the Swedish insurance industry's institutional development, 1850–2011

Period	Characteristics of the epoch	Key legislation	Front actors	Key values in the debate	Key self-regulatory body
1850–1902	Self-regulation		Companies	Solidity	
1903–1947	Increased state governance	Insurance act: 1903, 1917. Contract act: 1927	Companies and state	Financial security, transparency	Accident and medical insurance board in the industry, 1942
1948–1983	Strict regulation	Insurance act: 1948, 1982	State	Greater democracy	Customer ombudsman in the companies, starting in 1970s
1984–1999	De- and re-regulation		State and companies	Expanded market economy	
2000–	Increased self-regulation *and* government regulation	Insurance act: 2010. Contract act: 2005, 2011	Companies and state (and doctors)	Integrity, fairness, transparency	

Source: The 1850–2000 period adapted from Larsson et al. (2005a, p. 262).

extensive nationalizations in Sweden (Lewin 1970; Grip 1987, Chap. 6; Englund 1993, pp. 207, 315; Stenlås 1998; cf. Appelqvist 2000, p. 116), but government regulation of the market increased.

In that state governance and control was given a more prominent role in the new insurance business act adopted in 1948, the sensitive question of socialization of the industry got pushed into the background. A key reason for the insurance industry being willing to accept certain restrictions to the freedom of firms was a fear that even more extensive restrictions to corporate freedom might be introduced if the industry was not accommodating and did not mollify some radical interests. Hence, the socialization issue was disarmed, yet a rhetorical threat of socialization would nevertheless be present in the debate in the coming decades as well, and the threat contributed to the continued attempts by the insurance market to adapt to the various societal demands (Grip 1992, pp. 108–109, 157; Larsson et al. 2005a, pp. 56–57, 77; Larsson et al. 2005b, p. 348). The second wave of proactive efforts to self-regulate, the review boards that emerged within the companies from the 1970s onward (Legal Committee 2004, pp. 46–54, 77) surged forward at a time when the social democratic government – after intense public debate on the downsides of advertising and consumption in the late 1960s and early 1970s – had advanced their consumer policy positions. A radical proposal to give the newly established Swedish Consumer Agency (Konsumentverket) a statutory 'right to information' in private companies' product development and marketing scared many entrepreneurs (Ministry of Trade 1980). The proposal was later rejected, however, by a conservative government in 1980 (cf. Funke 2004, pp. 18, 55).

In the early 1980s, a de- and re-regulation of the insurance market began. A more market-oriented Swedish social democracy returned to power and now proposed a transition to a system where the companies themselves proactively took responsibility to both identify consumer problems and come up with their own measures to solve them (Legal Committee 2004, pp. 6–7; Haglind 2001, pp. 264–265). Just as the state and the companies had agreed about increased statutory regulation at the beginning of the 1900s, they were in agreement about increased self-regulation at the end of the 1900s. The changes that occurred during the deregulation epoch, 1984–1999, were also fuelled by the fact that the internationalization of Swedish insurance firms had accelerated during the 1970s and 1980s. This meant that the national legislation was perceived as outdated (Larsson et al. 2005a, Chapter 9).

Similarly to the deregulated era at the end of the 1800s, the deregulated era at the end of the 1900s was followed by a period of new state regulations. Unlike the situation at the turn of the century, 1900, when it was those who represented insurance interests that stepped forward as active market organizers and demanded government legislation that underlined solidity, it was representatives with, above all, health care interests who demanded legislation that highlighted and protected the values of fairness (a ban on denying personal insurance on non-objective grounds) and integrity (restricting insurance firms' access to sensitive information in patient records) in the early 2000s (cf. Swedish National Council on Medical Ethics 2002). Both of these demands were addressed by amendments to the law in 2005 and 2011 (SFS 2005:104; SFS 2011:12). Finally, the self-regulation parallel to the legislated regulation at the beginning of the 2000s was a 'softer' attempt on the part of the companies to manage the value conflicts that had begun to be articulated during the 1980s and 1990s. There was a 'significant problem with confidence' in Swedish business and industry, concluded a government commission in charge of restoring confidence (Förtroendekommissionen) in 2004 (SOU 2004:47, p. 134). That the confidence in large Swedish corporations had fallen dramatically at the end of the 1900s was due to various reasons, from deregulation and globalization to excessive executive salaries and the narrow recruiting pool for corporate boards (ibid., pp. 105, 109–110). Of particular interest here is that the commission included the large corporations' 'upper hand with respect to information' in relation to customers as one of the causes of the confidence problem (ibid., p. 138). In the personal insurance market, it became particularly evident where the products were becoming increasingly complex (and therefore less transparent to customers) at the same time as the customer's 'disclosure' requirement from 1927 remained (the statutory obligation for customers to be transparent to the companies). How could confidence be restored? 'Through various kinds of organizing', was the response of the confidence commission, above all through vigorous and proactive self-regulation (ibid., p. 152).

In the next section, I look more closely at contemporary attempts of the insurance industry to handle value conflicts in and through these self-regulatory bodies, which have been successively constructed to handle the value conflicts that flared up during the reported 150-year period. Today, I argue, the organization of the field tends to hide some conflicting values and preclude open conflicts.

MARKET ORGANIZING HIDES VALUES AND VALUE CONFLICTS

The basic argument in this second half of the chapter is thus the reverse of that of the first half. Now the question in focus is not of how value conflicts have affected market organization, but how the (historically structured) organization of the market affects which value conflicts that become visible in the (contemporary) debate.

Self-Regulation of Consumer Disputes in the Early 2000s

There is no generally accepted definition of 'self-regulation', but roughly speaking it has to do with measures taken in a systematized form by a company, an industry, or business and industry as a whole, to prevent or solve a problem in relation to consumers or other customers (Haglind 2001, p. 263; Heuman 1980, pp. 32–37). 'This means that the market regulates itself without the intervention of legislators' (Committee on Civil Affairs 2010, p. 8). Although this type of organizing has a long history in Sweden, it gained importance as confidence in market solutions became increasingly common in the 1980s (Josefsson 2001, p. 211; Haglind 2001, p. 265). Flexibility and positive support among the companies concerned, as well as simpler and less expensive application (for the state at least) are often cited when the advantages of self-regulation are discussed. The disadvantages include doubtful effects, weak penalties, and a risk of reduced legitimacy in the eyes of the public due to poor insight into the boards and/or a power imbalance between the parties affected by the activities (Jonson 2001, p. 298; Josefsson 2001, p. 209; SOU 2004:47, pp. 151–152; Government Bill 2010, p. 25). This type of organizing, where the companies administer the justice themselves (Heuman 1980, p. 849), cannot deepen democracy (compare the values listed in Table 6.1). On the contrary, there is a conflict between the so-called 'subsidiarity principle' that is often cited in support of self-regulation and democracy. According to this principle, regulation should be decentralized and transferred to those affected, but democracy entails that citizens have the ability to influence also issues that do not directly concern them, and thus be able to take part in determining societal development as a whole (Mattsson 2001, p. 313). The state's threat of more 'hard' legislation, on the other hand, is expected to drive attempts at 'soft' self-regulation by the companies and the industry, as a means of preventing state intervention (Haufler 2001, p. 21). What is at stake for the privately organized review boards, as I highlight below, is essentially 'control over how criticism is handled' (Josefsson 2001, p. 214), the power to determine which issues make it onto the agenda (for example, Lukes 1974). How is the system constructed more precisely (cf. Haufler 2001, p. 3)?

As shown above, the Swedish insurance companies employ a privately organized system that emerged during the 1900s. It is a system in which customer issues and complaints are handled at different levels, first by

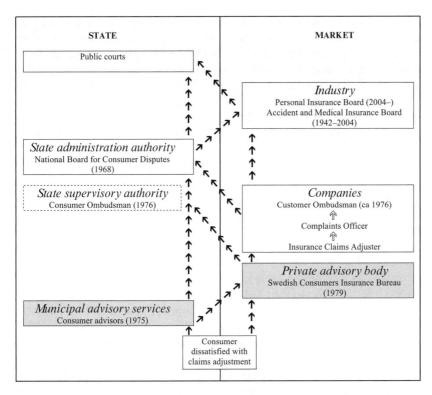

Figure 6.1 Possibilities to appeal decisions concerning claims adjustment:
advisory bodies and review boards of the state and in the market

instances within the companies, and then by instances within the industry. Most dissatisfied consumers who have sought to have their insurance settlement claims reviewed appear to have never left the market domain (see right-hand side of Figure 6.1) to visit instead review bodies of the democratic state (see left-hand side of Figure 6.1). The typical procedure for these active and dissatisfied consumers is as follows (right-hand side, Figure 6.1): when they disagree with the firm about an insurance claim, they contact the 'insurance claims adjuster' handling the case again. If the customer is still dissatisfied after speaking with the adjuster, he/she may take the matter further to a 'complaints officer' and thereafter, if the dispute is still not resolved, to the company's 'customer ombudsman' (see the bodies within the companies at the right in Figure 6.1). Less easily resolved issues between insurance customers and insurance firms may be taken to meta-organizations at the industry level ('Accident and Medical Insurance Board', Olycksfalls- och sjukförsäkringsnämnden, founded in 1942, with a subsequent name change to 'Personal Insurance Board', Personförsäkringsnämnden, at the top right in Figure 6.1). Very few cases seem to make it all the way up to the public courts (top left in Figure 6.1), the only instance with no private counterpart. There are also a few public bodies where dissatisfied consumers can turn if they want to leave the market (see left-hand side of Figure 6.1): consumers may have their cases reviewed partly by the National Board for Consumer Disputes (Allmänna reklamationsnämnden, established in 1968), and partly by a public court.

Figure 6.1 also shows that consumers can move between the public and private spheres. A consumer can seek the advice of a municipal 'consumer advisor' (shaded box at lower left in figure), but because few municipalities have the expertise to advise consumers in more complicated cases regarding financial services, the municipality often refers to the industry-financed joint body (shaded box at lower right in figure), the Consumers Insurance Bureau (Ministry of Finance 2005, pp. 28–29),[4] constituted by the Swedish Consumer Agency (Konsumentverket) and Swedish Financial Supervisory Authority (Finansinspektionen),[5] both state agencies, and the insurance companies' industry organization, Insurance Sweden (Svensk Försäkring).[6] The Consumers Insurance Bureau can offer qualified advice about where the dissatisfied consumer can turn to have his/her case reviewed, but does not act as the dissatisfied customer's legal representative (Swedish Consumers Insurance Bureau 2010, p. 4). The power balance between the public and private bodies is the same at the next level in Figure 6.1: because the state administration agency, the National Board for Consumer Disputes, lacks medical expertise, many cases are referred to the private industry body, the Personal Insurance Board. I will come back to the division of tasks between the two boards, both of which review disputes between companies and consumers free of charge.

That the private companies' internal bodies that provide assistance to customers (the 'Customer Ombudsman' at the centre right of Figure 6.1) appear to be named after the state supervisory authority that ensures that companies comply with consumer affairs laws (the 'Consumer Ombudsman' at the centre left of Figure 6.1) is not surprising. By imitating names of government agencies, along with their organizational features, private companies makes themselves appear more legitimate (Brunsson 1991/2011, p. 245). The odd customer may certainly also get lost in the private organizational jungle and believe that he/she is in the domain of the democratically governed state. There is also a potential source of value conflict here, which may ultimately lead to reduced legitimacy for the companies. Because these bodies are formed, executed and financed by the companies affected, there is a risk that the public will think that there is a confusion of roles in self-regulatory bodies (SOU 2004:47, p. 151). The Folksam insurance company's own 'Deputy Customer Ombudsman' illustrates the problem of possible role confusion when she tells about how she helps Folksam customers by way of 'impartial' review of cases where customers 'feel unfairly treated' by Folksam itself (Rahn 2011). 'The firm maintains its position' is a similar example from another company group. 'The case has even been submitted to the firm's customer ombudsman who found no cause to change the firm's decision' (Personal Insurance Board, Archive, Ref. 770-2004).

The contrasts between how different parts of the Swedish personal insurance market are organized are striking (compare Figure 6.1 and Figure 6.2). While there is a number of different review bodies available – all free of charge – to customers dissatisfied with insurance firm decisions regarding claims adjustment (Figure 6.1), there is only one instance that captures the dissatisfaction of people that the insurance companies have refused to insure (Figure 6.2), namely, the public court (cf. SFS 2005:104, Chap. 16, §7). In isolated cases of principal importance, the state 'Consumer Ombudsman', who is also the Director-General of the state Consumer Agency, has represented insurance policyholders in court actions, for example in December 2011, when the Consumer Ombudsman represented a 1-year-old girl denied insurance based on the child's low birth weight (Swedish Consumer Agency 2011; cf. Stockholm District Court 2011). But it is only in cases of exception that the state Consumer Ombudsman can take on individual disputes. That private individuals who have been denied personal insurance do not find the thought of meeting the big firms and their lawyers in court especially appealing is

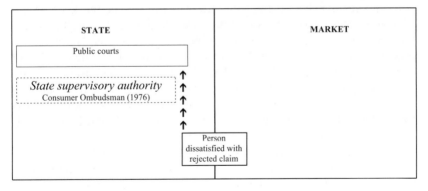

Figure 6.2   Possibilities to appeal a rejected insurance claim regarding entrance to the market: advisory bodies and review boards of the state and in the market

due to the fact that disputes such as these can be costly, both financially and socially. Moreover, from a European perspective, Swedish insurance customers stood out for their high lack of confidence in their chances of winning a case against a private firm in a public courtroom:

> Court proceedings concerning disputes are seldom tempting to consumers, in part because of the time factor and risk of being hit with high legal costs. A questionnaire survey conducted on behalf of the European Commission shows that Swedish people feel it is more difficult to win a dispute with an insurance company than other EU citizens on average. In Sweden, as many as 57 percent believe it is 'very difficult' to win a dispute with an insurance company, compared to an average of 40 percent in the EU. (SOU 2004:47, p. 323)

As there is no alternative to the public courts to capture and channel the dissatisfaction with firms that deny families with child insurance protection, as has been shown, it seems it is this very dissatisfaction that leaks out to the media now and then. Because a qualified majority of the people who seek child insurance, about 75 percent (Swedish Consumers Insurance Bureau 2012), are actually approved, it would at the same time seem that the insurance firms' focus on bodies that review claims adjustment disputes between customers and companies is understandable. The number of potentially dissatisfied customers wanting to dispute compensation levels is higher, and has better resources, than the number of potentially dissatisfied people wanting to dispute that they have been denied insurance.

From Transparent Public Forums to Poorly Illuminated Private Realms

After having sketched in the contours of the insurance market's organizing with respect to claims adjustment and entrance to the market, I now examine how the state and insurance industry review boards are used in practice. Are there a lot of customers who utilize the multitude of different review bodies to help settle their claims? What does the relationship look like between cases handled by the state bodies (with public transparency) and cases handled by private bodies (where the results are not transparent to the customer community or citizens in general), and how has this relationship changed over time? And who usually comes out on top in the battles waged in the various instances for dispute resolution – the customer or the firm? The study complements the discussion related to Figure 6.1 by taking a closer look at what parts of the system actually process the most cases. This adds more depth to the analysis of the ability of organizing to hide value conflicts: the more disputes handled and resolved in the non-transparent market domain, the fewer disputed values one would expect to appear in the general societal debate. The analysis also tells us something about how the market organizing affects and addresses two values – transparency and fairness – that have indeed risen to the surface and been subjected to public debate, which in turn relates to discussions about the mutual trust between firm and customer that, according to the opening argument, is fundamental to the industry's legitimacy (cf. Larsson et al. 2005a, p. 17).

Figure 6.3 shows among other things the number of cases concerning child insurance reviewed between 1995 and 2010 by the statue authority, the National Board for Consumer Disputes (ARN), where consumer- and

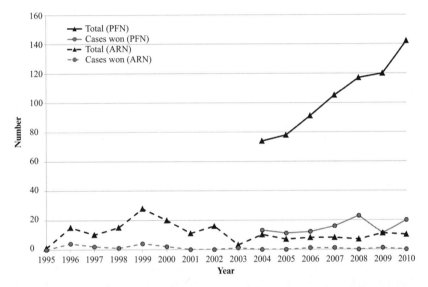

Note: The material from disputes within PFN – where children and youth insurance cases are not separated, as within ARN, from other insurance cases with a specific code – consists partially and especially of all cases where the paediatrician has been involved in the decision meetings (approximately one quarter of these cases are classified as 'child and youth insurance' in the archives, but most are registered in the more age-neutral and general term 'medical and accident insurance') and partly by a small number of cases (about 5–10 percent of the total), which was decided without a present paediatrician, but then explicitly labelled as health and accident insurance for 'children and youth' in the records.

Source: Data from disputes relating to child and youth insurance (Code 3630) at National Board for Consumer Disputes (ARN), and medical and accident insurance where paediatricians have been in attendance at meetings of the Personal Insurance Board (PFN).

Figure 6.3   *Number of cases concerning child and youth insurance handled by ARN 1995–2010 (n = 180) and PFN 2004–2010 (n = 727), and number of cases where consumer complaints have won*

business and industry interests are represented in equal numbers.[7] The figure shows, firstly, that the number of cases processed by this instance, where access to information for the public – and researchers – is legislated, is exceptionally low for the entire 15-year period and has decreased over the years (broken black line with triangles). Secondly, the figure shows that virtually none of the child insurance consumers were granted approval in disputes in this state instance during the years 1995–2010 (broken grey line with circles). Most of the cases that made it as far as ARN were either dismissed or were rejected (not shown in Figure 6.3).[8] That ARN dismisses many of the few child insurance cases that reach the instance is due to the lack of medical expertise often needed to complement the expert legal knowledge in disputes relating to personal insurance. The dismissed cases were referred to the corresponding – but much more resource-rich – private industry body, the Personal Insurance Board (Personförsäkringsnämnden, PFN), where members representing the business interests of industry outnumber members representing the interests of consumers.[9]

'There is no information on how large a proportion of the rulings are entirely or partially in favour of the complainant', reads one parliamentary report on the private Personal Insurance Board in 2010 (Committee on Civil Affairs 2010, p. 109).[10] Normally, moving from a public to a private instance (from left to right in Figure 6.1) also means moving from a transparent world, that is, one governed by the principle of access to public information in Sweden, to a less well-illuminated one in that there is no corresponding statutory right to transparency into private companies in Sweden (cf. Wijkström and Einarsson 2006, pp. 82–83). Because the insurance industry's trade organization has shown a welcoming attitude toward research in the area, however, I was given access to anonymized data from the private regulatory body PFN for the period 2004–2010 – the first seven years of the PFN board in its existing form. That is, this is material that is not covered by Sweden's access to public information principle and which is therefore normally hidden and not accessible. An analysis of this material yields several important insights.

Firstly, Figure 6.3 shows that the number of cases processed by the well-resourced private instance (solid black line with triangles) increases markedly in comparison with the number of cases at the resource-weak state instance (broken black line with triangles).

Secondly, the figure illustrates that the child insurance consumer complainants only very rarely won against their insurance firms in the industry instance (solid grey line with circles). The number of rejected cases in the private instance is increasing at about the same rate as the total number of cases (not shown in Figure 6.3).

Thirdly, Figure 6.3 indicates a strikingly low total number of disputes relating to child insurance even in the private review board – just between 100 and 140 per year toward the end of the period studied. This finding should be seen in relation to the fact that a large proportion of the country's families with children are customers in this market. According to one estimate, 70 percent of Swedish children under the age of 10 had some form of private insurance coverage in 2001 (see Weilenmann 2001b).

A probable explanation for the small number of disputes in ARN and PFN is that the vast majority of insurances cases are solved informally, at the local level within the companies (see centre right of Figure 6.1), before they reach the industry or state review instances higher up in the organizational hierarchy. The exact number of cases handled by the companies cannot be determined. Companies' internal instances for handling complaints, which began to appear in the second half of the 1970s as a complement to the industry bodies, are completely hidden from view.[11] The statutory right to transparency discussed above in the historical background section, which would make it possible for the state to require information on the companies' internal complaint statistics and so on, never materialized (SOU 1979:5, pp. 93, 97). Although transparency is a central value in the rhetoric, in practice, these instances help to block or hide controversies that might give the insurance firms a bad reputation and, in the long run, problems with legitimacy, if the information were to reach the arenas governed by public transparency, such as state review bodies and the mass media. The type of organizing developed by the insurance market thus has a concealing effect on the values that make it into the public debate. Even though there is no further information available, everything suggests that the insurance firms themselves handle 'a large number of cases' (Committee on Civil Affairs 2010, p. 21) and that their own boards have 'a great deal of importance for dispute resolution in the area of insurance law' (Heuman 1980, p. 98).

That consumers rarely win the few cases that are handled by ARN (a mere 15 percent of disputes in the entire insurance field in 2002) has previously been explained by the fact that 'the companies, through competent internal handling, are able to resolve misunderstandings or make good with the consumer directly' at an earlier stage (SOU 2004:47, p. 323; cf. SOU 1979:5, p. 85; Ministry of Finance 2005, p. 57). Only cases where misunderstandings remain unresolved, and those that the companies can be fairly certain of winning, are passed on to a higher instance (cf. Ericson et al. 2003, p. 354). The same argument has been put forward to explain the low percentage of decisions in favour of the complainant in the public courts. According to a study of Stockholm District

Court, the claims of injured parties who pursued court actions against insurance firms were successful in 33 percent of the cases in 1999–2000, and in only 7 percent of the cases in 2003–2004 (Johansson 2005, p. 24). 'A key purpose of the private administration of justice', writes procedural law professor Lars Heuman, 'is that one have wanted *to prevent disputes from being dragged before the courts*'. Because court proceedings can incur a business substantial costs, not least in the form of negative publicity, there is an interest on the part of firms to avoid giving dissatisfied consumers reason to take matters to a higher decision-making instance (Heuman 1980, p. 458).

The fact that few cases get to the National Board for Consumer Disputes (ARN) and the Personal Insurance Board (PFN) is thus explained by how the hierarchy of review bodies is organized (many cases at the bottom, few at the top). That the consumer complainants tend to lose against the firms in the few cases that do reach these two instances, the public instance with transparency (ARN) and the private instance without transparency (PFN), is explained by how the insurance product is organized. The information on what the consumer actually purchased can in many cases, as the above-mentioned state confidence commission (Förtroendekommissionen) expressed the problem, be 'so complicated or difficult to understand that only someone who is an expert in the field can understand and draw relevant conclusions about it' (SOU 2004:47, p. 156). Only once the case has been reviewed by legal and medical experts does the consumer understand, incisively expressed, that he/she did not understand what he/she purchased. Many cases reviewed by ARN and by PFN also show how the everyday language of customers clashes with the insurance companies' – and board members' – 'expert language'. One woman who appealed an insurance firm's decision, claiming that the child insurance most certainly should apply to her son who had accidently injured his knee while playing indoor bandy found, for example, that special linguistic exercises were needed to work out what constituted – in technical insurance language – an applicable accident, and that her definition of 'accident', although reasonable, was wrong in the context. 'According to common language use', explained the ARN board members in an interpretation regarding the probable cause of this linguistic confusion:

> the injury would be considered an accident. According to the terms of the insurance policy, however, an 'accident' is defined as a sudden external event. In the case in question, the Board assumes that the child's foot was caught due to friction against the floor rather than as a result of a crack or other fault in it [the gym floor]. Based on this, it is not a question of an external event, and therefore the injury is not covered by the insurance. (National Board for Consumer Disputes, Archive, Code 3630, Case no. 1998-0810)

The way in which both the product and the dominant review bodies are organized consequently contributes to the market for child insurance becoming less and less transparent for customers and citizens, a trend that paradoxically is occurring parallel to the values of openness and transparency being increasingly emphasized in discussions about how the market should be organized (cf. for example, SOU 2004:47, p. 155). Another effect of the market organization is that conflicts are resolved in the companies' home territory and therefore do not make it into the public eye. Hence, the organizing has a concealing effect that means that some values are not leaked to the mass media or managed in state bodies with transparency.

Less Public Debate on Power Relations Between Customers and Firms

A reasonable assumption is that the number of open and visible conflicts between customers and firms in the insurance market has remained low in the post-war period, since the private arenas for conflict management – both in the companies and their industry organizations – have increased over time, in some parts of the market. The analysis can be taken a step further by a somewhat more systematic testing of the opening argument that the debate about 'claim adjustments' is absent from the mass media, that is, has been organized out by way of a large number of self-regulatory bodies, while the debate about 'rejection of prospective consumers' applications for entrance to the insurance market' has a larger presence in the public media, since there is a lack of self-regulatory bodies in this area. The argument is based on my reading of newspaper clippings collected by the chief physician of paediatrics, Margareta Blennow, during the 2000s when she herself was engaged in the issue of the insurance firms' access to the public medical records of patients (cf. Gustavsson forthcoming). Below, I complement these readings with a systematic search for articles about 'child insurance'[12] in Mediearkivet, a digital media archive covering all the big dailies, local newspapers and journals in Sweden.[13] Is the working hypothesis supported even when confronted with a larger media base? Is it true that highly charged values – such as integrity and fairness – threaten to rise to the surface and create conflicts with other values – such as solidity and financial security – only at the gates to the child insurance market, while value conflicts relating to claims adjustments do not become visible in the same way?

In 1974, one of the big Swedish insurance firms, Skandia, introduced a new variant of child insurance that covered both accidents and childhood diseases (children's accident insurance had long been in existence). However, it took a long time before customers found their way to the new product, which did not really begin to spread in the population until

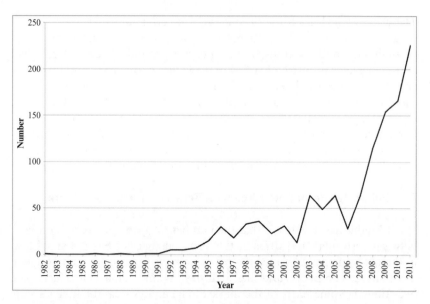

Source: Mediearkivet (2012). Note that the same article may appear in several newspapers.

Figure 6.4   *Search results for 'child insurance' in Mediearkivet. Number of hits for the publication period 1982–2011 (n = 1 257)*

the 1990s (Gustavsson forthcoming). The delayed but fairly rapid spread appears to be reflected in the mass media, where child insurance was a topic that slowly made its way into media conversations toward the mid-1990s, to receive considerably more attention a decade later (see Figure 6.4).

Here, I conduct two cross-sections and study all of the articles containing the term 'child insurance' for the years 2001 and 2011, the two years used in spots to illustrate the debate at the beginning of the chapter. Most of the articles deal with child insurance in a general sense, (19 of 31 articles in the Swedish media in 2001 and 124 of 226 articles in 2011), for example about the importance of buying private insurance such as this. It is interesting to note in this context that the articles rarely had to do with claims adjustment (only 1 of 31 articles in 2001 and 3 of 226 articles in 2011), but quite often had to do with the unfairness that not all people are allowed the opportunity to purchase insurance (11 of 31 articles in 2001 and 99 of 226 articles in 2011), which provides further support for the working hypothesis presented.

As one journalist wrote in *Dagens Nyheter* in the autumn of 2000,

Table 6.3   Search results for 'child insurance' in Mediearkivet. Number of hits in 2001 and 2011, broken down into different categories

Theme	Number of articles: 2001	Number of articles: 2011
Critical regarding new subscription	11	99
Critical of claims adjustment	1	3
Other	19	124
Total	31	226

Source: Mediearkivet (2012).

a common question among insurance policyholders is: 'Why was the company so eager to accommodate when selling the insurance and why are they being so obstinate now when an injury has occurred?' (Löfberg 2000). There is, suggested the head of Swedish Consumers Insurance Bureau (Konsumenternas försäkringsbyrå) in Sydsvenskan ten years later, 'often a large discrepancy between those who sell insurance and those who settle claims' (quoted in Birgersson et al. 2010; cf. Ericson et al. 2003, Chap. 9). But the irritation of policyholders about how they have been treated by unhelpful claims adjusters seldom finds its way into the mass media. Everything suggests that potential conflicts in this part of the market – whether about the generally value-laden issue of integrity or about values more specifically linked to the agreements, such as honesty and reasonable compensation – are captured and handled somewhere in the hierarchy of private dispute resolution instances.

CONCLUSION: CONFLICTS ORGANIZED OUT OF EXISTENCE?

The organizational history maintains a large presence in the value-laden Swedish personal insurance market. On one hand, disputed values constantly affected the organizing of the market. On the other hand, the market organization affected what values became visible in the debate in different time periods. I have shown how the self-regulatory apparatus established at the industry level during the 1940s in an aim to avert a far-reaching threat of socialization from dissatisfied citizens, and which was complemented by company-level bodies during the 1970s as a response to threats of sweeping statutory rights to transparency into companies for state consumer bodies, was put into use in the 2010s to prevent and solve problems relating to dissatisfied customers. The self-regulatory bodies built up in this way over a 70-year period were, among other things, capable of reducing open value conflicts concerning claims adjustments in the child insurance market. The disputes about new purchases of child insurance – an area where there is a lack of proactive self-regulatory bodies that can solve discrepancies at an early stage – were, however, much more visible in the mass media. Here, customer integrity and insurance firm solidity were central values that stood in conflict.

An overall impression, however, is that the total number of disputes in the private child insurance market in Sweden was strikingly few. This could be explained in part in that the vast majority of cases, not least the value-laden cases that could create very negative publicity, appear to have been resolved informally at the local level within companies, before they reached the numerous private and few public review instances higher up in the organizational hierarchy. Another explanation for the relatively limited number of disputes may naturally be that very few customers are dissatisfied with the product and compensation levels. An equally plausible explanation, however, is that the power resources of the firms are too big, and those of the consumers too small, for many open conflicts to come about. The likelihood of open conflicts between two parties is greatest when the power resources of the parties are fairly equal, and is reduced when the difference in power resources increases (Korpi 1987, p. 98). The firms' practice of requiring access to the customer's medical records in connection with purchasing a new insurance policy and in connection with insurance claims, appears also to be an extremely cost-effective system for control. This contributes to both prospective consumers and accepted consumers – knowing that there is complete transparency, body and soul exposed to the all-seeing eye of the insurance companies – being largely steered away from confrontational solutions and toward a self-imposed adaptation to, among other things, the rulings of the firms' legal and medical experts (cf. discussion of panopticism in Foucault 1987, p. 228; Garsten and Montoya 2008, pp. 6–7).

In its entirety, it would seem that this largely privately organized system for authoritative dispute resolution has thus been able to mute the value conflicts in the market. At the same time, around the turn of the century, 2000, public doctors and nurses began to demand legislation to protect the value of integrity (which was threatened by the firms' access to information in patient medical records) and that of fairness (which was threatened by those in most need not being able to obtain insurance). Although some of the demands have been addressed in amendments to the law, at the time of writing, spring 2012, it does not look as if potential conflicts concerning these values have been stably organized out of existence. That the central value in the rhetoric – transparency – does not extend to the companies' business activities in practice may also end up creating more tensions. Therefore, the same type of legitimacy crisis that threatened the more unregulated market of the 1800s, due to a lack of trust between firms and customers, could very well arise in the tightly state- and industry-regulated market of the early 2000s.

NOTES

1. The to-be or not-to-be debate about compensation for whiplash injuries in Sweden and other countries shows that there by no means needs to be a constant media silence on claims adjustment issues; see, for example, Ericson (2007, pp. 74–76).
2. Rejected customers have only the public courts to turn to, but it is costly to pursue matters in these courts if the complainant loses, which is often the case – see further discussions below.
3. The discussion on the institutional development of the insurance industry, 1850–2011, partially overlaps the background painted in Gustavsson (forthcoming; a sister study that looks at reviews carried out in connection with the purchase of new personal insurance policies and not, as here, disputes between firms and actual customers in connection with insurance claims).
4. The Swedish Consumers Insurance Bureau is a joint body run in the form of a foundation. However, because the advisory bureau is financed by the insurance industry and considered an expression of 'business and industry's own measures' (Ministry of Finance 2005, p. 27), it is placed under 'market' in Figure 6.1 (and not in civil society, in between market and state, which could be an alternative placement).
5. The state Financial Supervisory Authority is responsible for the supervision, setting regulations and licensing process for companies operating in financial markets.
6. An industry organization started in 1937 under the name of Swedish Insurance Companies Federation (Svenska Försäkringsbolags Riksförbund). At year-end 1990/91, the organization changed its name to the Swedish Insurance Federation (Sveriges Försäkringsförbund), and again in May 2011 to Insurance Sweden (Svensk Försäkring).
7. When ARN takes a decision, five board members and one rapporteur take part: the government appoints the chairperson and decides which authorities and industry organizations may appoint the other board members. Among the organizations that appoint members to represent consumer interests (two people) is the cooperative body Swedish Consumers' Association (Sveriges Konsumenter), and among the organizations that appoint members to represent the business interests of the insurance industry (two people) is the industry group Insurance Sweden (Svensk Försäkring, previously Sveriges Försäkringsförbund). The rapporteur, who is either a lawyer from the ARN office or an external lawyer, is appointed by ARN (SFS 2007:1041, §12, §25; Government Decision 2010). Myndigheters och organisationers representation i Allmänna reklamationsnämnden 2010).
8. A popular Swedish magazine for parents (*Vi föräldrar*) wrote that the ability to appeal a decision by one's insurance firm in child insurance cases ceased in February 2001. 'The National Board for Consumer Disputes [ARN] cites reasons relating to a lack of resources and expertise as an explanation for the decision . . . in the case of child insurance, "it is often a matter of medical expertise, which we lack here at ARN. So now consumers may lodge their complaints directly with the firms instead"', says an administrator from ARN (Nejman 2001, p. 55). The review of child insurance was later administered, however, on a modest scale as shown in Figure 6.3.

Configuring value conflicts in markets

9.   When PFN takes a decision, six board members, four of whom are appointed by the industry organization Insurance Sweden (Svensk försäkring), take part: the chairperson, two people with extensive experience of claims adjustment in insurance firms, and one medical advisor (a physician). Since 2004, there are also consumer representatives on the PFN board: two people appointed by a consumer advice association (Konsumentvägledarnas förening, a member organization of the Swedish Consumers' Association, Sveriges Konsumenter, a cooperative body that appoints members to ARN – cf. note 7) (Personal Insurance Board 2011; cf. Legal Committee 2004, pp. 68–69).
10. Based on the diverse underlying data available to the investigators from self-regulatory bodies in various Swedish industries, they concluded that the proportion of cases where decisions went in favor of the complainant had increased between 2002 and 2009 (Committee on Civil Affairs 2010, p. 28). The data I had access to, however, points in the other direction (see Figure 6.3).
11. Anna Augsburger, acting head, Customer Ombudsman (Kundombudsmannen), Skandia bank & försäkring, says in an email from 27 October 2010 that 'at present, there is no time to extract the information you are looking for', which could perhaps be interpreted as if the company might possibly open the door to its archives at some point in the future (Augsburger 2010).
12. Note that the search was done in Swedish, thus the actual search word used was the Swedish: *barnförsäkring**, with truncation [*] to get all grammatical forms of the search word.
13. Mediearkivet Svenska AB (a Retriever Research database) is a media archive containing approximately 450 Swedish print dailies, journals and trade publications. All of the big dailies are covered, as well as 95 percent of local newspaper circulations monitored by Tidnings Statistik AB (a firm that reviews and compiles circulation and distribution statistics). Mediearkivet contains a total of over 20 million articles in full-text or PDF format, the oldest dating back to January 1981 (Mediearkivet 2012).

REFERENCES

Archives

National Board for Consumer Disputes (Allmänna reklamationsnämnden, ARN), Stockholm.
Tvister om barn- och ungdomsförsäkringar [Disputes concerning child and youth insurance] (Code 3630), 1995–2010.
Personal Insurance Board (Personförsäkringsnämnden, PFN), Stockholm.
Tvister om sjuk- och olycksfallsförsäkringar där barnläkare har varit med på mötena [Disputes concerning medical and accident insurance, where paediatricians have been in attendance at meetings of the Board], 2004–2010.
Mediearkivet, Retriever Sverige AB, Stockholm.

Email

Augsburger, Anna (2010), Acting head, Customer Ombudsman (Kundombudsmannen), Skandia bank & försäkring, Stockholm, Sweden, 27 October 2010.

Literature

Appelqvist, Örjan (2000), *Bruten brygga: Gunnar Myrdal och Sveriges ekonomiska efterkrigspolitik 1943–1947*, Stockholm: Santérus, Diss. Stockholm University.
Arbetarrörelsens efterkrigsprogram: sammanfattning i 27 punkter (1944), Stockholm.
Baker, Tom and Jonathan Simon (2002), 'Embracing Risk', in Tom Baker and Jonathan Simon (eds), *Embracing Risk: The Changing Culture of Insurance and Responsibility*, Chicago, IL: University of Chicago Press, pp. 1–25.
Birgersson, Petter, Anna Bank and Ingemar D. Kristiansen (2010), 'Billig försäkring kan bli dyr', in *Sydsvenskan*, 13 October.
Brunsson, Nils (1991/2011), 'Politisering och företagisering – institutionell förankring och förvirring i organisationernas värld', in Rolf Lind and Anders Ivarsson Westerberg (eds), *Ledning av företag och förvaltningar: former, förutsättningar, förändring*, 4rd edn, Stockholm: SNS förlag, pp. 231–255.
Committee on Civil Affairs (Civilutskottet) (2010), *Näringslivets självregleringsorgan – utvecklingen sedan 2003*, Swedish Parliament (Riksdag), 2009/10:RFR12, Stockholm.
Ds 2005:13 (2005), *Försäkringsbolags tillgång till patientjournaler*, Ministry of Justice, Stockholm.
Englund, Karl (1993), *Skandiamän och andra försäkringsmän 1855–1970. Femtio biografiska studier*, Stockholm: Försäkrings AB Skandia.
Ericson, Richard V. (2007), *Crime in an Insecure World*, Cambridge UK: Polity.
Ericson, Richard V., Aaron Doyle and Dean Barry (2003), *Insurance as Governance*. Toronto; Buffalo: University of Toronto Press.
Fligstein, Neil (2001), *The Architecture of Markets: An economic sociology of twenty-first century capitalist societies*, Princeton, NJ: Princeton University Press.
Forslund, Petter and Anders Haraldsson (2011), 'Barnens skydd måste ses över. Bolagens barnförsäkringar får hård kritik av politiker', in *Svenska Dagbladet*, 9 September.
Foucault, Michel (1987), *Övervakning och straff: fängelsets födelse*, Lund: Arkiv.
Funke, Mikael (2004), *Att göra reklam för reklamen. Reklambranschens opinionsbildning 1965–1977*, Student thesis, advanced level, Fall 2004, Stockholm: Department of History, Stockholm University.
Garsten, Christina and Monica Lindh de Montoya (eds) (2008), 'Introduction: examining the politics of transparency', in Christina Garsten and Monica Lindh de Montoya (eds), *Transparency in a New Global Order: Unveiling organizational visions*, Cheltenham, UK and Northampton, MA, USA: Edward Elgar, pp. 1–21.
Government Bill (2010), *Prop. 2009/10:241 Ett förstärkt integritetsskydd i försäkringssammanhang*, Swedish Government, Stockholm.
Government Decision (2010), *Myndigheters och organisationers representation i Allmänna reklamationsnämnden* 2010-09-09, IJ2010/1527/KO, Swedish Government.
Grip, Gunvall (1987), *Vill du frihet eller tvång? Svensk försäkringspolitik 1935–1945*, Uppsala: Diss. Uppsala University.
Grip, Gunvall (1992), *Den försäkringsbehövande allmänhetens förtroende: sju uppsatser om svensk försäkring*, Stockholm: Assurans.

Gunnartz, Kristoffer (2007), *Välkommen till övervakningssamhället*, Stockholm: Bokförlaget DN.

Gustavsson, Martin (forthcoming), 'Protecting the Customers' Privacy – Attempts to Reform the Market for Personal Insurance', in Nils Brunsson and Mats Jutterström (eds), *Forming and Reforming Markets* (prel. title).

Haglind, Lars (2001), 'Lagstiftning eller självreglering – vad tycker lagstiftaren?', *Svensk Juristtidning*, 86 (3), 263–271.

Haufler, Virginia (2001), *A Public Role for the Private Sector: Industry self-regulation in a global economy*, Washington, DC: Carnegie Endowment for International Peace.

Haufler, Virginia (2003), 'Globalization and industry self-regulation', in Miles Kahler and David A. Lake (eds), *Governance in a Global Economy: Political authority in transition*, Princeton, NJ: Princeton University Press, pp. 226–252.

Heuman, Lars (1980), *Reklamationsnämnder och försäkringsnämnder*, Stockholm: Norstedts.

Johansson, Bengt H. (2005), 'Svårt för skadad få rätt mot försäkringsbolag. Domar i personskademål vid Stockholms tingsrätt 2003–2004', *Advokaten*, 71 (5), 24–25.

Jonson, Lars (2001), 'Marknadsrätten, särskilt regleringen av reklam', *Svensk Juristtidning*, 86 (3), 293–299.

Josefsson, Carl (2001), 'Lagstiftning eller självreglering? Olika aspekter på frågan om när och hur lagstiftningsinstrumentet bör användas', *Svensk Juristtidning*, 86 (3), 206–218.

Korpi, Walter (1987), 'Maktens isberg under ytan', in Olof Petersson (ed.), *Maktbegreppet*, Stockholm: Carlsson, pp. 83–117.

Larsson, Mats (1991), *Den reglerade marknaden: svenskt försäkringsväsende 1850–1980*, Stockholm: SNS.

Larsson, Mats, Mikael Lönnborg and Sven-Erik Svärd (2005a), *Den svenska försäkringsmodellens uppgång och fall*, Stockholm: Svenska försäkringsföreningen.

Larsson, Mats, Mikael Lönnborg and Sven-Erik Svärd (2005b), 'Staten, försäkringsbolagen och marknaden – svensk försäkring efter andra världskriget', *Nordisk försäkringstidskrift (NFT)*, 86 (4), 345–355.

Legal Committee (Lagutskottet) (2004), *Näringslivets självregleringsorgan: en uppföljningspromemoria*, Swedish Parliament (Riksdag), 2003/04:URD5, Stockholm.

Lewin, Leif (1970), *Planhushållningsdebatten*, 3rd edn, Stockholm: Almqvist and Wiksell.

Löfberg, Kjell (2000), 'Alla får råd hos försäkringsbyrån', in *Dagens Nyheter*, 9 October.

Lukes, Steven (1974), *Power: A Radical View*, London: Macmillan.

Mattsson, Dag (2001), 'Genteknik och försäkringar', *Svensk Juristtidning*, 86 (3), 309–313.

Mediearkivet (2012), 'Leverantör: Mediearkivet Svenska AB', available at http://www.kb.se/bibliotek/centrala-avtal/databaserna/mediearkivet/ (accessed 5 March 2012).

Ministry of Finance (2005), *Konsumentskyddet inom det finansiella området*, Memo by Anders Eriksson, Fi 2005/1958, Stockholm.

Ministry of Trade (1980), *Konsumentverkets uppgiftsbehov: betänkande från Insynsutredningen*, Stockholm: LiberFörlag.

Nejman, Fredrik (2001), 'Barnförsäkring – hitta den bästa för er!', *Vi föräldrar*, (13), 53–58.

Personal Insurance Board (Personförsäkringsnämnden) (2011), 'Nämndens sammansättning', available at http://www.forsakringsnamnder.se/templates/Page____203.aspx (accessed 19 December 2011).

Rahn, Anna (2011), Deputy Customer Ombudsman of Folksam, 'Vad klappar ditt hjärta för?', available at http://www.youtube.com/watch?v=XVWzkyBRzvA (accessed 20 December 2011).

SFS 2005:104 (2005), *Insurance Contracts Act*, Swedish Code of Statutes, Stockholm.

SFS 2007:1041 (2007), *Förordning med instruktion för Allmänna reklamationsnämnden*, Swedish Code of Statutes, Stockholm.

SFS 2011:12 (2011), *Lag om ändring i försäkringsavtalslagen (2005:104)*, Swedish Code of Statutes, Stockholm.

SOU 1979:5 (1979), *Konsumentinflytande genom insyn? En rapport från insynsutredningen*, Report of the Commission on Transparency for Consumers, Swedish Government Official Reports, Stockholm.

SOU 2004:47 (2004), *Näringslivet och förtroendet*, Report of the Commission on Business and Confidence, Swedish Government Official Reports, Stockholm.

Stenlås, Niklas (1998), *Den inre kretsen: den svenska ekonomiska elitens inflytande över partipolitik och opinionsbildning 1940–1949*, Diss. Uppsala University, Lund: Arkiv.

Stockholm District Court (2011), 'Judgement, Equality Ombudsman (DO) vs. Trygg-Hansa Försäkringsaktiebolag', Case no. T 20377-09, 8 March.

Swedish Consumer Agency (Konsumentverket) (2011), *KO företräder ettårig flicka i tvist med Skandia*, Press Release 16 December.

Swedish Consumers Insurance Bureau (Konsumenternas försäkringsbyrå) (2010), *Verksamheten 2010*, Stockholm.

Swedish Consumers Insurance Bureau (Konsumenternas försäkringsbyrå) (2012), 'Guide vid val av barnförsäkring', available at http://bankforsakring.konsum enternas.se/Forsakring/Barn/Barnforsakring/Guide-vid-val-av-barnforsakring/ (accessed 8 March 2012).

Swedish National Council on Medical Ethics (2002), *Angående försäkringsbolagens tillgång till och hantering av journaluppgifter*, Written Communication 18 December (Ref. 42/02), Stockholm.

Trosdahl, Kristian (2007), 'Sosialiseringsspøkelset – bare et knirk i trappen?', *Nordisk försäkringstidskrift (NFT)*, 88 (3), 273–289.

Weilenmann, Leni (2001a), '4-åring nekats teckna försäkring', in *Dagens Nyheter*, 9 January.

Weilenmann, Leni (2001b), 'Sjuka får inte försäkra sig', in *Dagens Nyheter*, 17 October.

Wijkström, Filip and Torbjörn Einarsson (2006), *Från nationalstat till näringsliv? Det civila samhällets organisationsliv i förändring*, Stockholm: Ekonomiska forskningsinstitutet (EFI), Handelshögskolan i Stockholm.

Zelizer, Viviana A. Rotman (1979), *Morals and Markets: The development of life insurance in the United States*, New York, NY: Columbia University Press.

Zelizer, Viviana A. Rotman (1994), *Pricing the Priceless Child: The changing social value of children*, Princeton, NJ: Princeton University Press.

7. 'The word' and 'the money': balancing values in the online newspaper market

Karolina Windell

INTRODUCTION

> The problem is finding a way to defend journalistic quality – there is a risk that quality deteriorates in the commercial media landscape. (Editor-in-chief of *Svenska Dagbladet*'s culture section, Publicistklubben website, 15 April 2009)

The quote above reflects the escalating debate about the newspaper market and its recent transformation. The challenges that the newspaper market has witnessed over time have raised concern. The media is commonly described as the fourth estate, referring to its role as an objective auditor and scrutinizer of government as well as an important information provider in society (Thurén 1988). Newspapers are therefore often understood as a public good central to the formation of opinion and the democratic conversation in society – that is values worth protecting for the benefit of the common good (Hvitfelt 2008). In the debate about the newspaper crisis, it is therefore often underlined that it is not only an economic crisis for newspaper owners but also a societal problem, as the democratic conversation is thereby endangered (cf. Greer 2004; Bergström et al. 2005; Berte and De Bens 2008; Hvitfelt and Nygren 2008). The institutionalized idea about the value of newspapers for the democratic conversation distinguishes the newspaper market from many other markets in terms of that it is not only commercially driven but that it also serves a role as provider of a public good. In Sweden, this distinctive role has, for example, been manifested in attempts by the government to prevent the 'death' of newspapers (Gustafsson 2007).

The newspaper market is characterized by and organized around strong ideas about how newspapers uphold the values of the democratic conversation and the formation of opinion. The newspaper market in Sweden was initially dominated by private companies but popular movements and political parties have also contributed to the establishment of newspapers

– often prioritizing the formation of opinion over commercial success (Gustafsson 2007). In the newspaper market, the value of economic prosperity is therefore complemented by or, as some would even argue, competes with the values of the formation of opinion and the democratic conversation. Over the years, the tension between 'the word' and 'the money' has been manifested in different ways. For example, newspaper organizations have commonly been separated into an editorial unit with a chief editor, and an administrative unit led by a CEO (Engwall 1985; Nygren 2008). This division of work demonstrates a clear idea that the word – the editorial work – must be separated from the economic work. In previous research, it has even been argued that a newspaper organiza- tion is characterized by two contrasting cultures – the editorial culture, which prioritizes content and thoughts, and the economic culture, which highlights values about economic results (Nygren 2008: 48). The borders between the editorial and economic have become blurred over time, however, as economic issues have come to play a greater role in the news- paper organization, not seldom resulting in conflicts between the editorial and economic cultures. This development has been called market-driven journalism, referring to the establishment of a stronger managerial culture even in the editorial work (Nygren 2008).

As I show in this chapter, in today's changing media landscape, the fric- tion between journalistic ideals and financial performance has increased. The chapter demonstrates how the introduction of new technology – that makes it possible to track readers' reading preferences online – makes it difficult to separate the 'the word' from 'the money' in the online newspaper market. This in turn raises questions about how co-existing values about the formation of opinion and the democratic conversation on one hand, and the importance of financial soundness on the other, are managed in the Swedish online newspaper market. How do these values relate to one another and to what extent is one value prioritized over the other?

VALUES GUIDING JOURNALISTIC PRACTICE

Values outline which actions are desirable, accurate and worthwhile within a particular social sphere (see Chapter 1). In previous research, journalism and the production of news have been described as being permeated with values that give news producers a shared perception of why news production is important, who news producers are, what con- stitutes news, and how news production is practiced (cf. Bourdieu 1996; Cook 1998). It has been noted that journalism is driven by ideals about the value of contributing to the formation of opinion and the democratic conversation (cf. Thurén 1988; Hvitfelt 2008; Nygren 2008). This can be seen as an overarching value in news production, answering the question of why journalism is performed. As argued by Torsten Thurén (1988: 18), 'The mass media has an important function in democratic society, they are indispensable. If the mass media do not do their job – democracy cannot function'. Journalists share common ideas about their professional role and work – both in terms of why journalism is important and how it ought to be performed.

Mark Deuze (2005: 447) argues that journalism can be understood as an occupational ideology comprising five building blocks that define journalism and journalists as: (1) providing a public service; (2) neutral, objective, fair and (thus) credible; (3) autonomous, free and independent; (4) having a sense of immediacy, actuality and speed; and (5) having a sense of ethics, validity and legitimacy. Other researchers have argued that journalists not only share common ideas about who they are and what purposes journalism serves, but also that their day-to-day work is guided by common values that serve as 'organizing principles' of what to cover and how to cover it – often described as 'news valuation' or 'media logic'. Several researchers have tried to capture this process of news selection, and to categorize what types of issues become news. For example, it is argued that issues have a news value if they: (1) have consequences for the readers; (2) have geographical proximity to the reader; (3) are unexpected; (4) include celebrities; and/or (5) include crimes, conflicts or traumas (cf. Hvitfelt 1985; McManus 1994; Nygren 2008). However, what ends up in the newspaper is also influenced by two overarching and contrasting ideas found in the journalistic occupational role: (1) that news produc-tion means giving the readers what they want to read; and (2) that news production is about giving the readers what they ought to read; where the first idea reflects a more market-driven journalism and the second a more ideal-driven journalism (cf. Nygren 2008: 228). Thus, research has demon-strated that journalism and news production are not only about publish-ing news based on journalistic ideals about the importance of contributing to the democratic conversation. On the contrary, research has indicated that news production always implies a negotiation between commercial realities and journalistic ideals (cf. Hultén 1999).

Based on previous research, it is therefore apt to argue that news production is both guided by overarching values about the core of news journalism, that is, contributing to the democratic conversation, and about producing a newspaper that can sustain itself on commercial grounds. Recent research has indicated that the managerial culture is entering the editorial work and contributing to an evolution toward a more market-driven journalism (cf. Nygren 2008). And, moreover, it has been argued that the journalistic profession is undergoing change, indicating that journalistic ideals and values are being interwoven with market values (Andersson and Wiik 2012). For these reasons, it is relevant to explore how the introduction of new technology – that makes it possible to measure the commercial value of editorial content – influences the value balance in the online newspaper market.

METHOD

In order to capture how values are upheld and how potential value conflicts arise in the online newspaper market, the chapter is based on interviews, documents and online video clips from media conferences. A total of 17 interviews were conducted in the spring of 2010 with representatives of Swedish media organizations (that is reporters, editors and CEOs of newspaper organizations), media analysts, representatives of trade associations and trade journals, and with representatives from the Ministry of Culture. The interviews with media representatives served the purpose of developing knowledge about how new technology transforms online news production, and provided informative accounts about potential value conflicts. I carefully selected interviewees, who were key actors engaged in using and developing new technology in online news production.

Against this backdrop, interviews were conducted with representatives from some of the largest Swedish online news media organizations (Aftonbladet.se, DI.se, DN.se, E24.se, Expressen.se, SvD.se and VA.se). Interviews were conducted with newspaper reporters, editors, editors-in-chief and business managers specifically responsible for the news sites or insights into online news production. In addition, interviews were conducted with other key actors that could give important accounts of the transformation of the online newspaper market. Interviews were therefore also conducted with the CEO at the Swedish news agency TT.se, the head of future and media at the Swedish media company Bonnier, the editor-in-chief of the trade journal *Medievärlden* ('The Media World'), representatives from Tidningsutgivarna (a trade association for newspaper publishers), the head of digital media at Tidningsstatistik (TS, a trade association that tracks newspaper statistics), and a political advisor from the Ministry of Culture.

The chapter also draws on document studies of trade magazines, reports from media research institutes, literature from research groups and trade associations, and official documents from the Ministry of Culture and Press Subsidies Council, as well as online video clips from media conferences and panel debates with journalists, editors and media experts from the spring and autumn of 2010.

TRANSFORMATION OF THE MEDIA LANDSCAPE

The long-term developments of declining subscriptions and recent withdrawal of advertisers from the newspaper market have resulted in headlines announcing the impending death of newspapers. Pronouncements predicting the death of newspapers are, however, not new. As far back as in 1961, a chronicle with the headline 'Newspapers dying' was published in the Swedish daily *Svenska Dagbladet* (see Engwall 1983). Being among the oldest mass media, newspapers have time and time again faced the challenge of other newer media: in the 1920s, when the radio broadcast was born; when the television broadcast had its breakthrough in the 1970s; when local radio broadcasts began in Sweden; and finally, in the 1990s, when free dailies were launched in Sweden (Bergström and Wadbring 2005; Weibull 2005).

The reason behind the current debate about the future of newspapers stems from the expansion of digital technology, which has led to radical transformations in the newspaper industry. Firstly, newspapers are witnessing a decline of subscribers as well as increasing competition for advertisers. The expansion of new forms of media has given journalists as well as citizens in general new tools for producing and distributing news. This also implies that readers can find news not only in print newspapers, but also via digital channels, where the news or information is available free of charge (cf. Berte and De Bens 2008). This has been manifested in decreasing consumption of newspapers over recent decades and in particular since the introduction of online news. Between 1970 and 2009, the circulation figures for dailies (issued 4–7 days a week) fell by 15 percent (TS Industry Statistics 2010). In the last decade alone, when the online papers made their entry into the market, the circulation of dailies dropped 12 percent and evening press circulation figures by 19 percent. However, as stressed above, it is not only the decrease in readers that has created difficulties, but also the increasing competition for advertising. As the number of digital media channels increases, so too does the ability to attract advertisers, which increases the competition over advertisers. All in all, this leads to falling revenue for newspaper organizations.

Secondly, as new ways of consuming news and distributing news have been introduced, it is no longer self-evident that news content is produced by professional groups such as journalists (see for example Kline 2005; Grafström and Windell 2012a). Instead, an increasing number of actors take part in online news production and it is often carried out in interaction between journalists, readers and bloggers. The entrance of digital technology has made it possible for everyone to take part in news production. And it has also become possible for newspaper organizations to take their newspaper outlets online. This means that the number of news producers as well as news outlets is expanding. The technological changes in the media landscape that enables anyone and everyone to publish their own news contributes to a diversification of the democratic conversation in society. However, it is at the same time argued that this may undermine journalistic identity as well as endanger the quality of journalism (cf. Singer 2003; Karlsson 2010). As readers can put together their own news, journalism's role as gatekeeper is challenged (Nygren 2008). Such concerns were expressed at a seminar arranged by the Swedish Publicists' Association (Publicistklubben) in April 2009 entitled 'Journalism – What's the problem?' where one of the participating journalists expressed his worries with the following words:

> There is a traditional form; a classical definition of journalism – to inform, to entertain, and to scrutinize some kind of power. If we take this as our point of departure, the question is how we are to do this. The way I see it, there've never been so many qualified and well-educated journalists as today. At the same time, never before have so many written so much about so little. And here I think there is much more we can do. We [journalists] have an advantage compared to those other people who are trying to compete with good journalism. (Knut Kainz Rognerud, reporter, *Dagens Nyheter*)

Thus, the industry's vulnerable financial situation as well as the entrance of other news producers has given rise to an intense debate about the future of newspapers and their role in society. Concerns are expressed that the uncertain financial situation of newspapers will not only lead to their death, but also affect the journalistic quality of news production, which will have consequences for the formation of public opinion and the democratic conversation.

The 'Click Spiral' and its Consequences

The introduction of online newspapers is one of the more influential shifts in the newspaper market in the past 10–15 years. During this period, over 100 dailies have launched online versions of their print newspapers in Sweden (Hedman 2008) and, in concert with this trend, online news readership has increased dramatically (Nilsson et al. 2008; Nordicom 2009). When newspaper organizations introduced their online papers, however, few had business plans in place; instead, the web was seen as just another channel through which PDF versions of the printed news could be distributed (Greer 2004; Alström and Hedman 2008). This meant that the same news that readers had to subscribe to in the print edition was distributed for free at news sites. The early development of online papers has therefore become a drawback for the newspaper market. The consumers' willingness to buy print newspapers has decreased as news content has been made available at no cost on the web.

Newspaper companies in Sweden and elsewhere have therefore experimented and tested new ways to charge readers for online news (Hedman 2008). For example, in October 2009 the US-based daily *Newsday* began to charge readers for the online news content. Three months later, however, there were only 35 subscribers (Stampen 2010). In 2010, two German news sites in the Axel Springer Group, *Berliner Morgenpost* and *Hamburger Abendblatt*, and the French daily *Le Figaro*, put their websites behind a pay wall. The same year, the Swedish evening tabloid *Aftonbladet* launched a subscription service, *Plustjänst*, enabling readers to subscribe to premium articles and news content. Few attempts have been successful, however, and online news production has thus become more or less entirely dependent on advertisements (Hedman 2008). In Sweden, more than half of print newspaper sales revenues stem from advertising, and for online newspapers advertisements are crucial since advertising is often their only source of income (Nordicom 2009). Online newspapers are not only competing against each other for advertisers but, as described above, against other internet channels such as Google and Facebook. In the Nordic countries, newspapers' share of the advertising market used to be around 50 percent; however, this share has fallen over the past decade to the benefit of other internet channels (Nordicom 2009).

Newspapers have always been dependent on two income sources – readers and advertisers. These two income sources are highly dependent on one another. In previous research, the relationship between advertisers and readers has been described as the 'circulation spiral', which underlines how high circulation numbers attract advertising, allowing newspapers to flourish and making them even more attractive to readers, and thus also even more attractive to advertisers (Engwall 1983). One reason behind this relationship is the development of tracking statistics for circulation figures of print newspapers. Sweden began to track circulation statistics in the 1940s, clearly exposing newspapers' possible competitive advantages (Gustafsson 2007). It became possible for advertisers to access the circulation figures of all of the newspapers in Sweden, and they could easily evaluate where they would get the most exposure.

Today, we are seeing a similar development with news sites. As stressed above, advertising is often the only source of income for online newspapers. In order to attract advertisers, however, just as print newspapers, they must present high readership numbers. One could therefore argue that the circulation spiral is just as valid for describing the relationship between readers and advertisers in online journalism – though a more proper name for it would be the 'click spiral', referring to the measurement of the number of clicks on news items at news sites.

The establishment of tracking clicks of all Swedish websites – the so-called 'KIA Index' – has made it possible for journalists and editors not only to keep track of their readers' habits and evaluate what type of news items are read the most, but it also implies that the commercial value of editorial content can be evaluated. In other words, it is now possible to collect detailed information about readership statistics that are compiled in the KIA Index and distributed to advertisers, providing them with information about where to advertise. Hence, it has become important to attract readers to news sites since reader numbers also attract advertisers and secure the financial situation of the online newspaper.

Briefly stated, the KIA Index can be described as the 'official measurement currency' for Swedish websites (www.kia-index.net), controlled and managed by the Association of Swedish Advertisers (Sveriges Annonsörer). The KIA Index publishes a weekly index based on three types of data from Swedish websites: (1) the number of visitors; (2) the total number of visits; and (3) the total number of clicks on items on the websites. The index is distributed for free to advertisers, customers and other stakeholders. Results from the weekly index can also be downloaded from the KIA Index website (www.kia-index.net). One can also download and view statistics of the most visited websites in Sweden for a particular week, or compare the most visited sites in a particular industry. For example, one can compare the most visited nationwide online newspapers on a weekly basis. The KIA Index also has detailed information about the number of visitors at different parts of websites. It is therefore possible to access data about which parts/pages of an online newspaper – for example, business section, culture section or sports pages – that receive the most visitors.

The KIA Index has thus become an important tool in the competition for advertisers. The development of the KIA Index also has implications for the everyday work of online newspapers. The index has made it possible to calculate the exact number of readers of each news item on a news site. As stressed above, this makes it possible to evaluate what kind of news items readers like to read. And, thus, it also becomes evident what news items have a commercial value. In the editorial work, this creates new incentives to follow reader patterns in real time on the web and to edit news items in order to make them more attractive to readers. More clicks on news items make the online newspaper even more attractive to advertisers. Attracting more readers to the news sites therefore means better performance in the KIA Index and, consequently, better chances of attracting advertisers. This raises questions about the value balance between journalistic ideals and commercial realities. To what extent is new technology influencing the online newspaper product in terms of content and presentation?

Giving Readers What They Want or What They Ought to Read?

Today, newspaper sites have their own so-called 'traffic systems', which are used to track reader visits to their news sites. This implies that the editorial staff can follow this traffic minute by minute, and that they can observe exactly how many readers an online news site has during the course of the day and, moreover, exactly how many readers click on each news item. The ability to track readers' behavior in real time influences how the journalistic product is evaluated and developed; in other words, it influences how news is selected and presented. Publishing decisions are based on data from the traffic systems.

In the interviews with journalists and editors, they state that it has become increasingly important to monitor reader habits and attract readers to the news sites. Editorial staff at the news sites follow the reader traffic on a daily basis and observe the extent to which articles are being clicked on. If an article receives fewer clicks than expected for an article placed in a certain position on the news site at a certain time of the day, the article may be pulled or revised. This can mean changing the headline or the introduction, or perhaps adding a picture. If the number of clicks on the news article is still not satisfying, the article may eventually be removed. The manager of research and development at *Svenska Dagbladet* explains that it is important to constantly monitor the traffic at the news site in order to revise articles if the number of clicks needs to be increased.

> Readers influence the news articles at the news site to a much greater extent than in the print newspaper. The readers at the news site influence both what we publish and where we place the article on the news site. This is one of the things that the web allows. It allows us to measure . . .. We are aware of the fact that the number of clicks is so important and that we therefore need to keep track of them. (Interview with manager of research and development, *Svenska Dagbladet*, 11 March 2010)

The business manager for Aftonbladet.se gives a similar account of the editorial work at the news site. He explains that the traffic system is of importance and, for this reason, at least one person in the editorial staff keeps a constant eye on the number of clicks on the news site. Based on this information the editor of the site decides how long a news item can be posted on the site and when it should be revised or deleted. Following the traffic on news sites means that the site editor needs to make decisions about whether or not to revise articles in order to increase the number of clicks. The business manager explains the procedure for revising articles that have fewer clicks than expected.

> We try to find a new angle, a new headline or a new picture. . . . Sometimes we don't have the resources to find a new angle and therefore the article might be deleted instead. . . . It is fantastic how something can be changed. Some of our co-workers are so skilled at revising articles. We can have a news item that has been lagging behind all day and then suddenly one of our co-workers notices this and changes the headline and the article is just overloaded with clicks. (Interview with business manager, Aftonbladet.se, 16 March 2010)

Similar accounts can be found in previous literature about online journalism. For example, a study of the editorial work at di.se (the online edition of *Dagens Industri*, a daily business newspaper) demonstrated that the content as well as the prioritization of news articles – where they are presented on the news site and for how long – is based on reader behavior data from the traffic system (Lord and Malicki Jakobsson 2008).

It is also evident, however, that journalists are reluctant to admit that they are giving the readers what they want to read. Instead, the argument is often that journalists need to balance news that they consider important and that the readers ought to read, with news that 'sells', that is gets readers to click on the news item. For example, the editor-in-chief at the business news site di.se argues that, even though they track reader behavior, it is the news site's journalistic ambition that determines what gets published and what does not. Listening only to what the readers want would erode the newspaper brand:

> [Based on the information from the traffic system] we know pretty instinctively what our readers are interested in. However, this doesn't mean that they always get what they want. If that were the case, they would only get articles like 'your apartment is worth 50 billion' or nude shots of his Majesty the King, and that would kill our brand in two weeks. But the traffic system is very important to us. (Interview with editor-in-chief, di.se, 9 March 2010)

The business manager for the Aftonbladet website also underlines the importance of not basing their decisions about the editorial content solely on readers' clicks, since that would give the news site an in appropriate editorial profile.

> If a celebrity loses his or her pants, that news item gets a lot of clicks, but we can't make a big deal out of it on the news site, though we may decide to keep the news item up for a while since it has lots of clicks. . . . But we can't only go on the clicks, because then we'd only have one type of news content. For example, if we did that we wouldn't have any news about the EU, which we also have to have. (Interview with business manager, Aftonbladet.se, 16 March 2010)

A similar argument is presented in a handbook about online journalism written by journalist Kristian Lindquist (2010: 17). In the book Lindquist offers the advice that: 'if a puff doesn't get any clicks, it may be a signal that it needs to be revised', and 'the clicks may influence your work, but never let them govern your work' (author's translation).

It is thus argued that listening only to the readers would result in what is often called 'click journalism' – meaning that the journalistic production is adjusted in order to increase the number of 'clicks' by online readers (cf. Karlsson 2010). The interviews indicate a certain ambivalence towards the traffic systems. On one hand, they make it easier to evaluate what readers want to read – what sells; and on the other hand, it becomes even more important for journalists to determine what they think readers ought to read. The problematic relationship towards the new technology is expressed by an editor in a previous study of an online newspaper (Lord and Malicki Jakobsson 2008: 173):

> You are faced with increasing pressure to do that [give the readers what they want]. It's good because the readers are given what they want. It can also be bad if it means that it goes against your own opinion about what is important. But do I have the right to decide what they want to read? Yes, it is my role as an editor to tell them – this is what we're interested in. And then I realize they [the readers] are not interested in this, they're interested in Britney Spears' new car.

As suggested in the interviews as well as in previous literature, the journalist's role as gatekeeper – deciding which issues are to be presented as news in the newspaper – is challenged by new media (cf. Nygren 2008; Lindquist 2010). The journalist's occupational role, as discussed earlier in the chapter, builds on the idea that journalists are autonomous, free and independent, and that they have a sense of what types of news should be published in order for the newspaper to contribute to the democratic conversation. However, at the same time, journalists are limited by the commercial reality and, as new technology makes it possible to track reader behaviour and more or less evaluate the commercial value of each news item, journalists face a situation where they need to balance their ideas about what readers want to read with their ideas about what they think readers ought to read. As discussed above, journalists and editors are engaged in a constant negotiation between these two ideas. News items with few readers are revised in order to attract more readers. But news items are not adjusted entirely according to what readers want. Indirectly, this means that in their daily work journalists balance values about commercial success with values about the importance of producing news that furthers the democratic conversation.

As a consequence of the KIA Index, online newspapers struggle to attract readers in order to improve their web traffic statistics and thus attract advertisers. Even though the interviewees stress that journalists need to listen to their own ideas about what news should be published, it is evident that the quest for advertising influences the news content. It is a fact that online journalists monitor reader behaviour and revise articles in order to attract readers. And journalism is hereby bound to change. As Lindquist put it in his handbook for online journalism (2010: 96):

> The ability to interact with readers is influencing journalism. . . . Researchers argue that news journalism needs to develop from being more of a lecture to being more of a seminar. Or, to express it differently: to go from monologue to dialogue. (Author's translation)

In order to attract readers, online newspapers not only revise articles but they also seek a dialogue with readers on their news sites. This is often done by allowing comments and blog links to articles, and some news sites even encourage readers to send in their own news stories and to upload their own photos. This so-called 'user-generated' content is sometimes also used by journalists and reporters to create news. For example, reader comments and reader polls are sometimes turned into news stories. One of the interviewees gives an account of how reader polls are becoming an important feature in the news-producing process:

> Mr. Reinfeldt [the Swedish prime minister] makes a statement and we publish what he said, and then the readers say something about that. For us it's very interesting to know what the readers say. It enables us to summarize what they say, and then we can call Mr. Reinfeldt back and tell him what our readers think. . .and ask for his response. And then he answers the readers, and the readers react again, and we can continue on like that and be somewhat of a bridge between the people and the power. (Interview with business manager, Aftonbladet.se, 16 March 2010)

The goal is to keep the discussion going about that issue all day, as reader interaction itself is argued to attract other readers to the news site. In this way, content created by actors other than journalists themselves is seen as valuable and as something that is a key part of the emerging practice of online news production. As newspaper organizations invite their readers to comment on articles and participate in reader polls, readers thereby also become part of the news-producing process. That means that more actors contribute to the democratic conversation. This is, to some extent, valued but it also means that the gatekeeping role of journalists is reduced and thus, news selection becomes an interactive process between the professionals and their audience.

CONCLUDING DISCUSSION

The online newspaper market has undergone several dramatic changes. The competition for readers as well as advertising has intensified and several voices have announced the impending death of newspapers. As described in the introduction, these problems are not considered merely a market problem for the newspaper organizations. It is commonly argued that a democratic society needs an ongoing conversation with several voices – that is several media producers – that give different versions of what is happening (Hvitfelt 2008). Ideally a multitude of newspapers secures the democratic conversation in society. As newspapers struggle to survive, concerns are expressed about how to protect journalism's freedom and independence as the competition for advertisers and readers increases. As stressed in the quote in the introduction of this chapter: 'The problem is finding a way to defend journalistic quality – there is a risk that quality deteriorates in the commercial media landscape' (Editor-in-chief of *Svenska Dagbladet*'s culture section, Publicistklubben debate website, 15 April 2009). Thus, in the debate, concerns are voiced both about the survival of newspapers and about how the quality of journalism can be protected. In other words, the increasing commercialization of the media landscape has raised questions about how this will influence the character of journalism and the occupational role of journalists.

This chapter set out to explore how co-existing values about the formation of opinion and the democratic conversation on one hand, and the importance of financial soundness on the other, are managed as new technology is introduced in the online newspaper market. New technology has made it possible to calculate the exact number of readers of each news item in online journalism, thereby enabling newspapers and advertisers to evaluate the commercial value of editorial content.

The findings indicate that there is a value conflict between journalistic ideals and commercial realities. To some extent, the respondents in this study indicate that what is measured, counts. As reader traffic is measured and compiled into an index, which is then used by advertisers when deciding where to advertise, it has become important to monitor reader behaviour at news sites and to actively increase the number of readers at these sites. The measurement of news site traffic has thereby come to influence news production practices. The focus in online journalism is not only on news production in terms of what news to produce, how to present it, and how to keep up the pace of the flow of news on news sites. The new technology has also made it important and worthwhile to monitor how articles are consumed and to revise them in order to make them more palatable for readers.

The reader has always played a central role in news production. In the newspaper market, the formulation and presentation of news is governed by the journalists and their professional ideas about what types of news ought to be published and how they ought to be presented (cf. Bourdieu 1996; Cook 1998). These ideas are of course also based on ideas about what readers ought to read and, thus, the reader has always been at the center of journalists' minds. However, in online journalism, the reader has come to play a more active role in news production as journalists follow reader habits online and adjust the presentation of news in order to attract readers. Through blog links and comments, readers are active on news sites and, at times, their comments are turned into news. Online news is consequently adjusted according to readers' habits and readers even indirectly take part in the presentation and making of news.

This has also contributed to a change in how readers are looked upon – previously, there was a more or less we-write-and-you-read attitude. Today, however, news production has become a more interactive process between journalists and their readers. We can also observe a process where the journalist's occupational identity is changing and a new form of online journalism is being established, governed by other norms and values than those of traditional journalism, stressing the importance of shorter deadlines and social interaction with the readers (cf. Grafström and Windell 2012b). Although we see changes in the journalistic identity, previous studies indicate that journalistic ideals and values about the purpose of journalism and what journalists do are maintained (cf. Andersson and Wiik 2012). For example, in the commercialized media landscape, there is an increased debate among journalists about the importance of protecting newspapers' role in contributing to the democratic conversation. Moreover, the editorial staff of online newspapers interviewed in this study emphasize the importance of not renouncing journalistic values for commercial gain. In today's online newspaper market, the value of contributing to the democratic conversation therefore seems to be accentuated rather than omitted. For this reason, it is apt to raise the question of whether and to what extent values about commercial success are prioritized and receive increased influence over journalism and journalistic ideas?

However, there is an obvious contradiction here. On one hand, the respondents in this study as well as other studies (cf. Lord and Malicki Jakobsson 2008) underlined the importance of publishing what readers ought to read rather than what they want to read. This indicates that journalists are trying to maintain their autonomy and role as gatekeepers in the newspaper market – since it is believed that professional journalists are trained to protect the journalism standards and to select and present news that contributes to the democratic conversation. Journalists seek to manifest the idea that online journalism contains quality that cannot be found in other web forums authored by non-professional journalists (Grafström and Windell 2012b).

Still, it is obvious that the growing quest for advertisers has an influence on the product – the news sites. In order to make oneself attractive in the market where online newspapers earn their money – the advertising market – they need to be relevant and need to attract to readers. This makes it difficult to sustain ideals about producing news that readers ought to read for the greater good. Instead, what we see is a constant – minute-by-minute – negotiation between news that readers want to read and news that journalists want to give the readers. This dual role of newspapers has also been stressed elsewhere; for example, Gustafsson (2007: 58) argues that:

> Newspapers often play a double role. They play an important role in the democratic system, but at the same time play a central role as media in the commercial system. They seek their success in one market, the circulation market, but are reworded in another, the advertising market. (Author's translation)

With today's technological advances, the link between the readers' market and the advertising market becomes even closer. It is therefore inevitable that online newspapers end up in a 'click spiral', seeking as many clicks as they can to secure advertisements that will in turn secure their survival. What we see is that commercialism does not emerge as more important than contributing to the democratic conversation – at the rhetorical level. In other words, journalistic ideals seem resistant to technological changes. However, the practice of news production may become more affected by commercialism. As emphasized in previous research, what people say about what they do is not necessarily the same as what they actually do (cf. Czarniawska 2004). These findings may serve as a fruitful point of departure for further studies, of ethnographic design perhaps, that seek to explore how values about journalism and democracy are reconfigured, and how this in turn influences editorial work and market practices.

REFERENCES

Alström, Börje and Hedman, Lowe (2008). Medieföretag utan strategier. In Hvitfelt, Håkan and Nygren, Gunnar (eds), *På väg mot medievärlden 2020: Journalistik, teknik och marknad*. Lund: Studentlitteratur.

Andersson, Ulrika and Wiik, Jenny (2012). Synen på journalistikens drivkrafter. In Asp, Kent (ed.), *Svenska journalister 1989–2011*. Göteborg: Department of Journalism, Media and Communication, University of Gothenburg.

Bergström, Annika and Wadbring, Ingela (2005). Introduktion till en 25-åring. In Bergström, Annika, Wadbring, Ingela and Weibull, Lennart (eds), *Nypressat – en kvartssekel med svenska dagstidningsläsare*. Gothenburg: Department of Journalism, Media and Communication, University of Gothenburg.

Bergström, Annika, Wadbring, Ingela and Weibull, Lennart (2005). *Nypressat – en kvartssekel med svenska dagstidningsläsare*. Gothenburg: Department of Journalism, Media and Communication, University of Gothenburg.

Berte, Katrien and De Bens, Els (2008). Newspapers go for advertising. New challenges in the media landscape. *Journalism Studies* 9(5): 692–703.

Bourdieu, Pierre (1996). *The Rules of Art*. Cambridge, UK: Polity Press.

Cook, Timothy E. (1998). *Governing with the News. The news media as a political institution*. Chicago: University of Chicago Press.

Czarniawska, Barbara (2004). *Narratives in Social Science Research*. London: Sage Publications.

Deuze, Mark (2005). What is journalism? Professional identity and ideology of journalists reconsidered. *Journalism* 6(4): 442–464.

Engwall, Lars (1983). *Den dubbla spiralen. En betraktelse över dagstidningarnas konkurrensvillkor*. Working Paper 1983/4, Department of Business Studies, Uppsala University.

Engwall, Lars (1985). *Från vag vision till komplex organisation: En studie av Värmlands Folkblads ekonomiska och organisatoriska utveckling*. Uppsala University.

Grafström, Maria and Windell, Karolina (2012a). Newcomers conserving the old: Transformation processes in the field of news journalism. *Scandinavian Journal of Management* 28: 65–76.

Grafström, Maria and Windell, Karolina (2012b). *Going Online: The transformation of normative ideas in the professional field of journalism*. Conference paper presented at the 28th EGOS Colloquium 2012, Helsinki.

Greer, Jennifer D. (2004). Advertising on traditional media sites: Can the traditional business model be translated to the Web? *Social Science Journal* 41: 107–113.

Gustafsson, Karl Erik (2007). *Det svenska presstödets marknadskonsekvenser*. Analysis commissioned by the Swedish Ministry of Culture, 13 February 2007.

Hedman, Love (2008). Internet utmanar. In Hvitfelt, Håkan and Nygren, Gunnar (eds), *På väg mot medievärlden 2020: Journalistik, teknik och marknad*. Lund: Studentlitteratur.

Hultén, Lars J. (1999). *Orden och pengarna: om kamp och kapitulation inom journalistiken*. Stockholm: Natur och Kultur.

Hvitfelt, Håkan (1985). *På första sidan – en studie i nyhetsvärdering*. Stockholm: National Board of Psychological Defence.

Hvitfelt, Håkan (2008). Det går allt snabbare – om medieutveckling och demokrati.

In Hvitfelt, Håkan and Nygren, Gunnar (eds), *På väg mot medievärlden 2020: Journalistik, teknik och marknad.* Lund: Studentlitteratur.

Hvitfelt, Håkan and Nygren, Gunnar (2008). *På väg mot medievärlden 2020: Journalistik, teknik och marknad.* Lund: Studentlitteratur.

Karlsson, Michael (2010). *Nätnyheter: Från sluten produkt till öppen process.* Stockholm: Institute for Media Studies.

Kline, David (2005). I Blog, therefore I am. In Kline, David and Burstein, Dan (eds), *Blog! How the newest media revolution is changing politics, business, and culture.* New York: CDS Books, pp. 237–252.

Lindquist, Kristian (2010). *Webbjournalistik.* Stockholm: Norstedts.

Lord, Camilla and Malicki Jakobsson, Karoline. 2008. Snabb, vass och växande. In Nygren, Gunnar (ed.), *Nyhetsfabriken: journalistiska yrkesroller i en förändrad medievärld.* Lund: Studentlitteratur.

McManus, John H. (1994). *Market-driven Journalism – Let the citizens beware?* Thousand Oaks, CA: Sage Publications.

Nilsson, Åsa, Ohlsson, Jonas and Sternvik, Johanna (2008). Pressande tider för den prenumererade morgontidningen. In Holmberg, Sören and Weibull, Lennart (eds), *Skilda världar. Trettioåtta kapitel om politik, medier och samhälle.* SOM Report 44, pp. 343–358. Gothenburg: University of Gothenburg.

Nordicom (2009). *The Nordic Media Market. Media companies and business activities.* Complied by Eva Harrie. Gothenburg: Nordicom, University of Gothenburg.

Nygren, Gunnar (2008). *Nyhetsfabriken. Journalistiska yrkesroller i en förändrad medievärld.* Lund: Studentlitteratur.

Publicistklubben (2009). Journalism – What's the problem? Seminar held by the Swedish Publicists' Association in Stockholm.

Singer, Jane B. (2003) .Who are these guys? The online challenges of the notion of journalistic professionalism, *Journalism* 4(2): 139–163.

Stampen (2010). Omvärldsnyheter. Newsletter. Available at: http://www.stampen. com/sv/index.php?mact=News,cntnt01,detail,0&cntnt01articleid=128&cntnt01 origid=15&cntnt01detailtemplate=News&cntnt01dateformat=%25Y-%25m-% 25d&cntnt01returnid=86 (accessed 10 April 2010).

Thurén, Torsten (1988). *Ljusets riddare och djävulens advokater. En bok om den journalistiska yrkesrollen.* Finland: Tiden.

TS Industry Statistics (2010). Stockholm: Tidningsstatistik (TS).

Weibull, Lennart (2005). Sverige i Tidningsvärlden. In Bergström, Annika, Wadbring, Ingela and Weibull, Lennart (eds), *Nypressat – ett kvartssekel med svenska dagstidningsläsare.* Gothenburg: Department of Journalism, Media and Communication, University of Gothenburg.

8. Polarization and convergence of values at the intermediary position

Anette Nyqvist and Renita Thedvall

INTRODUCTION: FLO AND KPA AS INTERMEDIARIES IN MARKETS

This chapter focuses on a particular kind of market actors: the intermediaries. The intermediary position has a particular character. It is one that connects, joins, helps, enables and serves as a channel between buyers and sellers, and between the local and global (Wolf 1956; Geertz 1960; Callon 1994; Spulber 1999; Popp 2000; James 2011). Intermediaries are nodes that disseminate knowledge, work as gatekeepers and enable participation (Wolf 1956; Geertz 1960; Popp 2000). In the marketplace, as we will demonstrate in this chapter, intermediaries are able to reconfigure values of both their own markets and markets in general. Our two cases, the Fairtrade International (FLO) and the Swedish pension fund company KPA are used to illustrate how economic, social and environmental values are arranged and rearranged by intermediaries in value configuration processes. FLO and KPA continuously and strategically use value configurations with the express object to both make money and change the world. We shed light on their organizational efforts to promote the idea that not only economic values, but also social and environmental values should be part of market transactions. We use here the term polarization to describe the widespread idea of a division between the economic, the social and the environmental (WCED 1987). We argue that FLO and KPA make use of and reproduce notions of polarization between these values and make this their particular business idea. At the same time, they also aim to converge economic, social and environmental values. In other words, FLO and KPA strive to make the distinction between these values obsolete. This simultaneous use of value polarization and value convergence evokes questions as to why they do this and how they are able to combine seemingly contradictory organizational processes of polarization and convergence. The aim of the study is to examine how the intermediary position in the marketplace opens up for value configurations in the form of both polarization and convergence.

We begin with a brief note on the methodology before we go on to describe FLO and KPA as intermediaries. We then give examples of the tools used when FLO and KPA polarize economic, social and environmental values. This section serves as an empirical background to the analytical discussion that is thematically divided into two parts. The first sheds light on what values are prevalent in the tools used in the seemingly contradictory organizational processes of polarization and convergence. Focus is placed on the intermediary position and how it makes it possible to 'gently force' other market actors to follow the values of FLO and KPA. In the second part of the analysis, we examine how these intermediaries do their missionary work by presenting themselves as role models trying to reshape and foster market actors in general to converge economic, social and environmental values.

The chapter draws on data collected off and on since 2006 (FLO) and 2009 (KPA). It includes mainly studies of policy documents such as standards documents, certification documents, investment guidelines and commercial campaigns. We have also conducted interviews with key actors in the respective organizations as well as performed instances of participant observation (FLO).

THE INTERMEDIARY POSITION OF FLO AND KPA

As mediators of both money and values, FLO and KPA are illustrative examples of intermediaries that affect the value configurations and organization of markets, both their own and markets in general. In the case of FLO, it mediates the idea of sustainable development through its standards and certification tools. FLO's notion of sustainable development entails that, in order to make money in a sustainable fashion, social and environmental considerations must be assigned equal significance as economic matters. FLO is an organization that puts forward its version of sustainable development and how it can be achieved (see also Thedvall 2010; Casula Vifell and Thedvall 2012). This is also something that FLO-Cert, the company that certifies FLO's standards, makes a profit on. FLO-Cert certifies producers and traders that follow FLO standards, including ideas such as transparency, democracy and non-discrimination.

In the case of KPA, it mediates the vision of responsible investment (RI) through screening instruments. Large international and transnational organizations such as the UN, OECD, ILO and WWF have gained substantial importance and influence by drawing up guidelines for responsible investments (Hasselström 2008; Nyqvist 2009; Gold 2010).

The idea of responsible investment when investing in the financial market is commonly traced back to religious congregations of 19th century USA (Skillius 2002; Sandberg 2008). More generally, it can be traced back to 'Christian values', where financial support or investments in 'sinful' businesses such as weapons, gambling, tobacco, alcohol and pornography were considered unethical and thus prohibited (Skillius 2002; Sandberg 2008). As an organization in the responsible investment industry, KPA highlights issues such as human rights, animal rights, labour conditions, corruption and environmental concerns in its investment strategies. FLO and KPA here serve as examples of intermediaries in the market place. Through these examples we discuss what the intermediary position makes possible in terms of value configurations.

Polarizing Tools

FLO and KPA use standards, criteria and screening instruments through which they filter their notions of sustainable development and responsible investment, respectively. In the case of FLO, the tools used are the Fairtrade label and the standards and certification processes that follow from applying a label. The Fairtrade label is mainly used on food items such as chocolate, coffee, tea and juices. In order to use the Fairtrade label, there are certain conditions that have to be fulfilled. First, the product or the ingredients of the product must be grown or manufactured in the Global South, which is part of FLO's so-called geographical scope. From its intermediary position, FLO aims at changing working conditions in the Global South and trading conditions between the Global South and the Global North (FLO 2008), and in its effort to do so focuses on the producers in the Global South.

The conditions that need to be fulfilled are put forward in standards documents set up by FLO and implemented through certification criteria evaluated by FLO-Cert. FLO has several different standards. The standards aimed at producers in the Global South include: a generic standard for small producer organizations; a standard for hired labour; and a standard regarding contract production. Furthermore, there are specific product standards depending on whether products are produced by small producer organizations, contract production, or hired labour. The standards aimed at traders and producers in the Global North are the trade standards. Each standard has its own value configuration, where, for example, the trade standards emphasize the trade between the Global North and Global South with a focus on traceability, price, sustaining trade and pre-financing, while the standards for the producers in the Global South include other issues. In the standards for the Global South,

FLO's focus is on working conditions such as labour rights, democratic procedures and exposure to chemicals.

The standards for traders and producers in the Global North have a different aim. They are focused on the economic transaction, mainly on the price that producers in the Global South are given for their products. In other words, the standards aimed at producers and traders in the Global North focus on the traceability of ingredients so that it can be shown that the ingredients are Fairtrade-labelled products. If traders and producers can show that the ingredients in their products – that can be labelled as Fairtrade – have the Fairtrade label, they can become certified according to FLO's trader standards and use the Fairtrade label. In the case of a chocolate bar manufactured in the Global North, for example, there are FLO producer standards for sugar, cacao and nuts. This means, for example, that the cacao must come from a Fairtrade cacao grower in the Global South. If the cacao is traded and refined on its way to the chocolate bar manufacturer, all traders and refiners along the way, for example a cacao butter manufacturer, also have to be certified according to the standards.

FLO-Cert certifies the producers, traders and retailers throughout the entire commodity chain in both the Global North and the Global South.[1] The certification is sold to producers and traders by FLO-Cert. The fees for certification vary depending on whether the producer or trader is based in the Global South or the Global North. There are two categories of trade fees: trade certification fees[2] and licensing fees. The two fees are paid by manufacturers and retailers in the Global North, who also license the Fairtrade label from FLO directly, or via their national Fairtrade Labelling Organizations' affiliate. In the category of producers in the Global South, there are seven different fee systems based on organizational type, ranging from a first grade small farmer organization to a factory. Each fee system is then dependent on the number of members in the organization.[3] There is a price that needs to be paid for sustainable development and FLO-Cert serves as an intermediary between buyers and sellers through the sale of Fairtrade certifications.

In the case of KPA, the tools used are different screening strategies for responsible investments. In their written information, KPA claims to use 'definite' and 'strict' responsible investment criteria. By this they mean that they offer nothing but responsible investments, and that the screening instruments used are strict and narrow. KPA invests capital in firms 'whose activities make a positive contribution to social developments, and that, conversely, 'avoid investments in companies whose operations, products and services are plainly detrimental to people and the environment' (www.kpa.se).

Swedish legislation requires that all fund management companies provide customers with detailed information of the investment products offered. Such information includes a description of not only the content of a fund's portfolio and the fees charged, but also of the kind of investment strategies and selection tools used to assemble the fund's investment portfolio. Fund managers offering any kind of responsible or ethical investment alternative must provide information on the investment criteria used when selecting which stocks are to be included in the fund.

Fund companies in the responsible investment industry commonly adopt one or more screening strategies as they create ethical funds. These strategies are seen here as tools used in value configuration processes in attempts to shape market actors. The market actors here are companies whose stocks are to be included (or not) in the ethical fund. There are three basic selection strategies, all with a set of varying labels: one is called 'positive', 'including screening' or 'supportive screening'; another 'negative screening' or 'excluding screening'; and the third is commonly known as 'active engagement' or 'engaged participation'.

Simply put, in positive screening, fund managers actively choose to invest in certain companies judged to be ethical and responsible in particular ways. In negative screening, fund managers opt not to include the stocks of certain companies in their responsible funds after deeming them unethical, or not ethical enough. Negative screening can also entail the sale of particular holdings – in this case stocks – previously included in a portfolio. In other words, they are excluded from the fund's portfolio if, after being subjected to screening, the company fails to meet the fund company's criteria for responsible investment.

The third investment strategy, active engagement, means that, instead of selling the more or less unethical stocks that might be a part of the investment portfolio, the fund company keeps them in order to change the particular company for the better. Such an investment strategy entails working from the inside, so to speak, where the fund managers involved in responsible investments place specific demands on companies. In the responsible investment industry, combinations of different screening strategies are often used when assembling ethical funds.

VALUE CONFIGURATIONS GENTLY FORCED FROM THE INTERMEDIARY POSITION

It is the intermediary position of FLO and KPA that enables them to channel and gently force different values such as transparency, democracy, environmental considerations, human rights and labour conditions on market actors in their respective markets.[4] In their capacity as intermediaries, they constitute a node not only between buyers and sellers, but also between globally constructed policy concepts and local practices.

In the case of FLO, how the values in FLO standards are configured determines and shapes the users of the Fairtrade label. While the trade standards have remained relatively stable, focusing on trade relations and compensation, the standards for producers in the Global South have undergone redefinition with some regularity. There has been continuous discussion about what new areas the Fairtrade label should enter and what the label could mean. This means that the standards aimed at the Global South are much more up for debate. Still, there are certain values that are constant, though of different weight (see also Thedvall 2010; Casula Vifell and Thedvall 2012).

Key values such as democracy, participation, transparency, non-discrimination, freedom of labour, freedom of association and collective bargaining, environmental management and biodiversity are visible in the standards. 'Democracy, participation, and transparency' and 'non-discrimination' are buzzwords that can be seen in policy documents from all sorts of national, transnational and international organizations. FLO standards also focus on labour conditions and prescribe freedom from discrimination, freedom of association and collective bargaining, as well as occupational health and safety, and freedom from forced labour and child labour. The choice of these values is clearly inspired by ILO conventions on labour conditions.

Furthermore, environmental values are focused in the standards in terms of regulating the use of agrochemicals, waste, soil and water, and so forth. All of the values in the standards documents are recognizable from other areas of the global discourse on how market production and exchange should be performed. The notion of fair trade is thus connected to general ideas and values of how to organize markets. However, FLO not only uses and translates these values by way of its standards documents, it is also an important actor in promoting and spreading certain value configurations. In doing so, it aims to contribute to the general understanding of what fair trade means in global markets.

More importantly, the standards also change how business may be conducted in markets such as, for example, cotton. From its intermediary position, FLO is able to do this by way of positive and negative sanctions. FLO gently forces producers and traders into following the standards as translated in FLO-Cert's certification criteria, through positive sanctions. In this way, FLO mediates its vision between producers and traders on one hand, and consumers on the other. By following the standards, producers from the Global South can use the Fairtrade label on their products and gain goodwill in relation to traders and consumers in the Global North. But more importantly perhaps, they can also charge the current Fairtrade Minimum Price for their products and receive the Fairtrade Premium to invest in their business or community. The Fairtrade Minimum Price is a floor price that covers average production costs. If the minimum price is higher than market price, buyers of the Fairtrade-labelled product in question must pay the minimum price in order to be permitted to use the Fairtrade label (www.fair trade.net). Buyers in the Global North are also required to pay a Fairtrade Premium that the producers in the Global South must invest in their business, workers, if any, and/or their local communities (www.fairtrade.net). Producers and traders in the Global North make a niche for themselves in the marketplace by creating goodwill and often selling Fairtrade products for a higher price than similar conventional products.

A negative sanction is exclusion from the use of the Fairtrade label. This is, however, aimed to be avoided. Certified producers and traders are often given the opportunity to correct non-compliance, which is reflected, for example, in a specific fee of 1260 EUR for a follow-up audit for a trader in the Global North (FLO-Cert 2010a). Certification is also performed in stages. There are basic compliance criteria that all producers must comply with. Then there are two sets of compliance criteria that must be fulfilled within three and six years. Development is built into the system so that producers are shaped into becoming Fairtrade producers in the sense prescribed by FLO's standards. In this way, FLO gently forces its members to comply with the standards, filtering FLO's version of sustainable development.

Turning to KPA, for a company to be included in KPA's investment portfolio it needs to meet certain criteria in the areas of environment, anti-corruption and human rights. In explaining what these criteria entail, KPA refers to its ethics consultants as well as to large international organizations and their guidelines for responsible investments. In the quote below, we see how KPA first refers to negative screening, stating which companies it excludes from its investments, then directly follows this with an example of the results of positive screening, stating which companies KPA chooses to include in its responsible investments: 'KPA Pension does not invest in energy companies related to energy production that use non-renewable energy sources, unless they are listed on the Dow Jones Sustainability Index and have also received the highest certification, in other words, an "A" from GES's[5] environmental assessment' (www.kpa. se). When it comes to anti-corruption criteria, KPA refers to the business principles developed by Transparency International and, regarding basic human rights, KPA invests only in companies ascribing to the guidelines set out in ILO conventions.

In this way, the screening instruments for responsible investments are constructed on the basis of guidelines issued by large national, transnational and international organizations such as Transparency International, International Labour Organization (ILO) and the Dow Jones. When referring to these organizations, KPA situates itself within a larger framework of ethical, responsible and morally good values created within the global discourse of international organizations. In its intermediary position, KPA acts as both a follower and a leader, distancing itself from the responsibility of shaping the actual value-based criteria. At the same time, it positions itself as a mediator of values: from entities larger than itself, to companies that must comply if they want to continue to be included in the product KPA is selling – the ethical and responsible investment fund.

KPA's 'strict' investment strategies and the use of positive and negative screening strategies lead to positive or negative sanctions. That is, after a positive screening, certain companies are defined as 'ethical' and 'good', and therefore fit to be included in the responsible investment fund, while others are deemed 'unethical' and therefore excluded from the selection of stocks in the portfolio. For example, KPA actively chooses to invest in companies that work specifically with human rights issues, environmental issues and anti-corruption when they conduct business. The excluding or negative sanction after screening for 'unethical' companies means that KPA chooses not to include such stocks in its responsible investment funds. In fact, KPA sets out to shape market actors by negative sanctions, such as exclusion, as when it excludes entire industries from its investment strategies.

The strict investment criteria adopted by KPA means that no stocks from companies involved in the four industries of tobacco, alcohol, gambling and weapons are to be included in the portfolio of the fund company. KPA, and many other fund companies in the responsible investment industry, sometimes use a kind of double negative sanction in order to shape market actors. Such a double-edged fostering tool is used when KPA not only excludes certain 'bad' companies from its fund portfolios, but also shames them by publishing 'blacklists' and alerting the media to the bad behaviour of such companies. Such naming and shaming practices have been referred to as 'corporate governance by public embarrassment' (Hawley and Williams 2000) and can be seen as deterrent examples of what happens to 'bad' companies if they do not better themselves according to the values of, in this particular example, KPA.

With regard to the third investment strategy presented earlier, active engagement, the sanction in this case is a positive one, whereby the fund company keeps the stocks even though they were deemed not quite up to the ethical standard. But here the fostering and reshaping process is emphasized in processes commonly called 'dialogue'. Using the broadly- and rather ill-defined process of 'dialogue', responsible investors such as KPA attempt to gently force companies to work with human rights, environmental or anti-corruption issues, or in other specified ways better their behaviour according to responsible investment standards and guidelines.

MISSION TO RESHAPE MARKETS IN GENERAL

This part of the analysis deals with how FLO and KPA work within their respective markets and, at the same time, how both organizations strive in various ways to reshape and foster markets in general. We argue that FLO and KPA are market actors with a mission. And as 'missionaries', they are dedicated not only to reshaping and fostering other market actors in their own markets (the markets for standards and funds, respectively), but also to spreading their ideas of sustainable development and responsible investment to markets in general. In their own markets, they profit from and legitimize their existence by polarizing economic values with social and environmental values. Their missionary aim for markets in general, however, is to make these values converge. In other words, they want to make consideration of economic, social and environmental factors intrinsic to doing business. Their intermediary position makes their missioning feasible in that they work as, and are recognized as, value configurators in the marketplace. In the next section, we focus on FLO's and KPA's attempts to mission their vision of a convergence of economic, social and environmental values.

In the case of FLO, its mission is to contribute to better working and trade conditions for the poorest of the poor, here – producers in the Global South (FLO 2008). FLO has its particular version of what better working and trade conditions are and this is visible in its standards. The main tool that it uses to mission is the Fairtrade label, but it makes the label known through various practices. In its efforts to make itself known in the labelling market, FLO missions its message of what fair trade is by using different communication tools depending on the recipient. FLO actively lobbies policy-makers through its involvement in conferences such as the United Nations NGO Conference, and also through its lobby organiza- tion in Brussels, the Fair Trade Advocacy Office (FTAO). FTAO is made up of Fairtrade International, the World Fair Trade Organization Europe (WFTO-Europe), and European Fair Trade Associations (EFTA), and lobbies the EU via writing policy papers, following policy processes and liaison with policy-makers. FLO also works towards producers and traders to make the Fairtrade label known through different trade fairs, such as Biofach Organic Trade Fair.

At the local level in the Global North, national Fairtrade labelling organizations such as Fairtrade Sweden missions in the form of conferences, campaigns and ambassadors aimed at convincing individuals and organizations to buy Fairtrade products. The campaign methods are recognizable from social movements. During campaigns, such as at the World Fair Trade Day in May 2011, activists, for example, put up signs with the Fairtrade mark saying 'Choose Fairtrade labelled. At our place'[6] at hotels, restaurants and cafés in Sweden that serve Fairtrade products (www.fairtrade.se). Or during the national 'Fairtrade Focus'[7] campaign in October 2011, retailers, manufacturers, ambassadors, Fairtrade Sweden, politicians and consumers together launched a campaign aimed at increasing sales and consumption of Fairtrade products (www.fairtrade.se). Fairtrade Sweden also organizes courses for people wanting to become Fairtrade ambassadors, where they are taught what Fairtrade means and hopefully go on to spread the message. The use of ambassadors and campaigns are ways of spreading the idea of fair trade that differ from commercial campaigns and advertising as a means of spreading a message of convergence.

At the local level in the Global South, FLO uses 'liaison officers' to mission its version of sustainable development. The liaison officers are posted in the Global South and their task is to provide information and advice to producers who would like to join or, are already part of, Fairtrade. They also offer training and help producers to comply with the Fairtrade standards (www.fairtrade.net). As explained on FLO's website: 'The role of a liaison officer is to: seek new suppliers and products; introduce Fairtrade to producers; support work following inspections; source and liaise with support agencies; help coordinate the pricing process; provide information about local networks; represent Fairtrade in local workshops/conferences' (www.fairtrade.net).

In the case of KPA, it markets its products, responsible investment funds, through different communication tools such as required written investment strategies and documents that state and specify the content of the product. The responsible investment funds are also marketed in the same ways as any other product is marketed – through commercial campaigns and advertising. The marketing costs for fund companies in the responsible investment industry are said to be high compared to marketing costs for investment management companies in general (Nyqvist 2009). Over the past decade, KPA's advertising campaigns have gained substantial public and media attention and been subjected to both criticism and praise.

A review of some of KPA's marketing campaigns from the past decade shows how the tone and message communicated have changed over the years. At the outset, KPA's TV commercials for ethical and responsible investment were outspokenly polarizing and positioned, where KPA was presented as the do-gooders in an evil world of unethical financial investment companies. After having established themselves as an ethical alternative in an unethical business, KPA's next marketing campaign emphasized how, as a fund company, it made a difference in the world, communicating to potential customers how KPA's funds do good while others, presumably unethical fund companies, still do harm. KPA's intermediary position is highlighted by the fund company's next set of TV commercials aimed more specifically at showing potential customers the benefits gained by investing in KPA funds rather than other (here again, presumably unethical) fund companies. The latter marketing campaign shows how the KPA customer can rest assured that their money is doing good while the customer herself can sit back and do nothing. KPA has established itself as a company that makes social values profitable and, while doing so, has participated in the configuration of values that polarize good from bad, ethical from unethical, responsible from irresponsible. From its intermediary position as a fund company, KPA has not only used its screening instruments as tools in the value configuration process, but has also set out to shape and foster both companies and customers according to the values of responsible investments.

FLO and KPA spread the message that social and environmental values are profitable, through engaging in dialogue with other market actors. They do this in different ways, however, and with the help of different communication tools, in accordance with their different backgrounds. FLO originates from the world of aid and social movements, which makes its way of missioning different from KPA, which stems from the corporate world.

CONCLUSION: INTERMEDIARIES, POLARIZATION AND CONVERGENCE

In this chapter, we have shown how the seemingly contradictory organizational processes of polarization and convergence are handled by FLO and KPA. On one level, FLO and KPA use the polarization of economic, social and environmental values to stake out a position for themselves as sellers within their own markets. In their respective markets they are able to make profit by positioning themselves as the 'good' alternative. From the intermediary position, FLO and KPA bring forward certain values

– social and environmental ones – as opposed to economic values. They do so by formulating standards and criteria that separate certain values from others and then evaluate them accordingly. Using negative and positive sanctions to promote values such as democracy, labour rights, environmental sustainability and anti-corruption, they gently force companies to change their behaviour towards FLO's and KPA's visions. These tools are thus constructed so that they polarize the values at stake. In this way, FLO and KPA aim to shape producers by including some and excluding others in their markets.

On another level, both FLO and KPA aim to change the way market transactions are performed in markets, in general, by missioning the convergence of economic, social and environmental values. This missionary work is conducted by means of communication tools such as activist campaigns and commercial advertising used to spread FLO's and KPA's visionary aim of convergence rather than polarization of economic, social and environmental values. In doing so, they claim to hope that in the long run this will contribute to making their own organizations, or at least their sales of standards and funds, redundant. FLO and KPA thus have a vision of making their own existence obsolete, while making profit in the meantime. In this way, both polarization and convergence are at work in the intermediary position of these market actors.

FLO's role as a configurator and mediator of values is underlined by the fact that it shapes global policy concepts into its specifications of what sustainable development and fair trade entail. KPA's role as a mediator of values is emphasized by the fact that the organization situates itself within a larger framework of ethical, responsible and morally good values created by much larger, and international, organizations.

The intermediary position makes this possible, since FLO and KPA work as nodes between buyers and sellers, determining the contract between them. At the intermediary position between producers, traders and consumers, FLO uses tools such as standards, certification and pricing to configure values, turning Fairtrade products into FLO's version of sustainable development. As a fund company, KPA is by definition in an intermediary position between investors and companies, using different screening strategies that configure values in particular directions and here, specifically, in polarizing processes where some are established as 'good' and others 'bad'. We argue that it is their intermediary position that enables FLO and KPA to gently force market actors in the direction of their preferred values.

NOTES

1. FLO has a particular geographical scope that includes greater parts of Africa, Latin America, the Caribbean, Asia and Oceania, often referred to as the 'Global South'. For specific details on what countries are included, see www.fairtrade.net.
2. As an example, the annual fee for trade certification for an operator that imports more than 1000 tons of bananas directly from a grower in the Global South is 2730 EUR per year (FLO-Cert 2010a).
3. As an example, a first grade small farmer organization with fewer than 50 members pays an annual certification fee of 1170 EUR (FLO-Cert 2010b).
4. Similar to standards, the FLO label is voluntary, as it is published by the standard-setter. In practice, however, standards are often made compulsory – they are 'gently forced' – by third parties for various reasons (Brunsson and Jacobsson 2000; Brunsson et al. 2012).
5. GES Investment Services is one of the ethical consultant firms within the responsible investment industry.
6. In Swedish: Välj Fairtrademärkt. Hos oss (authors' translation).
7. In Swedish: Fairtrade Fokus (authors' translation).

REFERENCES

Brunsson, Nils and Jacobsson, Bengt (2000). *Organizing the World*. Oxford: Oxford University Press.

Brunsson, Nils, Rasche, Andreas and Seidl, David (2012). The dynamics of standardization: Three perspectives on standards in organization studies. *Organization Studies* 33(5–6): 613–32.

Callon, Michel (1994). Is science a public good? *Science, Technology and Human Values* 19: 395–424.

Casula Vifell, Åsa and Thedvall, Renita (2012). Organizing for social sustainability. Governance through bureaucratization in meta-organizations. *Sustainability: Science, Practice, and Policy*, 8(1): 50–58.

FLO (2008). Constitution of the Association. http://www.fairtrade.net/our_vision. html.

FLO-Cert (2010a). FLO-Cert Trade Certification Fees. Explanatory document. www.flo-cert.net.

FLO-Cert (2010b). Fee System Small Producer Organization 1st grade. Explanatory document. www.flo-cert.net.

Geertz, Clifford (1960). The Javanese Kijaji: The changing role of a cultural broker. *Comparative Studies in Society and History* 2(2): 228–249.

Gold, Martin (2010). *Fiduciary Finance. Investment funds and the crisis in financial markets*. Cheltenham, UK and Northampton, MA, USA: Edward Elgar.

Hasselström, Anna (2008). '. . .what gets measured gets managed!' Sorting out 'the social' in socially responsible investing (SRI). In Christina Garsten and Monica Lindh de Montoya (eds), *Transparency in a New Global Order: Unveiling organizational visions*. Cheltenham, UK and Northampton, MA, USA: Edward Elgar.

Hawley, James P. and Williams, Andrew T. (2000). *The Rise of Fiduciary Capitalism. How institutional investors can make corporate America more democratic*. Philadelphia: University of Pennsylvania Press.

James, Deborah (2011). The return of the broker. *Journal of the Royal Anthropological Institute* 17(2): 318–338.

Nyqvist, Anette (2009). Att skapa pengar och en bättre värld. En studie av aktörerna kring etiska fonder. Score Report Series 2009:12. Stockholm: Score, Stockholm University.

Popp, Andrew (2000). 'Swamped in information but starved of data': Information and intermediaries in clothing supply chains. *Supply Chain Management* 5: 151–161.

Sandberg, Joakim (2008). *The Ethics of Investments. Making money or making difference?* Gothenburg: University of Gothenburg.

Skillius, Åsa (2002). *Etiska fonder. Kategorier, metoder och finansiell utveckling.* Stockholm: Folksam.

Spulber, Daniel F. (1999). *Market Microstructure: Intermediaries and the theory of the firm.* Cambridge: Cambridge University Press.

Thedvall, Renita (2010). The role of bureaucratisation in organising 'fair' markets. The case of the Fairtrade Labelling Organizations International (FLO). Score Working Paper Series 2010: 11.

WCED (1987). *Our Common Future.* Oxford: Oxford University Press.

Wolf, Eric (1956). Aspects of group relations in a complex society. *American Anthropologist*, 88(6): 1065–1078.

9. Values aligned: the organization of conflicting values within the World Economic Forum

Christina Garsten and Adrienne Sörbom

INTRODUCTION

Once a year, the global elite gather in Davos, the Swiss ski resort, for the World Economic Forum to mull over the state of the world. In this snowy mountain town, the world's leaders in industry and finance present their views on the world economy, their visions, and argue for the best solutions. During this week in late January, Davos changes character – from being a sleepy alpine town, to become the hub of influence, power and prestige. At the 2012 meeting, the global economy and capitalism itself topped the agendas. The sense of urgency caused by the financial crisis sprinkled the town with a certain frenzied activity and nervousness. But there was also a sense of possibility in the transformation of capitalism, the opening of new markets for innovation and profit, for global collaboration and mutual benefit.

The streets of Davos were filled with delegates in elegant business suits and overcoats, easily identifiable by their badges and briefcases sporting the World Economic Forum logo. BMWs, Mercedes and other pricey car brands were conspicuously abundant, as were the middle-aged business-men stepping out of them. Banners with the World Economic Forum logo decorated buildings, hotel lobbies and café menus. Buses and houses also hosted ads for individual countries, such as India, Brazil and Mexico. On a busy street corner, Canadian mounties in red posed in front of a stand serving free 'beaver tails' (pastry). There was little chance visitors could miss the major event of the week.

The meeting area occupied a large part of the town, around it were high barbed-wire fences. Armed guards manned the few gates into the secured area, and anyone who came close was asked to produce his or her meeting badge and registration papers. Having shown these, they then passed through a security zone, resembling those of contemporary airports. And high above all the buzz at street level, numerous helicopters circled and hovered around the town and between the mountaintops to secure the area from potential trouble.

During this week, the mountain village of Davos became the locus of urgent and pressing global concerns. A wide array of differing values and priorities, and different ways to reach defined goals, were articulated and discussed. Lines of convergence and divergence, of community and exclusion, were drawn as the World Economic Forum made its presence felt. In this winter week, Davos became the junction of clashing values and priorities, but also of negotiation and collaboration.

THE ORGANIZATION OF MARKETS – A POLITICAL AFFAIR

In this chapter, we will analyse the World Economic Forum (WEF) as a political arena where market actors of different sorts take part. The picture of Davos, with its security systems and hovering helicopters, indicates that this arena is not entirely calm and quiet. It has to be ready to fend off possible violent offenders. Fundamentally, the WEF has to deal with a number of conflicting values in order to become legitimate as a global actor. In this chapter we analyse how the WEF as an organization works to align some of the core values that they defend and develop, values that represent different and sometimes contradictory positions.

Our point of departure is that – apart from being 'a social structure for the exchange of rights in which offers are evaluated and priced, and compete with one another' (Aspers 2011: 4) – markets should be seen as arenas for political struggles where values are negotiated, and conflicts arise and are handled (see Chapter 1). As recognized by Miller and Rose (1997: 174), political power today is exercised 'through a profusion of shifting alliances between diverse authorities in projects to govern a multitude of facets of economic activity, social life, and individual conduct'. Modern political rationalities and practices are seen to be intrinsically related to new forms of knowledge-seeking and expertise. Hence, to understand how politics, in the wider sense of the term, operates, we need to take into account the value struggles that take place in markets.

Moreover, how markets are organized, how values are transposed into rules and regulations, affect people in various ways. There are social consequences related to how they are constructed and framed. If we compare a so-called 'free' market with little regulatory intervention to a market that is more highly regulated, by state directives and legal structures, for example, we find that some of the conditions for the actors that operate in these markets will differ. For instance, the free market provides an unstable environment for business corporations, which, on the other hand, may entail higher revenues, since there are no negative externalities. For workers, the situation is reversed. Acting in a market that is regulated in line with their interests in matters such as wages and working conditions constitutes a situation that, at least along these parameters, makes for a better environment for them. As market actors, employees therefore have an interest in how these markets are organized. In this sense, a market is not only an arena for political struggles, but also a reflection of power relations in the market. The actors that are involved in the organizing efforts have different interests and strive to attain a number of values, such as economic revenue, social security, justice, equity and stability. Different actors also have different power resources to draw upon, such as financial capital, human capital or other (cf. Korpi 1983), and use these to further their chances of surviving and developing the interests of the organization.

We analyse the WEF as an organization involved in attempts to organize, that is to coordinate, structure and shape global markets. Committed to 'improving the state of the world,' the WEF is not a direct actor but an intermediary or broker (cf. Bierschenk et al. 2002; Mosse and Lewis 2006; James 2011), attempting to set the agenda for the future global regulation of markets, be it rules for buyers, sellers or products. Corporate and political leaders meet at WEF activities, such as the event in Davos, to discuss probable future scenarios and to suggest achievable solutions. These possibilities are realized and pursued, for example in the form of joint projects among participants or by way of individual actors pursuing the ideas in national or international decision-making bodies.

The WEF members, 1000 of the world's largest or most influential corporations, finance the WEF and exert a heavy influence on the organization. However, the master frame of the WEF, the understanding that guides all their activities, does not one-sidedly reflect the interests of the funders. Rather, it is the improvement of the state of the world at large that is of interest (www.weforum.org). According to the WEF, this can best be achieved by taking a dual perspective, where the interests of business meet the interests of politics. Economic development is seen as impossible to achieve without social development, at the same time as social development is described as dependent on economic development. This understanding has provided a firm point of departure since the birth of the organization in 1973, and has been continuously refined. It is therefore seen as essential that representatives from business corporations meet with representatives from governmental and political organizations to deliberate on issues of common concern.

The purpose of this chapter is to analyse how different values are balanced and aligned within the WEF (also called 'the Forum'). Of interest here are values in the sociological sense of the term, as conceptions of what is good, proper or desirable in life (Graeber 2001). While Davos and the Forum as an organization leave much room for business actors to debate economic values, that is the degree to which objects are desired (as expressed in pricing), this is not our prime concern here. Different organizations, such as business corporations, civil society associations and state agencies, may be seen to represent different sets of values. In themselves, each organizational type also houses a number of differing values. Value plurality is essentially a fact that every kind of organization has to deal with, for example, by way of corporate culture, bureaucratic rules and procedures, or by providing an ideological vision. Our interest is focused on understanding how different sets of sociological values are articulated and balanced at the WEF. Here, the value of 'economic growth' is fundamental. Equally important is the value of 'social development'. The WEF positions these as integrally linked and interdependent. How the WEF bridges this divide, how different logics and values are aligned, is our chief interest.

Empirically, we will illustrate this alignment with three examples of how this is worked on in the Forum and its activities. The first two examples are two interrelated founding ideas of the WEF, in which the tension between economic and social values is defined as non-existent: the multistakeholder model and the 'Davos Equation'. The third example derives from a panel discussion in Davos regarding the restructuring of capitalism, during which harsh criticism of the Forum was raised. In line with Forum logic – that all stakeholders are needed to solve the problems that the Earth is facing – this criticism was, however, quickly incorporated by the Forum and thereby also somewhat diminished. The analysis of the panel is based on transcripts from the discussion, which we attended in 2012.

We begin by discussing the role that WEF has in the global organizing of markets. Inspired by Weber (1946) and his argument that there is an inherent risk in politics that politicians enrich themselves rather than the public, we show that similar tensions exist within the Forum. To be a legitimate actor at the level of global governance, the Forum must align the values of its funders with the values of its invited guests, the politicians. Thereafter, we present and discuss our empirical examples, and conclude with a discussion of the alignment of values as a contemporary example of what Laura Nader (1990) terms 'harmony ideology'.

A MARKET INTERMEDIARY

The World Economic Forum has since its creation in the early 1970s emerged as an important shaper of global economic and security matters. Organizationally, the WEF is a non-profit organization, headquartered in Geneva with regional offices in Beijing and New York. The organization employs more than 450 people in total, who undertake the many large- and small-scale events and activities that the WEF organizes every year all around the globe. The activities are funded by the WEF's 1000 member companies, which are ranked the top in their fields of business. Of these companies, those who contribute the most in financial terms and are seen as the most influential have a stronger voice in the decision-making. The highest governing body is the Foundation Board, consisting of a smaller number of highly influential members. The WEF describes itself as politically neutral, in the sense that it is not tied to any national, political or partisan interests.

The WEF is not a decision-making body in the international political arena. Rather, it operates as a platform for networking and influencing among corporate leaders as well as top politicians, NGO representatives and academics. The Annual Meeting in Davos represents the prime event on the Forum's global agenda. Apart from the Annual Meeting, the WEF also sponsors several regional meetings, the Annual Meeting of the New Champions (targeting emerging economies), the Young Global Leaders Meeting (focusing on promising young leaders), meetings on the topic of social entrepreneurship, and scenario planning. It also works via Strategic Insight Teams, who produce reports of relevance in the fields of economic competitiveness, global risk and scenario thinking. Moreover, the WEF strives to be (and already functions as) a private organizer for diplomatic efforts in a range of topics. North and South Korea held their first ministerial-level meetings in Davos, Hans Modrow and Helmut Kohl met in Davos to discuss the reunification of Germany, and the first joint appearance of F.W. de Klerk and Nelson Mandela outside South Africa took place in Davos (WEF 2009). Reports, ratings and indexes are some of the specific outcomes from these activities, but most importantly the Forum works as the provider of the arena itself and its agenda. In the words of Geoffrey Pigman (2007: 2), 'the Forum is fundamentally a knowledge institution; it affects the field of operations by causing the thinking of its members and interlocutors on problems and solutions to change and develop. The Forum's story is a story of the power of words, ideas, and discourse'.

Theoretically, the role of the WEF in relation to markets is best described as an 'intermediary organization'. It neither sells nor buys products, nor does it set rules for market actors, but it attempts to be of service for other actors, through its involvement as a third party at the level of discourse. In this role, the Forum promotes ideas and practices that relate to the organizing or reorganizing of markets in various ways. These promotion activities can be categorized into three general types: networking (bringing the right people together to meet and discuss the right subject), construction of organizational governance techniques (such as ranking and indexing) and diffusion of solutions (official and non-official in the form of reports, media contacts, projects, and so on). In all of these activities, the WEF is the hub where topics, solutions and people are chosen and decided upon. The participants, members or guests, are invited to a table that is set by the Forum. What they do at the table, and to what degree the Forum is able to steer or is interested in steering what happens at the table, is an empirical question. It varies from setting to setting. What is of importance here is the organizing role of the Forum.

Not all of these activities relate directly to the functioning of markets, but we can identify two basic ways through which they do relate. First, the WEF is a platform for market activities. A major interest at the Annual Meeting in Davos, for example, is for business to do business. The lion's share of meeting attendees is made up of representatives from many of the major corporations around the globe. They are there not only to contribute to solving the problems of the world, but also – and oftentimes primarily – to sell, buy and talk business. As described in the following quote from an editorial in *The Economist* the prime focus is to do business:

> Although 40 or so heads of state will troop to Davos this weekend, the event is paid for by companies, and run in their interests. They do not go to butter up the politicians; it is the other way around. Davos Man, finding it boring to shake the hand of an obscure prime minister, prefers to meet Microsoft's Bill Gates. ('In praise of Davos Man', *The Economist*, 7 February 1997)

A large share of the Davos frenzy is thus markets in action – selling and buying, but also embedding (trans)actions in social relations. Sometimes this is done with an interest in shaping the market in a specific way. One of our informants at a regional meeting participated in order to find new customers and partners for his hedge fund investment service, described on the company's website as 'alternative' and 'research-driven', and with 'thoughtful' risk management. In cases like this, the WEF functions as a market fair, but with an organizing interest.

At the same time, the WEF is an intermediary actor in activities aimed at shaping regulations for business. The fundamental role that the Forum attempts to create for itself is to provide a bridge and an arena between global corporations and nation-states. It provides spaces and defines topics around which involved parties from business and politics meet and discuss the pros and cons of market rules. That is to say, they clearly engage in global politics. This is the second and increasingly important market-related aspect of the WEF. In the capitalist and nation-state configuration, as it has evolved over the last centuries, business needs government just as government needs business. As was shown by Charles Lindblom (1977) in his influential analysis of the relationship between private enterprise and democracy in relation to the Western nation-state framework, a general tendency is that a large array of major social demands are handed over to businesses, both large and small. These demands are in this sense taken off the public agenda, and decisions on pivotal matters such as jobs, prices, economic security and so forth are left to the discretion of private business. Governments must therefore take into account the needs and concerns of businesses; they cannot afford not to. At the same time, business needs governments in order to set the framework for their practices (Polanyi 1989; Fliegstein 1996). As corporate actors, businesses are rarely in favour of harsh taxes and regulation. Still, they cannot operate without regulations, because markets need stability and predictability. The same dual relationship applies for global business, that is transnational corporations operating in a number of countries. The difference, though, is that at the global level there exist no governments. Organizations such as the WTO, the UN and the IMF do not exert the same institutional power as national governments. Global businesses operate, at least partly, in a regulatory void, in which soft law, standards and codes of conduct play an increasingly influential role (cf. Braithwaite and Drahos 2000).

The Forum recognizes this regulatory gap and the opportunity it provides. It works to facilitate solutions for contemporary societal and global dilemmas; dilemmas that involve market actors (buyers, sellers, regulators) as well as products sold in global markets. As one managing director noted, the WEF is filling a regulatory gap by trying to be 'a vehicle for gathering stakeholders for political action' (Interview, Geneva, 8 April 2004). Hence, the WEF does not aspire to be an organization that provides global regulatory frameworks. Transnational rules for markets are not set by the WEF (neither in Davos, nor at any of their other activities or events), but the WEF can certainly play a role in articulating them. For example, in the many informal meetings between stakeholders, in the reports issued from their working groups, and in the ratings of countries and businesses, the Forum articulates its preferred alternatives for how to regulate specific business sectors and issues. Attempting to measure how successful they are in these efforts would be futile, but that ideas formulated within the WEF are communicated to and used by high-level officials, politicians, business leaders and representatives from multilateral organizations, is indisputable.

One example of this kind of political activity is the background deliberations leading up to the decisions taken at the Cancun summit on climate change. This is how it was explained to us by one informant working at the WEF headquarters in Geneva:

> You remember Cop15 in Copenhagen? How everybody saw that as a failure? Well, one week later, all the key protagonists, apart from Obama, met in Davos. Without the political pressure. They met without any particular agenda. It was decompression. And our role? We, as organizers, pursue no particular agenda, but we provide space. And, after that meeting, Calderon suggested to get a move on with what later became the Cancun Agreement. At the top level, there is an increasing demand for this kind of space. It works as decompression. Here, it is possible to say things that can't be said at top meetings. (Interview, Geneva, 8 September 2011)

What happened at the actual meeting in Davos, we do not know. The informant might overstate the importance of the meeting, and we have not asked Prime Minister Calderon about where he got the ideas for the so-called Cancun Protocol. But the words of the respondent tell us how the Forum sees its own role in other words, as an intermediary in global politics, creating an arena for decision-makers to meet and deliberate.

In this sense, the WEF is an intermediary actor for global market actors. It does not directly allocate values, as does the traditional political organization (Sartori 1974), but it organizes an arena where this allocation is discussed among actors and where solutions may be suggested. Oftentimes, these discussions and recommendations relate to the operation of markets, how actors may or should behave, and what is to be sold and under what conditions.

The word 'intermediary' does not imply that the WEF functions as a neutral tool for those attending the meeting. On the contrary, as stated in the quote above, the WEF describes itself as a neutral and independent arena, without attempting to voice any particular interest, and an important part of how it frames itself as an organization is that it 'is not a global board of commerce seeking to impose its view and order onto the rest of the world' (Interview, 8 April 2004). However, from a social science perspective, it is evident that notions of value are part and parcel of political discussions of how markets should be regulated, or not regulated, as well as how priorities should be balanced in doing actual business. In fact, it is hardly conceivable to think of, let alone discuss, markets without introducing notions of values. As was stated in the opening chapter of this book, markets are embedded in contested, and therefore organized, values. Not surprisingly then, the Davos meeting and Forum events in general serve as condensed arenas for the clashing, balancing and aligning of values.

INHERENTLY CONFLICTING INTERESTS AND VALUES

The WEF is thus, in our view, a political organization, building its status partly on being funded by large business corporations, but inviting high-level politicians to deliberate on contemporary issues. As a political organization, it is somewhat unorthodox. In modern politics, even though business might have been invited from time to time (in corporatist and/or pluralist arrangements), it has generally been kept in at arm's length for fear of inappropriate connections. As described early on by Max Weber, in his 'Politics as a Vocation' (1946), there is an inherent and therefore universal contradiction in politics in that it can be used as a means for enriching individuals or groups. Thus, according to Weber, there exists a permanent risk that politicians, of all sorts, are involved in politics for personal economic gains, not for the realization of the common good. In order to maintain legitimacy politicians need to balance and overcome the tension that these two kinds of value pursuits represent. Political bureaucracy is, as Weber shows, basically about the handling of this tension.

Translating this to the case of the WEF, it is clear that this tension is at the heart also of their activities. First, because the activities of the WEF must be considered as politics, in spite of having no clear-cut political agenda and being set in a non-institutionalized context. Politics defined as the allocation of values (cf. Sartori 1974) is at the heart of WEF activities, albeit with this allocation only suggested and not decided on. Second, in line with Weber's analysis of politics as an activity in which different values and interests must be balanced (cf. Weber 1946), WEF activities balance between the principles of capitalism (and the interests of the member corporations), and the interests of solving societal issues. Third, the tensions between these two interests, and the pursuit of values related to them, have to be resolved in order for the Forum to be a legitimate actor. Business corporations are generally not seen as legitimate political actors (that is, you cannot vote for a corporation and corporate donations to political campaigns are often harnessed with legislation) since they act in the interests of the shareholders, who are not commonly representative of any electoral constituency. The WEF must therefore show that it is able to forge interests and values in a Weberian sense. It must construct and exhibit an ethic that blends the principles of capitalism with an ethics of social responsibility, and in practice show that the values it advocates are not merely of the economic kind.

This forging of interests and values, proving that it is trustworthy and earnest about 'improving the state of the world', has been and remains a challenge for the Forum. Armed guards watch the secluded headquarters in Geneva, key persons (like Klaus and Hilde Schwab) are also protected outside of headquarters, and the Swiss military and police secure the Davos conference hub, indicating a perceived constant threat from the outside world. This 'fencing in' is not endemic to the WEF, it is something they share with parliament and government buildings and officials around the world. A key feature of the WEF case, that is of the criticism against it, however, is that, due to its strong relation to corporate members and funders, it must continuously prove that it is a legitimate actor. The very same corporations are, at the same time, the source for economic survival and for realizing the WEF's multi-stakeholder vision. The ambivalent relation towards business is therefore inherent in the organization. As suggested by Barley (2010: 796), 'Organizational theorists have long recognized that legitimation is important for constructing organizational fields'. Establishing and protecting legitimacy, he maintains, 'may involve more than being tied to high-status others or deploying culturally legitimate logics. Sometimes, protection and enhancement of legitimacy may be built into the structure of the field itself'.

In the case of the WEF, the balancing and alignment of values is built into the very system of the organization. One way of disarming these tensions without changing the organization itself has been to forge the interests at the level of discourse. In line with the contemporary tendency towards 'post-politics', as discussed in somewhat different terms by Chantal Mouffe (1993, 2000) and Slavoj Zizek (1999), the WEF tends to emphasize consensual positions rather than conflicting ones. It frames its activities as reflecting the necessity of different actors, representing differing interests, to meet. In the post-political version of politics, conflicts between ideological visions, materialized in organizations competing for power, have been replaced (at least in part) by cooperation and a purported consensus between actors who were earlier antagonists (Zizek 1999).

The following three examples will show how the WEF constructs legitimacy for itself by aligning economic and social values, both at the level of discourse and in practice. The WEF manages the potential tension between different stakeholders' interests and values related to these interests by arguing the need for an inclusive stakeholder model, and by an agile and flexible organization that is quick to incorporate criticism.

ORGANIZING STAKEHOLDER VALUES

The core vision of the WEF is to bring together different types of major stakeholders from across the world to discuss global issues and to come up with ways of solving urgent problems. The approach was established already in 1971 when the first forum was arranged, at that time called the European Management Forum. The approach had been laid out the same year in a book by the founder of the WEF, Klaus Schwab: Moderne Unternehmensführung im Maschinenbau ('Modern Enterprise Management in Mechanical Engineering'). Schwab argued that the management of a modern enterprise must serve all stakeholders (die Interessenten), 'acting as their trustee charged with achieving the long-term sustained growth and prosperity of the company' (WEF 2009: 7). The stakeholders here include the enterprise's owners and shareholders, customers, suppliers and collaborators of any kind, as well as the government and society, including the communities in which the company operates or which may in any way be affected by it. In 1973, the participants of the forum codified the approach into a code of ethics, termed 'The Davos Manifesto'. The first point in the manifesto states that:

> The purpose of professional management is to serve clients, shareholders, workers and employees, as well as societies, and to harmonize the different interests of the stakeholders. (Code of Ethics – The Davos Manifesto)

The enterprise shall thus serve not only the shareholders and clients, but also employees and society at large. This is to be ensured by securing long-term profit for the enterprise, stated in the manifesto's last point:

> The management can achieve the above objectives through the economic enterprise for which it is responsible. For this reason, it is important to ensure the long-term existence of the enterprise. The long-term existence cannot be ensured without sufficient profitability. Thus, profitability is the necessary means to enable the management to serve its clients, shareholders, employees and society. (Code of Ethics – The Davos Manifesto)

As such, the multi-stakeholder model builds on visions of aligning key priorities and values from different actors. In the words of Klaus Schwab, corporations must align their economic activities with ethical principles:

> Companies and their decision-makers do not operate in an open space. They cannot command as they please. Business leaders must meet economic, ecological and social demands. They are liable not only to one but to various stakeholders. If enterprises want to succeed at long term they need the trust of all the relevant interest groups. This can only be achieved if they are willing to align

their actions with ethic principles. Those who believe that they can do without
it must sooner or later reckon with the negative consequences. (WEF 2009: 192)

A basic assumption underlying the multi-stakeholder model is thus that
the values of economic growth and social and environmental sustainability can and must be aligned and balanced, in order to reach the universal
goal of survival, or at least improving the state of the world.

Related to this assumption of the need to align values is the thought that
there are solutions that will benefit all, 'win–win' solutions. According
to this model, there are no winners, no losers and no power relations.
Instead, the multi-stakeholder approach signals horizontal and equal
relationships. If the 'leaders' from different parts of society simply meet
and talk, they will be able to find the solution that everybody will benefit
from. Divergent interests in how the very basic needs – of peace, food
and education, for example – are to be accomplished, are not part of the
model. It is a model devoid of power and conflict, built on assumptions of
trust, mutual understanding and consent, in other words, dimensions of
essentially harmonious or consensual relationships.

THE DAVOS EQUATION

The alignment of economic and social values has thus been a part of the
WEF since the first meeting in 1971. It has since been worked on and
argued for in different versions. In the 2000s, the WEF launched something called the Davos Equation, in order to show the bond between the
economic and social worlds:

> We live in a world which is uncertain and fragile. At the Annual Meeting in
> Davos, global leaders from all walks of life will confront one basic fact: We will
> not have strong sustained economic growth across the world unless we have
> security, but we will not have security in unstable parts of the world without
> the prospect of prosperity. To have both security and prosperity, we must have
> peace. This is the Davos Equation: security plus prosperity equals peace. (Klaus
> Schwab, Davos 2004)

The Equation aims to capture the idea of a balanced and neutral solution
to global problems of all kinds: peace, health, education and so forth.
The very notion of 'equation' implies symmetry, or balance. It implies
that radically diverging tendencies and interests may be reconciled and
brought into balance and harmony with each other. The multi-stakeholder
approach is fundamental to this idea, which ideally serves to articulate the
priorities and interests of each party. Even though parties cannot entirely

agree on responsibilities or priorities, they can reach a partial consensus about global issues and development problems.

Underlying the equation and the multi-stakeholder model is the understanding that economic growth can work in tandem with a responsibility for the social and natural environment. In fact, according to WEF discourse, in the long run one is not possible without the other. With the goal of building and sustaining economic development in mind, the WEF wants to promote ways to mitigate global risks, promote health for all, improve social welfare and to foster environmental sustainability. In this vision, economic growth and social and environmental sustainability are brought into alignment.

The idea of economic and social values as intricately related to each other, and as unattainable without each other, is something worked on in all Forum settings. As phrased in the motto, the WEF is 'committed to improving the state of the world by engaging business, political, academic and other leaders of society to shape global, regional and industry agendas', the Forum wants to play a role in the alignment of different and sometimes divergent interests and values by the bringing together of groups and people from different spheres of society. In the 2000s, the concept of 'global citizenship' was added as a way of describing the relationship between the various groups (WEF 2011). As an extension of the stakeholder concept, it seeks to express the interdependence of all the groups.

Overcoming the inherent risk of politics being pursued in the interest of the politician is thus managed through the discursive alignment of stakeholders and the values they are thought to represent. To be sure, this alignment can also be identified in the actual activities of the Forum. Next, we will give an example from the Annual Meeting in Davos (2012), exemplifying how the WEF's interest in organizing the coming together of different interests and values works in practice.

OPEN FORUM AS MANAGEMENT OF CRITIQUE

In the early and mid-1990s, the WEF was increasingly criticized for being an exclusive club for corporate leaders interested in governing the world according to their own interests. The criticism grew and, with the advent of the alter-globalization movement (cf. Pleyers 2010), the WEF saw it as imperative to relate to this growing movement, which in the first years of the new millennium managed to put criticism of (above all) economic globalization on the agenda (Pigman 2007; Stiglitz 2002). In 2003, the first Open Forum (OF) was held, as a separate event at the Annual Meeting in Davos. The OF was set up together with a number of NGOs and the Swiss Protestant churches in order to counter this criticism and show what WEF activities were all about. One of the managing directors at WEF, also organizer of the OF, describes how the WEF saw the need to open the annual meeting so that civil society 'would be less afraid of the global animals' (Interview, September 2011). After ten years of activity, the OF is still an attraction in Davos during the annual meeting. The WEF is now the sole organizer, even though NGOs are part of the OF advisory board, and the organizing manager describes the situation as much calmer nowadays.

The criticism against the WEF, of not being open and transparent, resonates with the inherent risk in politics, as framed by Weber, that the politician and the political organization live off but not for politics. The image of the WEF as a secluded arena where top politicians meet with the CEOs of transnational corporations leaves it open to this kind of interpretation. At the same time, the Forum as an organization sees the secluded character as being their chief advantage. In their view, it is a prime reason why 'the leaders of the world' choose to take part in WEF activities. The Open Forum is the organizational answer to this dilemma. As the managing director stated in his introduction to one of the sessions at the OF in 2011, they want to show that 'the World Economic Forum does open up to the public at large'. Apart from following the Davos event on Twitter and in other social media, the Open Forum wants to provide a good opportunity to engage in a 'dialogue based on the principles we are reenacting', mixing business with religion, science and civil society so that they can 'meet at the same table'. And as he went on to say, dialogue is about making sure that 'viewpoints that might appear irreconcilable are all heard' and 'engaging seriously with the arguments of others in order to measure one's own standpoint. . . . It is not the search for the lowest common denominator, it is rather the search for a space of engagement, which in itself facilitates change, movement and development, and in doing so avoids the danger of standstill'.

At the Annual Meeting in Davos, 2012, the Forum was criticized by the then-strong Occupy movement. Small 'igloos' were built and tents were raised in a Davos parking lot, close to the WEF conference arena, and 30–40 people started to 'Occupy the World Economic Forum'. In spite of being small in numbers, the group had a rather big media impact. Numerous journalists from all over the world visiting Davos hurried down to the parking lot to interview the occupiers. The criticism raised in Davos primarily concerned what was seen as dishonesty on the part of the Forum. As one of the occupants argued when we met her at the camp, 'their motto is "improving the state of the world", but they are responsible for the state of the world'. Even if the theme of the meeting that year was the rebuilding of capitalism, the occupiers used 'dishonesty' as their argument. 'I simply do not believe that they want to change anything, because they are gaining from the system', one of the occupiers explained to us when we visited the Igloo camp.

The criticism was thus framed in line with the Weberian analysis of the inherent risk of politics. And in line with the Forum's interest of showing that there are no conflicts between different groups in society, this criticism was quickly incorporated into the meeting. Firstly, by stating to the media that the Occupy group was invited to the Annual Meeting (something that the group itself disclaims); secondly, by letting them become part of the OF's programme. It was not planned for in the initial programme, but was set up during the week in Davos that the Occupy group could have one representative in the Friday night discussion on the theme 'Remodelling Capitalism'. The group hesitated but accepted the invitation.

In the initial read-aloud statement made by Maria (who presented herself as such, without a last name), it was clear that the Occupy group understood that there was a risk that their voices could be co-opted by their participation in the panel. Maria explicitly explained that the OF was only about controlling criticism. Therefore she and the other occupiers tried in a number of ways to do their own thing. First, Maria tried to be anonymous, avoiding being a 'representative'. Not only did she choose to merely call herself Maria (which may not have been her real name), but also, as soon as she had read the statement, she stepped down from the panel, offering her place to anyone in the audience. Second, as soon as Maria had stepped down, the Occupy group started using the 'human microphone', where the words of one participant are repeated out loud by all who heard them. This was a popular technique in the Occupy movement, and was used here in order to recast the order set by the Forum, that only those with a microphone can and should be heard. Third, the group suggested that the panel should be split up. Instead of only the panellists talking and the audience being able to ask questions at the end, the Occupy group suggested that the entire audience could discuss in small groups.

The dilemma of partaking or not is well known and analysed in movement and political science literature (cf. Young 2001). In this case, one could make the argument that the criticizers from the Occupy group failed. In spite of their attempts to reorganize the setting, the panel discussion was held as planned, in the same format as panel discussions are always held. After the brief intervention of the human microphone, a vote was held on how to conduct the discussion – a vote that the Occupy group (and others in the audience who shared their view) lost. WEF's idea of having all the stakeholders at the same table, literally, was again settled.

These voices of the OF neatly illustrate the argument that the Forum is trying to make regarding politics and economy. Politics and economy are constructed as separate by history and tradition, but, in order to deliver, they need to be aligned with one another. More importantly, the way in which WEF organizes the coming together of different voices and positions in the Open Forum shows how alignment works in practice.

ALIGNING VALUES AND THE ORGANIZATION OF MARKETS

In our view, markets constitute arenas for political struggles in which values are articulated, negotiated and contested. Markets are, as well, outcomes of political struggles. In these struggles, values are mobilized and allocated to different actors, issues and values. The WEF is an example of how an intermediary market actor takes part in the organization of markets and in shaping political outcomes. The Forum sees itself as an intermediary actor that refrains from taking an active stance on political issues, but that facilitates for actors with different interests to meet and to discuss. Its multi-stakeholder approach not only allows for, but encourages divergent perspectives to clash and collide. In the process, however, the very political edge of different positions, of diverging values, tends to soften in favour of pragmatic solutions and concrete issues. The underlying assumption is that of a win–win situation, in which all participating parties have something to gain from deliberation and propositions for further concrete action.

In order to fend off the risk of being seen simply as an instrument for the political interests of business, the Forum has to find ways to align actors in a harmonious way. This demands careful and continuous organizing efforts. In a sense, the Forum keeps its own organization flexible and agile in order to deal with diverse and conflicting demands and values. As an organization, it is nebulous and ever-changing, continuously reorganizing and adapting to changing circumstances in its wider environment, in response to the changing priorities of its leaders and stakeholders, to better accommodate its activities and initiatives.

The WEF's mission, to 'improve the state of the world', builds, as stated in the Davos Equation, on the conviction that the values of economic growth and social development are interlinked and interdependent. Hence, the value of social wellbeing should not be seen as in any way running counter to the value of economic growth. The initiatives and activities of the Forum build on this alignment to mobilize and gain support and leverage. The multi-stakeholder approach brings the different priorities of the parties into the process and ensures that they are sufficiently aligned for initiatives and activities to be realized. The Open Forum is an example of how the WEF strives to stretch alignment beyond the secluded space it has built for its activities. By so doing, it has taken yet another step to show that it wants to let all groups of society, even the public, be a part of the multi-stakeholder model.

The WEF alignment approach relies on what can be conceived of as a case of 'harmony ideology', in Laura Nader's sense (Nader 1990). As we have shown, the approach postulates that not only are the values of economic growth and social development reciprocally related, but that it would be dysfunctional and unproductive to encourage one without the other. The Forum therefore argues that all types of actors are needed at the table. This reflects an expansionist idea, in that potential adversaries and conflictual or divergent views are included in the discursive community and allowed articulation within the WEF space. This resonates well with Nader's analysis of harmony ideology, which centres on the Western belief that the existence of conflict is by definition a bad thing, and that healthy societies are those where conflicts and confrontation are minimized and there is harmony between people. Harmony ideology, Nader argues, has been an important ingredient in recent forms of conflict resolution in the US; forms that emphasize harmony, compromise and the language of therapy over talk of injustice.

To our minds, such a harmony ideology is reflected in much of contemporary political discourse, where conflicts and confrontations are considered outdated and the possibility of win–win solutions postulated, and most certainly in the WEF. The multi-stakeholder model as a figure of thought entails that different groups of actors can be combined without exerting force on one another, or the poor–rich distinction and idea that growth and trade will benefit all. Essentially, this is a pragmatic approach that relies on communicability rather than on shared assumptions and values (cf. Albrow 1997).

A fundamental point of departure for the understanding of the workings of harmony ideology and alignment of values in the WEF is the notion of 'one-worldism' (cf. Robertson 1991). The WEF departs from the idea that there is only one world, the resources of which are limited, and the risk scenarios and threats facing the Earth are tremendous and alarming. Hence, there is no other way forward but to join forces to engage constructively in these challenges. The multi-stakeholder approach is indicative of this approach, as is the Davos Equation. The Open Forum can enact this idea in practice, showing not only that the WEF is transparent but also that critics are welcome. In conjunction, these arguments and practices underline the perceived need to incorporate and align diverging views and priorities, and to understand the interdependence of economic and social issues. The harmony ideology thus enhances the alignment of values.

Hence, the WEF alignment approach encompasses its critical environment by inviting conflicting views to take part in the agenda. Articulating a different view is therefore difficult, since not wanting to take the hand that is offered is seen as unconstructive. The actor that does not accept this becomes the 'black sheep'. Laura Nader (1990: 2) expresses this problem succinctly:

> Apparently, the basic components of harmony ideology are the same everywhere: an emphasis on conciliation, recognition that resolution of conflict is inherently good and that its reverse – continued conflict or controversy – is bad or dysfunctional, a view of harmonious behavior as more civilized than disputing behavior, the belief that consensus is of greater survival value than controversy. Harmony ideology can be powerful even when it contradicts the common realities of disputing.

The World Economic Forum is both an interesting case of this discourse, and a pivotal driver of the same. By analysing examples of how it is working to construct and uphold harmony and consensus, we may understand more fully how this contemporary discourse is set into operation, as well as how the legitimacy of a global actor, active in the global regulatory void, can be constructed in practice. Furthermore, the organization of global markets needs its intermediaries, and the WEF is a key instance of mediation. As an intermediary, the WEF occupies an important role in the brokering and negotiation of values and priorities in heterogeneous organizational arenas. In the increasing diversification of sources of power and influence, via a proliferation of organizations and intermediary networks at the global level, the WEF has emerged as an important intermediary hub. The processes involved in organizing markets at the global level are, to a greater extent than before, reliant on the active involvement of such intermediary organizations. At this point of juncture, the clashing and colliding of differing values is avoided by discursive alignment.

REFERENCES

Albrow, M. (1997). *The Global Age*. Stanford: Stanford University Press.
Aspers, P. (2011). *Markets*. Cambridge: Polity Press.
Barley, S. (2010). Building an institutional field to corral a government: A case to set an agenda for organization studies, *Organization Studies*, 31(6): 777–805.
Bierschenk, T., Chaveau, J.P. and Olivier de Sardan, J.P. (2002). Local development

brokers in Africa: The rise of a new social category. Working Paper No. 13, Department of Anthropology and African Studies. Mainz, Germany: Johannes Gutenberg University.

Braithwaite, J. and Drahos, P. (2000). *Global Business Regulation*. Cambridge: Cambridge University Press.

Fliegstein, N. (1996). Markets as politics: A political–cultural approach to market institutions. *American Sociological Review* 61(4): 656–673.

Graeber, D. (2001). *Toward an Anthropological Theory of Value: The False Coin of Our Own Dreams*. Basingstoke: Palgrave Macmillan.

James, D. (2011). The return of the broker: Consensus, hierarchy and choice in South African land reform. *Journal of the Royal Anthropological Institute (N.S.)* 17: 318–338.

Korpi, W. (1983). *The Democratic Class Struggle*. London: Routledge.

Lindblom, C. (1977). *Politics and Markets: The World's Political Economic Systems*. New York, NY: Basic Books.

Miller, P. and Rose, N. (1997). Political power beyond the state: Problematics of government. *British Journal of Sociology* 43(2): 173–205.

Mosse, D. and Lewis, D. (2006). Theoretical approaches to brokerage and translation in development. In Lewis, D. and Mosse, D. (eds), *Development Brokers and Translators*. Bloomfield, CT: Kumarian Press, pp. 1–26.

Mouffe, C. (1993). *The Return of the Political*. London: Verso.

Mouffe, C. (2000). *The Democratic Paradox*. London: Verso.

Nader, L. (1990). *Harmony Ideology: Justice and Control in a Zapotec Mountain Village*. Stanford, CA: Stanford University Press.

Pigman, G.A. (2007). *The World Economic Forum: A Multi-Stakeholder Approach to Global Governance*. London: Routledge.

Pleyers, G. (2010). *Alter-Globalization: Becoming Actors in the Global Age*. Cambridge: Polity Press.

Polanyi, K. (1989). *The Great Transformation: The Political and Economic Origins of Our Time*. Boston, MA: Beacon Press.

Sartori, G. (1974). Philosophy, theory and science of politics. *Political Theory*, 2(2), May.

Stiglitz, J. (2002). *Globalization and Its Discontents*. London: Penguin Books.

Weber, M. (1946) 'Politics as a Vocation'. In Gerth, H.H. and Mills, C.W. (eds), *Essays in Sociology*. Oxford: Oxford University Press, pp. 77–128.

WEF (2009). *A Partner in Shaping History – The first 40 years 1971–2010*.

WEF (2011). *Entrepreneurship in the Global Public Interest*.

Young, I.M. (2001). Activist challenges to deliberative democracy. *Political Theory* 29(5): 670–690.

Zizek, S. (1999). *The Ticklish Subject*. New York: Verso.

10. Contestation in transition: value configurations and market reform in the markets for gambling, coal and alcohol

Susanna Alexius, Daniel Castillo and Martin Rosenström

INTRODUCTION

Commodities are not essentially or naturally contested. They move back and forth across moral and legal boundaries in response to social forces such as technological change, the mobilization of interest groups, or the efforts of moral entrepreneurs (Fourcade and Healy 2007: 22). Contestation of commodities is thus a political outcome of continuous negotiation and value-laden power struggles, debates and reforms involving a wide range of market organizers.

The purpose of this chapter is to scrutinize value conflict underpinnings of contested commodities to contribute to our understanding of how and why the contestation of some commodities is sustained over extended periods of time. In order to investigate this question, we turn our attention to three contested commodities: gambling, coal and alcohol. This chapter draws empirically on a comparative historical study of value discourse and organization from the 1800s onward in the Swedish markets for gambling, coal and alcohol (Alexius et al. 2011). In that study, we found that the three commodities, although contested for centuries, had been so for different reasons in different time periods (see Tables 10.1–10.3 below). In the theoretical language of this volume – it clearly mattered to the organization of these markets that the underlying value conflicts had been actively reconfigured. In this chapter, we illustrate and elaborate on these findings and specifically aim to contribute to the conceptualization of value conflict reconfiguration and its implications for market organization. Three modes of value conflict reconfiguration are presented and illustrated with empirical data from our three cases. The three modes are:

1. Addition – *adding* values to a value conflict, for example, adding health concerns to an environmentally focused debate.
2. Expansion – *expanding* the scale of contestation, for example, a shift from local to global environmental concerns.
3. Relocation – *relocating* the scope of contestation, for example, a shift from problem representations of sellers to problem representations of buyers.

TRANSFORMATIVE MOMENTS OF VALUE CONFLICT RECONFIGURATION

A more elaborate understanding of the dynamics of contested markets requires an historical account of the value conflict reconfigurations that have occurred. Comparing the contested commodities of gambling, coal and alcohol offers a fresh new possibility to break up traditional value-laden categorizations such as that of the 'Triumvirate of Sin' for alcohol, gambling and tobacco (Hong and Kacpercyk 2009) or that of commodities with 'negative externalities', a category to which coal is typically assigned (Katz and Rosen 1991/1994, and Steiner and Steiner 2008). In this chapter, we focus instead on the common denominator of these three commodities: their sustained contestation and the underlying dynamics thereof.

Aware of the complex patterns of change in values and market organization over the years, we focused our comparative study (Alexius et al. 2011) on transformative moments (Hoffman and Ocasio 2001). In Rothstein's words (1992: 17–18), transformative moments are critical junctures, more turbulent times characterized by attempts 'not only to play the political game, but also change the rules of the game'. Transformative moments offer a better opportunity to study open contestation, vivid engagement and various attempts of market organizers to reconfigure value conflicts and suggest market reforms in response to perceived contestation. As seen in Tables 10.1–10.3 in the next section, we identified 11 transformative moments in the Swedish gambling, coal and alcohol markets from 1800 onwards and found evidence to suggest that we are better able to understand both how contestation changes and may be sustained over time if we study how value conflicts are reconfigured by market organizers. The next section presents a case-by-case account of the empirical findings. Thereupon follows an analysis of each of the three modes of value conflict configuration. The chapter concludes with a summary and discussion of our findings.

CONTESTATION IN TRANSITION – THE CASES

Gambling

The exchange of gambling products – whether prohibited or legalized – has always been a sensitive, value-laden policy area (Reith 1999; de Goede 2005; Ihrfors 2007; Hong and Kacpercyk 2009; de Geer 2011). As seen in Table 10.1, we identified three transformative moments in the Swedish gambling market between the 1830s and today.

The first transformative moment, Immoral gambling – from the royal lottery to prohibition (approx. 1830–1844), stemmed from a societal discourse in which gambling was increasingly seen as an immoral, wasteful, sinful, unproductive activity – not to be encouraged, and particularly not by governments that were to act as good examples. A consensus against gambling grew among influential interest groups such as the church, the labor movement and employers. By the 1830s, the mobilization had become a serious force, and the Swedish parliament consequently joined the European trend and abolished its successful royal number lottery (Kungliga nummerlotteriet) in 1841 (de Geer 2011). Three years later a national law was passed, imposing a general ban on gaming and lotteries.

During the prohibition era, legalization proposals were up for debate on several occasions, but resistance remained strong (Ihrfors 2007: 51). The state was not to give in to temptation but rather was to nurture citizens to enjoy and take pride in abstinence, thrift, diligence and virtuous living – with success, judging from the public debate of the 1800s (ibid.). Gamblers were seen as morally weak victims in need of state guidance, education and protection from supposedly unscrupulous illegal gambling operators (ibid, Report 1910: 54: Husz 2004: 232–285).

However, the public debate shifted in the early 20th century. The number of advocates for a legal, restricted state monopoly grew (Husz 2004). Initially, this change in attitude came out of a neutralization of the value conflict, but the arguments for a restricted state monopoly did not heat up the conflict until gambling was remoralized. Remoralization of gambling paved the way for a new value conflict between immorality and a more hedonistic leisure ethic (ibid.). The conflict was particularly intense in the 1920s and early 1930s, fuelling a second transformative moment: Remoralization of gambling – from prohibition to state monopoly (approx. 1920–1940). The Swedish state was an important market organizer in the revitalization of the conflict due to financial motives. Following this new value configuration, restricted legalization was decided on in 1934, and the first legal operator, Tipstjänst, a private

Table 10.1 Transformative moments in the gambling market

Transformative moment	Time period	Contestation, values in conflict	Main market organizers
Immoral gambling – from the royal lottery (Rikslotteriet) to prohibition	1830–1844	Profits *vs* Protestant ethic, work ethic, gambling as sinful, wasteful and unproductive	State, church, labour movement, employer organizations
Remoralization of gambling – from prohibition to state monopoly	1920–1940	Profits and leisure ethic, sports, modernity *vs* safety/ anti-fraud, protectionism and charity	State, illegal and foreign operators, sports movement – sports organizations and sports media
Emerging health concerns	1995–	Profits, prevention and responsibility *vs* health risks	EU and European Court of Justice (ECJ), national prevalence Commission, illegal and foreign operators, researchers and consultants, state and state-owned enterprise operator (Tipstjänst/ Svenska Spel)

corporation, became fully state-owned in 1940. The Swedish gambling market then underwent decades of relative status quo (Husz 2004; Ihrfors 2007). De Geer refers to the 1945–1980 period as the period of the 'stable profit machine' (de Geer 2011: 122–208).

In the third transformative moment, Emerging health concerns (approx. 1995–ongoing), the potential adverse effect of gambling addiction and various related social health concerns came to dominate the discourse and organization (Helling 2003; Ortiz 2006; Alexius, 2011a, 2011b). Three interrelated events in the mid- to late 1990s pushed the value of health (represented in terms of gambling addiction) firmly onto the political agenda: EU membership in 1995, the first Swedish prevalence study on gambling addiction in 1999, and the internet boom that followed shortly thereafter. As a result, and along similar lines as in the Swedish alcohol market, the state-owned gambling operator Svenska Spel ('Swedish Games') began to emphasize 'responsible' gambling as a value, along with high-quality entertainment as the mission and competitive advantage, in a market where the state monopoly had been bypassed by the internet era (Alexius 2011a, 2011b).

Inspired by recent research on internal biological/chemical causes of gambling addiction, there is now an ongoing search for a 'gaming gene' (de Geer 2011: 33) that takes us far from the moral stigma of the late 1800s, but likewise contributes to sustaining the age-old contestation of gambling.

Coal

Just like gambling, coal has been a widely contested commodity for at least two centuries. Negative values have amassed throughout history, making coal into the highly controversial commodity it is perceived to be today. In our historical analysis, we identified four transformative moments in the coal market from the 1800s until present times (see Table 10.2).

In the case of coal the first transformative moment, Identification of health hazards (approx. 1810–1840), marks the time when coal started to be recognized as a commodity with adverse effects on health. This was due to the identification by scientists of a correlation between coal dust and pulmonary disease among the growing number of coal miners. Based on these early pieces of scientific work, it was soon possible to describe specific harmful effects of coal, such as the tendency toward changes in tissue structure within the lungs (Gregory 1831). Expressions such as 'black lung' emerged and paved the way for worker mobilization and eventually legislative changes to protect workers (Cummins 1927; Cummins and Sladden 1930; Meiklejohn 1951; McIver and Johnston 2007). The value

Table 10.2 Transformative moments in the coal market

Transformative moment	Time period	Contestation, values in conflict	Main market organizers
Identification of health hazards	1810–1840	Worker health *vs* Profit	Medical researchers, coal miners
Intensified health concerns and the entrance of economics	1915–1950	Community Health/Societal costs *vs* Profit	Medical researchers, state, economists, corporations
Identification of environmental harms	1960–1990	Environment/Health/Societal costs *vs* Profit/Individual rights and wealth	Environmental researchers, state, corporations
Global warming calls for global solutions	1990–	Global dimension of mentioned values by discovery of 'global warming'	Researchers, state, EU, trade organizations, environmental organizations, corporations, social movements

of monetary profit was questioned as the value of health was added to the market discourse.

The second transformative change, Intensified health concerns and the entrance of economics (approx. 1920–1950), came on the heels of research findings in medical research and economics, and added a new spark to the conflict. In medical research, terms such as 'coal miner's lung' were cemented, and coal was moreover now observed to be harmful not only to the workers directly exposed in the extraction process, but also to the local communities exposed to the emission of particles produced in coal combustion and the adverse social effects caused by the working conditions (Klotz 1914; Haldene 1917; Collis, 1923, 1925). Hence, the health hazards of coal were emphasized and expanded in scope. In the meantime, contemporary research in economics came to emphasize the plausible costs to society of externalities such as emissions (Pigou 1920; Knight 1924; Kahn 1935; Baumol and Oates 1975; Serret and Johnson 2005). Wider health hazards and economic arguments in particular called for political measures. The introduction of an energy tax in Sweden in the 1950s can, for instance, partly be explained by this development (DS 2005:55; SFS 1957: 262).

Up to this point, the environmental impact of coal had not been the topic of much debate. This changed with the third transformative moment: Identification of environmental harms (approx. 1960–1990). This time period is marked by the rise of technology that produced scientific evidence of the environmental impact of combustion. Studies came to underline the environmental harms from combustion of carbonaceous substances, with attention focused on the issue of carbon dioxide (CO_2). By the 1980s, technology had developed sufficiently to coherently monitor the effects of CO_2 emissions on the climate (Schlesinger and Mitchell 1987; Cess et al. 1989; Raval and Ramanathan 1989; Cline 1992; Bongaarts 1992). A new tax system for CO_2 was imposed in Sweden in 1991 (SFS 1990: 582). Still, international solutions were not feasible at the time, partly due to resistance from industry, and partly due to disagreement in the research community. This was to change in a next transformative moment starting in the 1990s.

The fourth transformative moment, Global warming calls for global solutions (approx. 1990–ongoing), occurred when CO_2 emissions from fossil fuels such as coal came to be increasingly discussed by researchers as a global environmental and economic dilemma (Nordhaus 1994; Hohmeyer et al. 1996; Hope and Maul 1996; Falkowski et al. 2000; Pearce 2003). The research community was more in unison in acknowledging the negative environmental effects of combustion, as there was increasing evidence that these were of global magnitude.

With the use of the term 'global warming' as an expression for the consequences of the 'greenhouse effect' and the various harms of coal being debated – expressed in terms of health, wealth, profit and environmental harm – these were collected under the umbrella of global concerns and increasingly brought into the political arena (Nordhaus and Boyer 2000; Demeritt 2001; Oreskes 2004; Epstein 2005). Suddenly the issue engaged multiple stakeholders, including researchers, international cooperation bodies, media, industrial lobbyists, and to a greater extent environmental organizations and movements that were growing global (Legget 1990; Benedick et al. 1991; Rootes 1999; Stern 2006).

The situation called for global political measures such as the Kyoto Accord of 1997, targets for the reduction of fossil fuel emissions, the United Nations Framework Convention on Climate Change (Werksman 1998; FCCC/SB/1999/8; Directive 2002/358/EC; Cutajar 2004), and the 2005 launch of a market for emission rights in Sweden and in the EU. However, the debate is not permanently settled, as seen, for instance, in the reactions to the so-called 'Stern Review' on the economical impact of climate change (Stern 2006; Tol 2006; Weitzman 2007; Yohe and Murphy 2007). As with alcohol and gambling, the contestation of coal remains in transition.

Alcohol

Alcohol has caused intense political debate for centuries. However, just like the contested commodities markets of gambling and coal, the value conflict underpinnings of the alcohol market have changed over time. As seen in Table 10.3, we have identified four transformative moments from the 1800s onwards and observed that it is difficult to determine a primary value conflict in the Swedish alcohol market. Although being a complex conflict over time, it is possible to discern some major value conflicts regarding both the product itself and how the market for alcohol should be organized (Alexius et al. 2011). For example, the role of market organizers, the supply of products and market competition are three aspects of the market that have been particularly targeted for reforms.

Until the 19th century, Swedish regulation of alcohol was closely connected to religion and specifically to the Protestant church, where alcohol had been seen as a root of sin and vice since the 15th century. With the spread of Christian morals, the drinking of alcohol was constructed as a social problem. From a state point of view, by 1830 this problem had made an impact on the state agenda (Båtefalk 2000: 204). One reason for this was the growing popularity of the temperance movement, which made a major breakthrough in the Swedish parliament in 1840–1841. One of

Table 10.3 Transformative moments in the alcohol market

Transformative moment	Time period	Contestation, values in conflict	Main market organizers
Prohibition of home distilling	1830–1855	Morality/Social discipline *vs* State and private economic interests Freedom *vs* Moral paternalism	State, church, farmers, industry, temperance organizations
Establishing of Motboken (ration system)	1910–1922	Morality/Social discipline/Health *vs* State and private economic interests	State, medical expertise, temperance organizations and individuals
Abolishment of Motboken (ration system)	1940–1955	Welfare paternalism *vs* Liberal democracy/Universalism/Fairness	State, temperance organizations
EU membership and liberalization	1990–	Welfare paternalism *vs* Freedom of choice	EU, state

the temperance movement's primary goals was to strongly proclaim the prohibition of home distilling, an intention it shared with the state (Bruun and Frånberg 1985: 14). The first transformative moment, Prohibition of home distilling (approx. 1830–1855), was characterized by a turbulent debate that eventually resulted in the Swedish Aquavit[1] reform that put an end to home distilling. The profits from the alcohol sales of large industrial distilleries, the bourgeoisie and the state (ibid.: 17; Bergman 1918; Båtefalk 2000: 95), and values associated with leading a moral, sober and healthy life with character and discipline (moral paternalism), stood in contrast to libertarian values and farmers' economic interests (Bruun and Frånberg 1985: 17; Knobblock 1995: 43). As the home distillery became a scapegoat for excessive drinking (Johansson 2008: 20), focus shifted from drunkenness in general to the specific act of producing alcohol in a domestic environment. After the 1855 reform, the production and sales of alcohol were separated. State income from Aquavit sales grew almost tenfold (Nycander 1996: 17). Municipal stakeholders could also benefit financially from alcohol sales, but the profits had to be used for the municipality or philanthropic purposes.

The second transformative moment, Establishing of Motboken (approx. 1910–1922), took place at the beginning of the 20th century, when the temperance movement had advanced its positions in its quest for absolutism. The value conflicts of the 1850s remained the centre of attention during this period, although with a few minor changes: a medical dimension of the drunkenness problem was added, reinforcing the value of health in the debate. Simply put, the main battle was between those who wanted to target alcohol abuse with individual state control of consumers (welfare paternalism) and those who wanted to prohibit the use of alcohol in all its forms, criticizing the state for having major economic interests in allowing a state-run market for alcohol (Johansson 2008: 138). There were naturally also opponents to these two stances who represented more liberal values of freedom of choice, but their ideas were quite suppressed in the debate. The debate of the early 20th century paved the way for an internationally unique solution to the value conflict: Motboken, a state-run ration system for alcohol purchases from municipal companies that was in operation from 1922 to 1955 in the Swedish alcohol market (see section on relocation below).

The period prior to the collapse of the Motboken system in 1955, the third transformative moment – Abolishment of Motboken (approx. 1940–1955) – identified in our study, was characterized by much criticism of the downsides of the system. Opponents argued that Motboken was a paternalistic, class-based system, as well as an arbitrary and irrational authority. The system inspired the addition of new values to the conflict, concerning the organization of the market rather than the product itself: universality and fairness, in the form of respect for democratic ideas and human rights (Rothstein 1992: 154; cf. SOU 1952/53: 34). In terms of market reforms, one crucial outcome of abolishing the ration system was that the state took control over almost the entire market, as all municipal companies selling or distributing alcohol merged, in 1955, into two new state-owned monopoly firms – Systemaktiebolaget and Vin & Sprit AB (Lundqvist 2002: 9).

The fourth and, at the time of writing, still ongoing transformative period observed, EU membership and liberalization beginning in approximately 1990, is marked by calls for state deregulation and privatization in a debate heavily influenced by neoliberal ideals. In terms of values, the fundamental conflict between welfare paternalism and liberalism was accentuated once again, as individual responsibility for alcohol consumption was highlighted in the debate and market practice. As the temperance movement's ability to influence the organization of the market for alcohol weakened, liberal market ideals moved in. This development has also been strengthened by Sweden's EC membership in 1995. However, despite large resources being devoted to portraying the individual consumer as an accountable and responsible actor in the market, the state-owned Systembolaget remains the monopoly supplier of alcohol in Sweden.

Following this brief account of the contestation in transition in the three markets (see further (Alexius et al. 2011), a selection of these transformative moments will now be used to illustrate how value conflicts have been reconfigured using three modes of reconfiguration: addition, expansion or relocation.

ADDING VALUES TO THE CONFLICT

Characteristics of Value Additions

Value addition is a value conflict reconfiguration mode in which additional values become part of an existing value conflict. As will be shown in the empirical illustrations below, values may be added to spur a conflict or to neutralize it. We observed value addition in seven of the 11 transformative moments in our three cases. In the case of alcohol, the values of universality and fairness were added when calls were voiced to abolish the criticized ration system in the third transformative moment in the early 1950s (see Table 10.3). In the case of coal, we identified the addition of several new values, such as social welfare/economy and environmental concerns (see Table 10.2). However, as one transformative moment in the gambling case offers the most illustrative examples of value additions and their influence

Table 10.4   Addition of values. Illustration from the gambling case:
*   remoralizing gambling – from prohibition to state monopoly*
*   (1920–1940)*

Initial contestation – values in conflict	Values added	Impact on contestation and market reform	Main market organizers
Profits *vs* Protestant ethic, work ethic, gambling as sinful, wasteful and unproductive	Wave 1: Leisure ethic, sports, modernity	Neutralization of value conflict brings on normalization of gambling	Illegal and foreign operators, Sports movement – sports organizations and sports media State
	Wave 2: Safety (anti-fraud), protectionism, charity	Revitalization of value conflict, justification for state monopoly	

on market reform, we will use this to illustrate the characteristics and possible impact of value addition (see Table 10.4).

Adding Values to Neutralize a Value Conflict – Leisure, Sports and Modernity

In the mature and increasingly secularized, industrial Swedish society of the 1920s, there was suddenly time for leisure thanks to improved living conditions. There was a widespread positive spirit and strive to modernize rather than dwell on problems of the past. As basic needs were met, citizens now demanded products and services that could help them realize a meaningful leisure time. Because the church was no longer as influential, gambling proponents were gradually able to remoralize and destigmatize gambling with reference to leisure, sports and modernity (see Table 10.4). At the turn of the century (1900), the state lottery had been perceived by leftist commentators as a relic of the Gustavian autocracy, something to be opposed (de Geer 2011). However, in the post-World War I era, American influence saw leftist critics abandon their previous opposition toward gambling, to embrace lotteries as part of the new, modern and future-oriented society (Husz 2004). At this time in the 'roaring 20s', the rigorous work ethic was being challenged and supplemented by a more hedonistic 'leisure ethic' (ibid.). Although still prohibited, gambling was gradually normalized during this time, as it became associated with the pleasures and joys of leisure time (ibid.). This development was made possible in part by the growth of organized sports and the positive associations between sports and gambling (Ihrfors 2007; de Geer 2011). In the late 1800s, soccer was introduced in Sweden and clubs and associations were founded, and systematic sports journalism was established around the time that the first national soccer league (Allsvenskan) was founded in 1924 (de Geer 2011). To sum up this development in our terminology, the 'upside' of the previous value conflict became intensified in the 1920s, as positive values of leisure, sports and modernity were added to the discourse. This value addition thus neutralized the conflict at hand, and the neutralization in turn opened the way for a reorganization of the market. After nearly a century, prohibited gambling products had begun the transition back to their previous status of legal yet contested commodities. Officially, betting on any sport other than horseracing was still illegal in Sweden (until 1934). But many were laying bets anyway as games were readily available. Both major and minor sports clubs found tipping an increasingly accepted alternative to the traditional fundraising like jumble sales and dances. Despite its remaining illegal status, tipping, playing cards or playing the lottery had become a pastime for much of the population. But the growing demand and supply of illegal yet licit gambling opportunities of the late 1920s highlighted a regulatory conflict – between current norms and the illegal status of the market exchanges. It became an unbearable burden to track down and prosecute all individuals, sports clubs and other associations and corporations that had been enticed into this expanding and lucrative market.

The sentence for a first-time offence for organizing illegal tipping was faced by a cigar dealer who had arranged illegal tipping in cooperation with the Västerås IK and Västerås SK sports clubs in 1926, but this did not deter a steady stream of sports clubs and other voluntary associations from entering the illegal but publicly accepted market (de Geer 2011). By about 1930, there were nearly 100 operators in Gothenburg alone (ibid.). Bookmakers were fined but quickly reappeared with new principals. In Stockholm, there were also foreign operators such as Liverpool Vernons pools, which the authorities could not handle within the framework of the national Lotteries Act. And as fines were not heavy enough to be a deterrent, the Swedish government sought instead new ways to organize the illegal yet increasingly accepted market.

Adding Values to Revive Conflict: Safety/Anti-Fraud, Protectionism and Charity

The previously infected value conflict in the gaming market seemed temporarily neutralized by the added leisure values – but not for long.

For who was to benefit from the profitable and expanding market? In a short period of time marked by the Depression, a window of opportunity opened for a redefinition of the downside of the gambling market, a window soon seized by the state. After the financial crisis of the early 1930s, the Swedish state wanted to regain control of the gambling market and its profits – and it did not have laissez-faire legalization in mind. Rather, it was after a strictly state-controlled legalization or, better yet, a state monopoly (de Geer 2011). But in order to justify such an ambition, notions of a normalized market exchange similar to any other leisure product were of little help. The value conflict had to be restored and, as immorality claims were no longer politically viable, a new value entered the conflict: safety as in protection from fraud and other gambling-related criminal offences. In retrospect, the period when illegal tipping flourished was rather short, about five years. It is clear, however, that the defiance exhibited by these illegal businesses (enabled by the conflict neutralization) was crucial, as it sparked the events that followed. Reports of the flourishing illegal gambling market in Sweden and the sentences faced by a small number of operators had not had the desired deterring effect on illegal operators and players. But reports of Swedes playing abroad – in Germany, England or Denmark – in times of economic crisis were used successfully in attempts to revitalize the value conflict with respect to nationalism and protectionism (ibid.). In line with the nationalist, protectionist frame of Privatgeschäft, private profits were described by the state as something to be suspicious of and notions of the trustworthy state were used to promote the idea of a tightly controlled state system or even state monopoly to shut out supposedly untrustworthy private actors from the marketplace, thereby safeguarding the citizens from gambling-related crime (ibid.) and keeping the gambling economy and its profits within Sweden.

The immoral connotations of gambling that still lingered among some citizens were also addressed, with reference to another value added: charity. This was a value that was reintroduced in order to justify the state monopoly. Following the example of Austria and Italy, state lotteries in Sweden had earmarked funding for education and voluntary work since the 1700s (de Geer 2011: 31). It was now suggested that a share of the yearly profits from the gambling monopoly should be allocated to finance youth activities such as sports clubs. The profits were distributed to needy youth and sports associations once a year, later this distribution took place in a ceremony broadcast live on Swedish television. In the early 1930s, the value conflict that had been neutralized in the 1920s had thus been intensified once more as foreign and private gambling operators were made into scapegoats. Not because their operations were formally illegal, but – as the state claimed – because of the supposed higher risk for fraud and so on, making these operators supposedly less trustworthy than the state.

State investigator Gösta Engzell of the Ministry of Commerce was called in to investigate a legal reform in early 1933. The respect for the rule of law had to be restored and Engzell claimed that the illegal gambling market had reached such proportions that there was no prospect of a continued enforcement of the ban. He proposed that, in the long run, a total ban could be considered, but as a temporary pragmatic solution the market ought to be legalized (de Geer 2011: 53). Hence Engzell advocated legalization under state control as the lesser of two evils – the other being a sustained total ban. The proposed legalization, which was adopted in early June of 1934 (ibid.: 50–53), involved a state-controlled gaming operator that could be run by a private owner but would supply a significant portion of the surplus to the Treasury. In a cabinet meeting on 24 September 1934, the government then decided to grant the job to the private company Tipstjänst. The permit, in the form of a concession, was limited to the first half of 1936 and could be revoked at short notice. But as Tipstjänst's operations were an immediate success, before long – much due to its considerable profits – the company passed into state hands as a state-owned enterprise in the early 1940s (ibid.). Needless to say, the legalization and eventual state ownership of both Tipstjänst and the Swedish lottery (Penninglotteriet) was a means to bring substantial amounts of capital to the Treasury (Ihrfors 2007).

To summarize, the contested games made a transition from being prohibited on grounds of immorality to being legally marketed by the state following a shift in a discourse that first neutralized the value conflict and then revitalized it. First, leisure values were added to the upside of the conflict in the 1920s, not least by civil sector sports clubs. In a matter of years, however, the state took great efforts to add values to reinforce the conflict once more, this time with reference to safety, protectionism and charity – as an alibi for state gambling profits. Here, we find evidence that values can also be added to the debate as an 'alibi strategy' by those in charge of market organization. In the cases of both alcohol and gambling, the Swedish state added charity to the conflict discourse in an attempt to balance the conflict and justify its dominant market position and profits. In the case of alcohol, this strategy was seen after home distilling was prohibited in 1855, when protected municipal producers' profits were required to benefit the municipality or philanthropic causes.

EXPANDING THE SCALE OF CONTESTATION

Characteristics of Expansion

The second mode of value reconfiguration identified – expansion – indicates that not only the values at stake but also the scale of contestation can be expanded. This mode was identified in five of our 11 transformative moments. For example, in the alcohol case, the debate about the adverse effects of alcohol expanded from being mainly concerned with the working class in the 1920s and 1930s to encompass all citizens in the 1950s (see Table 10.3). The leisure value of gambling, which was likewise associated with aristocracy in the early 1800s, was gradually expanded to the entire adult population in the 1920s (see Table 10.1). In the case of coal, the debate about adverse health effects expanded from pulmonary syndrome in workers to an urban community disease (see Table 10.2). Yet another transformative moment from the coal case is used below to illustrate the mode of expansion (see Table 10.5).

Expanding Environmental Concerns: from Local to Global Warming

The 1960s and 1970s marked the starting point for a wider and more structured interest in the correlation between the burning of carbonaceous substances and its probable negative effect on the environment (Dyson 1977; Weart 2003). And with new technology in the 1980s, environmental research came to encompass and describe environmental damage of carbon dioxide from burning fossil fuels such as coal (Schlesinger and Mitchell 1987; Cess et al. 1989; Raval and Ramanathan 1989; Cline 1992; Bongaarts 1992).

Novel findings on the matter of the so-called 'greenhouse effect' offered an explanation to the adverse environmental effects of emissions: the rise in average temperature affecting grain production and in the long run causing starvation in certain regions, and the diminishing animal species and the imbalance in the ecosystem, which contributed to the expansion of deserts and to raised sea levels (Cline 1992; Houghton and Woodwell 1989; Peter and Darling, 1985; Weart 2003). Nevertheless, many researchers remained skeptical of the findings and attributed temperature changes to other causes such as natural random variation and the position of Earth's orbit and axis tilt (MacDonald 1980; Rosenberg 1981; Houghton and Woodwell 1989). Neither was the political pressure significant enough to fuel any firm transnational political solutions, although national measures were taken in some countries, such as the carbon dioxide tax in Sweden (SFS 1990: 582).

In the 1990s, however, proof of global climate changes resulting from coal combustion had become more convincing thanks to advanced technology for measuring climate impact on a global scale and methods for calculating the cost of environmental harm (Nordhaus 1994; Hohmeyer et al. 1996; Hope and Maul 1996; Falkowski et al. 2000; Pearce 2003). The term 'global warming' thereupon became the common expression of the harms of CO_2 emissions, primarily relating to the environmental aspects of the damages of coal, but also other adverse effects. The term was the result of research in numerous disciplines focusing on different aspects of the value conflict: wealth, profits, environment, health, emotional perceptions of carbon emissions (Bongaarts 1992; Liaskas et al. 2000; Nordhaus and Boyer 2000; Oreskes 2004; Epstein 2005; Patz et al, 2000; Stern, 2006). Attention to the perceived downsides of coal and other fossil fuels also flourished: in findings from environmental research, but also in calculations on demographic predictions, reports on the future scarcity of coal, reports on health and the environmental effects, from the UN and the US, that had an impact on international environmental policy; and in economic theory on the ills of externalities (Raval and Ramanathan 1989; NAS 1991; Bongaarts 1992, Cline 1992; IPCC 1995).

Accordingly, the 1990s marked the start of an era in which environmental organizations and movements, although confronted with powerful industrial lobbyists, became increasingly powerful and better able to influence the political sphere, using arguments from research in structures increasingly adopted to a global world (Leggett 1990; Benedick et al. 1991; Bartlett et al. 1995; Rootes 1999; Luterbacher and Sprinz 2001). Environmental organizations such as Greenpeace made active use of the opportunity to depict coal combustion as a severe threat to life on earth (Leggett 1990).

Table 10.5   Expanding the scale of contestation. Illustration from the coal case: global warming calls for global solutions (1990–ongoing)

Initial scale of contestation	Expanded scale of contestation	Impact on market reform	Main market organizers
Incoherent and contradictory images of environmental and economic harm	More unified picture of a 'greenhouse effect' and a world problem of 'global warming'	Kyoto Accord, European market for emission allowances	Scientists, environmental organizations, transnational cooperation bodies, states, EU

By framing coal as a global problem, public opinion and environmental organizations increasingly called for political solutions that could tackle the negative sides of coal on a global scale. The global warming debate called for global political measures and can in retrospect be seen as a catalyst for the Kyoto Protocol, the agreement on targets for reduction of emissions from fossil fuels and the United Nations Framework Convention on Climate Change (Werksman 1998; FCCC/SB/1999/8; Directive 2002/358/EC; Cutajar 2004). Actual political outcomes can be seen, for instance, in the launching and organization of a market for emission rights in the EU, and thus in Sweden in 2005 – a trading system with property rights intended to achieve an economically efficient reduction of emissions, in line with economic theory (Crocker 1966; Dales 1968; Montgomery 1972; Directive 2003/87/EC).[2]

RELOCATING THE SCOPE OF CONTESTATION

Characteristics of Relocation

Relocation is a reconfiguration mode aimed at shifting the scope, the locus, of contestation – for example, from one market element to another. We observed relocation in four of the 11 transformative moments. One example is the gambling case, where the state-owned gambling operator Svenska Spel has been a driving force in attempts to relocate contestation from the games and gaming operators to the consumers and their consumption of games (see Table 10.1). In the alcohol market, the debate about home distilling (1830–1855) also entailed relocation, from an initial scope of contestation of general drunkenness to a new scope of contestation of home distilling. This relocation eventually contributed to the dominant view of industry as responsible producers in contrast to farmers' home distilling (Alexius et al. 2011). Below, another relocation process of the Swedish alcohol market, one from commodity to individual consumption, will serve as an empirical illustration (see Table 10.6).

Relocating the Value Conflict: from Commodity to Individual Consumption

At the beginning of the 20th century, the temperance movement had grown and the corridors of power echoed with demands for absolutism and prohibition. The Aquavit dilemma was now defined as the 'intoxicant misery' (rusdryckseländet) by both the state and the temperance movement, although the two took different stances, for or against the free sale of alcohol, respectively. It is apparent that several significant values, such

Table 10.6   Relocating scope of contestation. Illustration from the alcohol case: establishing of Motboken (1910–1922)

Initial scope of contestation	New scope of contestation	Impact on market reform	Main market organizers
Commodity	Consumption	Establishing of individual control systems for consumers	State, medical expertise, temperance organizations and individuals

as medical, health and social values were in the spotlight of the conflict between prohibitionists and their opponents. On the other hand, we also observe that the general political trend was leaning towards some form of temperance. Stakeholders were also keen on opportunities for profit, a value shared by both the state and private corporations.

In 1909, a doctor named Ivan Bratt published a series of articles in one of Sweden's major newspapers. These articles paved the way for an internationally unique solution to the alcohol dilemma. Bratt was against prohibition, as he maintained the idea that alcohol itself was not a problem, only its abuse (Bruun and Frånberg 1985: 52). He argued instead for a system based on individual control and the elimination of private profit motives from the alcohol market (Sulkunen et al. 2000: 22). The main idea of Bratt's system was inspired by war-time rationing, and launched as the Motboken, a ration book first introduced in his newly established firm AB Stockholmssystemet in 1914 (Knobblock 1995: 64). In 1919, the Bratt system was sanctioned by a decision in the Swedish Parliament (Riksdag), making the municipal companies selling alcohol legitimate monopolists as well as the sole assessors of the amount each individual could buy (Rothstein 1992: 151). The individual-based control system meant that individual consumers could apply for a ration book (though unmarried women and vagrants were exceptions), and the logic was based on a principle of individual need. Thus, alcohol was never prohibited in Sweden, although it was heavily restricted (see Table 10.6).

From our analytical perspective, the ration book system can be seen as a successful attempt to relocate the value conflict from revolving around alcohol as an inherently evil commodity, to bad drinking habits of the individual consumer as a social and health problem. Thus, relocation from the commodity to the consumer could be observed. This transformation of the value conflict between prohibitionists and liberals made it possible for Bratt to launch a system based on individual control and the elimination of private profit from the market.

The restrictions that followed the ration book system had major consequences for the organization of the market for alcohol. First, the system led to private actors who sold alcohol being forced out of the market, as only the municipal companies had the right to sell alcohol. Consequently, the common market element of competition was heavily affected, in this case reduced. We also see several attempts by the state to organize how exchanges occurred in the market – using organizational elements such as membership (application for a ration book), surveillance (of individual consumption) and sanctions (the ability to deny further purchases if misconduct was suspected). This implied that consumers came to be registered and subjects of somewhat repressive control when buying alcohol.

CONTESTATION IN TRANSITION

This chapter has brought forth empirical evidence to suggest that, in order to sustain their perceived high level of contestation over extended periods of time, the value conflict underpinnings of the contested commodities of gambling, coal and alcohol have had to change continuously. Our study has thus helped to confirm that taken-for-granted contestation of commodities and markets ought to be understood as a political outcome rather than a reflection of some presumed natural essence.

It is not surprising to find that attempts to shape and organize contestation are likely to become influential when they are in line with institutional trends and demands of the day. However, all cannot be explained by institutional logics, or by state regulation. Rather, the study demonstrates that contestation is often challenged and is continuously recreated in value-laden power struggles and debates that more often than not involve more or less entrepreneurial 'others', such as interest groups, scientists and researchers, the media, and certain influential individuals.

Our study suggests that individuals and organizations that wish to influence value conflicts to sustain contestation of a market typically do so through attempts to add values to the conflict. We found the conscious addition of values to both sides of conflicts – as a means to heat up a conflict, or the opposite – as a means to normalize and neutralize it. The study further illustrates contestation in transition in terms of a shifting scale and scope of contestation. Regarding scale, we have shown, for instance, how the scale of contestation of coal was expanded in several steps – from a local concern with 'coal miner's lung' to a community disease, and from a local environmental concern to a global environment issue. As for the shifting scope of contestation, we used the case of the alcohol market to illustrate how contestation was successfully relocated from a concern with alcohol as a commodity to a focus on individual consumption as the prime locus of conflict and target for reforms.

Furthermore, we have identified a number of market reforms that we believe to be clearly preceded and influenced by one or more of three value conflict reconfiguration modes: addition, expansion and relocation. In the case of the gambling market, the addition of safety/anti-fraud, protectionism and charity in the 1920s revived the value conflict and justified the introduction of a state monopoly. In the case of coal, an expansion of contestation occurred in the 1990s and coal combustion became perceived as a global problem ('global warming'), requiring a global, transnational solution. And in the alcohol market, the relocation of the conflict from the commodity itself to its consumption in the early 1900s, paved the way for the Bratt reform, the Motboken rationing system.

As our findings emphasize the processes of addition and expansion, it becomes relevant to ask why, despite a longitudinal design and covering three markets, we did not see any clear processes of a subtracting or contracting nature. Are values rarely actively removed from market discourse and practice? Is expansion of value conflicts more common than contraction of a contestation? If so, why? And is this pattern characteristic of value conflicts in markets? Rather than being consciously subtracted through formal decision-making, previous research has suggested that a value may slowly 'fade' from market discourse and market memory or become 'dormant' at times as a result of a loss of status or influence on the part of its proponents (Djelic and Quack 2007: 168, see also Crouch 2005; Schneiberg 2007; Sorge 2005; Streeck and Thelen 2005). In line with these findings, our data points to a complex 'layering' of values. However, we did find one interesting twist to this theme in our data. In the 1990s' coal market, when several value discourses were actively collected or accumulated under the common label of 'global warming', this unifying framework successfully contributed to mobilizing and directing the various stakeholders towards a common goal in a way we think would have been more unlikely had the value discourses remained openly 'layered' (see further Alexius et al. 2011).

In closing, we have proposed that the often taken-for-granted contestation of some commodities, such as gambling, coal and alcohol, may be better understood in terms of 'contestation in transition', the outcome of far-reaching processes involving a plethora of market organizers. However, as each of the identified value conflict reconfiguration modes – addition, expansion and relocation – and the potential reverse modes of subtraction and contraction invites further research, it is our ambition to continue to scrutinize the dynamics of these modes and the implications they have for the organization of contested markets.

NOTES

1. Aquavit is a distilled spirit.
2. The solution of an emission allowance market rests on the logic that every company is allowed to emit a certain amount of CO_2 corresponding to a specific number of allocated 'emission rights'. Emissions beyond this level require the purchase of allowances at a market price determined by supply and demand, from companies willing and able to emit less than their permitted allowance (COM 2001:581, COM 2000:87, EC/2002/358, EC/2003/87, 2004/156/EC). This was considered the special advantage of a market system: the reward from selling surplus allowances would hopefully lead to a reduction in emissions at a low cost. Such economically efficient reduction would thus balance the bad and the good of coal (Bohm and Convery 2004; Serret and Johnstone 2005).

REFERENCES

Alexius, S. (2011a). *Making Up the Responsible Gambler: Organizing self-control education and responsible gaming equipment in the Swedish gambling market.* Paper presented at the Nordic Academy of Management Conference Track 19: Self-control and self-organization in post-bureaucratic organizations. Stockholm University, Stockholm, 22–24 August 2011.

Alexius, S. (2011b). *Play Responsibly! A case about the Swedish state gaming operator Svenska Spel and its dual mission to balance profits and social responsibility.* Business case adapted for higher education. Available upon request from author at susanna.alexius@hhs.se.

Alexius, S., D. Castillo and M. Rosenström (2011). *Contestation in Transition. Value-conflicts and the organization of markets – the cases of gambling, coal and alcohol.* Score Report Series.

Bartlett, R.V., A.K. Priya and M. Malik (eds) (1995). *International Organizations and Environmental Policy.* Westport, CT: Greenwood Press.

Båtefalk, L. (2000). *Staten, samhället och superiet: samhällsorganisatoriska principer och organisatorisk praktik kring dryckenskapsproblemet och nykterhetssträvandena i stat, borgerlig offentlighet och associationsväsende ca 1770–1900.* Uppsala: Uppsala University, Department of History.

Baumol, W.J. and W.E. Oates (1975). *The Theory of Environmental Policy: Externalities, public outlays, and the quality of life.* Englewood Cliffs, NJ: Prentice-Hall.

Benedick, R.E., J.T. Mathews and J.K. Sebenius (1991). *Greenhouse Warming: Negotiating a global regime.* Washington, DC: World Resources Institute.

Bergman, J. (1918). *Den svenska nykterhetsrörelsens historia. En översikt.* Stockholm: Svenska nykterhetsförlaget.

Bohm, P. and F. Convery (2004). *Allocating Allowances in Greenhouse Gas Emissions Trading.* Dublin: University College Dublin (The Environmental Institute).

Bongaarts, J. (1992). Population growth and global warming. *Population and Development Review*, 18(2): 299–319.

Bruun, K. and P. Frånberg (eds) (1985). *Den svenska supen. En historia om brännvin, Bratt och byråkrati.* Stockholm: Prisma.

Cess, R.D. et al. (1989). Interpretation of cloud-climate feedback as produced by 14 atmospheric general circulation models. *Science* 245: 513–516.

Cline, W. (1992). *The Economics of Global Warming.* Washington, DC: Institute of International Economics.

Collis, E.L. (1923). An inquiry into the mortality of coal and metalliferous-miners in England and Wales. *Proceedings of the Royal Society of Medicine* 16: 85–101.

Collis, E.L. (1925). *The Coal Miner: His health, diseases & general welfare.* Glasgow: Industrial Health Education Society.

COM (2000:87). *Green Paper on Greenhouse Gas Emissions Trading within the European Union.* Brussels: Commission of European Communities.

COM (2001:581). Proposal for a Directive of the European Parliament and of the Council: establishing a scheme for greenhouse gas emission allowance trading within the Community and amending Council Directive 96/61/EC. Brussels: Commission of the European Communities.

Crocker, T.D. (1966). The structure of atmospheric pollution control systems. In Wolozin, H. (ed.), *The Economics of Air Pollution.* New York: WW Norton & Co.

Crouch (2005). *Capitalist Diversity and Change. Recombinant governance and institutional entrepreneurs.* Oxford: Oxford University Press.

Cummins, S.L. (1927). Effects of coal dust upon the silicotic lung. *Journal of Pathology and Bacteriology,* 30: 615–619.

Cummins, S.L. and A.F. Sladden (1930). Coal-miner's lung. An investigation into the anthracotic lungs of coal-miners in South Wales. *Journal of Pathology and Bacteriology* 33(4): 1095–1132.

Cutajar, M.Z. (2004). Reflections on the Kyoto Protocol – Looking back to see ahead. *International Review for Environmental Strategies* 5(1): 61–70.

Dales, J.H. (1968). *Pollution, Property & Prices.* Toronto: Toronto University Press.

de Geer, H. (2011). *Statens spel. Penninglotterier, Tipstjänst, Svenska Spel.* Atlantis.

de Goede, M. (2005). *A Genealogy of Finance – Virtue, Fortune and Faith.* Minneapolis, MN: University of Minnesota Press.

Demeritt, D. (2001). The construction of global warming and the politics of science. *Annals of the Association of American Geographers* 91(2): 301–337.

Directive 2002/358/EC of the European Parliament and of the Council of 25 April 2002.

Directive 2003/87/EC of the European Parliament and of the Council of 13 October 2003.

Directive 2004/156/EC of the European Parliament and of the Council of 29 January 2004.

Djelic, M.-L. and S. Quack (2007). Overcoming path dependency: Path generation in open systems. *Theory and Society* 36(2): 161–186.

DS (2005:55). *Sweden's Fourth National Communication on Climate Change.*

Dyson, J. (1977). Can we control the carbon dioxide in the atmosphere? *Energy* 2(3): 287–291.

Epstein, C. (2005). Knowledge and power in global environmental activism. *International Journal of Peace Studies* 10(1): 47–67.

Falkowski, P., R.J. Scholes, E. Boyle, J. Canadell, D. Canfield, J. Elser, N. Gruber, K. Hibbard, P. Hogberg, S. Linder, F.T. Mackenzie, B. Moore, T. Pedersen,

Y. Rosenthal, S. Seitzinger, V. Smetacek, and W. Steffen (2000). The global carbon cycle: A test of our knowledge of earth as a system. *Science* 290: 291–296.

FCCC/SB/1999/8 *Procedures and the Mechanisms Relating to Compliance under the Kyoto Protocol*. United Nations Framework Convention on Climate Change.

Fourcade, M. and K. Healy (2007). Moral views of market society. *Annual Review of Sociology* 33: 285–311.

Gregory, J.C. (1831). Case of peculiar black infiltration of the whole lungs resembling melanosis. *Edinburgh Medical Surgery Journal* 36: 389–394.

Haldene, J.S. (1917). *Organism and Environment as Illustrated by the Physiology of Breathing*. New Haven: Yale University Press.

Helling, S. (2003). *Det är som ett kärleksförhållande: spelmissbruk bland ungdomar*. Stockholm: Swedish Council for Information on Alcohol and Other Drugs (CAN).

Hoffman, A.J. and W. Ocasio (2001). Not all events are attended equally: Towards a middle-range theory of industrial attention to external events. *Organization Science* 12(4): 414–434.

Hohmeyer, O. et al. (1996). *Social Costs and Sustainability – Valuation and implementation in the energy and transport sector*. Berlin: Springer-Verlag.

Hong, H. and M. Kacpercyk (2009). The price of sin: The effects of social norms on markets. *Journal of Financial Economics* 93: 15–36.

Hope, C. and P. Maul (1996). Valuing the impact of CO2 emissions. *Energy Policy* 24(3): 211–219.

Houghton, R.A. and G.M. Woodwell (1989). Global climatic change. *Scientific American* 260: 36–44.

Husz, O. (2004). *Drömmars värde. Varuhus och lotteri i svensk konsumtionskultur 1897–1939*. Gidlunds.

Ihrfors, R. (2007). *Spelfrossa: spelets makt och maktens spel*. PhD Dissertation, Stockholm University School of Business.

IPCC (Intergovernmental Panel of Climate Change) (1995). *The Science of Climate Change*. Cambridge: Cambridge University Press.

Johansson, L. (2008). *Staten, supen och systemet. Svensk alkoholpolitik och alkoholkultur 1855–2005*. Stockholm/Stehag: Brutus Östlings Bokförlag Symposion.

Kahn, R.F. (1935). Some notes on ideal output. *The Economic Journal* 45(177): 1–35.

Katz, M.L. and H.S. Rosen (1991/1994). *Microeconomics*. Irwin Publishers.

Klotz, O. (1914) Pulmonary anthracosis – A community disease. *American Journal of Public Health* 4(10): 887–916.

Knight, F.H. (1924). Some fallacies in the interpretation of social cost. *Quarterly Journal of Economics* 38(4): 582–606.

Knobblock, I. (1995). *Systemets långa arm: en studie av kvinnor, alkohol och kontroll i Sverige 1919–1955*. Stockholm: Carlssons.

Leggett, J. (ed.) (1990) *Global Warming. The Greenpeace Report.* Oxford: Oxford University Press.

Liaskas, K., G. Mavrotas, M. Mandaraka and D. Diakoulaki (2000). Decomposition of industrial CO_2 emissions: The case of the European Union. *Energy Economics* 22: 283–239.

Lundqvist, T. (2002). *Den starka alkoholstatens fall*. Working Paper 2002: 3. Stockholm: Institute for Future Studies.

Luterbacher, U. and D.F. Sprinz (2001). *International Relations and Global Climate Change*. Cambridge, MA: MIT Press.

MacDonald, G.J. (1980). *Climatic Effects of Trace Constituents of the Atmosphere.* Paper presented at the Third International Conference on the Environment, Paris.

McIver, A. and A. Johnston (2007). *Miner's Lung: A History of Dust Disease in British Coal Mining.* Farnham: Ashgate Publishing Ltd.

Meiklejohn, A. (1951). History of lung diseases of coal miners in Great Britain. *British Journal of Industrial Medicine* 8(3): 127–137.

Montgomery, W.D. (1972). Markets in licenses and efficient pollution control programs. *Journal of Economic Theory* 5(3): 395–418.

NAS (National Academy of Sciences) (1991). *Policy Implications of Greenhouse Warming.* Washington, DC: National Academy Press.

Nordhaus, W.D. (1994). *Managing the Global Commons – The economics of climate change.* Cambridge, MA: MIT Press.

Nordhaus, W.W. and J. Boyer (2000). *Warming the World: Economic models of global warming.* Cambridge, MA: MIT Press.

Nycander, S. (1996). *Svenskarna och spriten. Alkoholpolitik 1855–1995.* Malmö: Sober Förlag.

Oreskes, N. (2004). Beyond the Ivory Tower: The scientific consensus on climate change. *Science* 306(5702): 1686.

Ortiz, L. (2006). *Till Spelfriheten! Kognitiv beteendeterapi vid spelberoende. Manual för behandling individuellt eller i grupp.* ('Toward Gaming Freedom! Cognitive behavioural therapy for gambling addiction. Manual for individual or group treatment') Stockholm: Natur och Kultur.

Patz, J.A., D. Engelberg and J. Last (2000). The effects of changing weather on public health. *Annual Review of Public Health* 21: 271–307.

Pearce, F. (2003). Heat will soar as haze fades. *New Scientist* 7: 7.

Peters, R.L. and J.D.S Darling (1985). The Greenhouse Effect and Nature Reserves. *BioScience* 35(11): 707–717.

Pigou, A.C. (1920). *The Economics of Welfare.* London: Macmillan.

Raval, A. and V. Ramanathan (1989). Observational determination of the greenhouse effect. *Nature* 342: 758–761.

Reith, G. (1999). *The Age of Chance.* London: Routledge.

Rootes, C. (1999). *Environmental Movements: Local, national and global.* London: Routledge.

Rosenberg, N.J. (1981). The increasing CO2 concentration in the atmosphere and its implication on agricultural productivity. *Climatic Change* 3(3): 265–279.

Rothstein, B. (1992). *Den korporativa staten: intresseorganisationer och statsförvaltning i svensk politik.* Stockholm: Norstedts.

Schlesinger, M.E. and J.F.B. Mitchell (1987). Model simulations of the equilibrium response to increased carbon dioxide. *Reviews of Geophysics* 25: 760–798.

Schneiberg, M. (2007). What's on the path? Path dependence, organizational diversity and the problem of institutional change in the US economy 1900–1950. *Socio-Economic Review* 5: 47–80.

Serret, Y. and N. Johnstone (2005). *The Distributional Effect of Environmental Policy.* Cheltenham, UK and Northampton, MA, USA: Edward Elgar.

Sorge, A. (2005). *The Global and the Local. Understanding the dialectics of business systems.* Oxford: Oxford University Press.

Steiner, G.A. and J.F. Steiner (2008). *Business, Government, and Society: A managerial perspective*, 12th Edition. McGraw-Hill.

Stern, N. (2006). What is the economics of climate change? *World Economics* 7(2): 1–10.
Streeck, W. and K. Thelen (eds) (2005). *Beyond Continuity*. Oxford: Oxford University Press.
Sulkunen, P., C. Sutton, C. Tigerstedt and K. Warpenius (2000). *Broken Spirits. Power and Ideas in Nordic Alcohol Control*. Helsinki: Nordic Council for Alcohol and Drug Research (NAD).
Systembolaget Ltd's website: http://www.systembolaget.se.
SOU 1952/53:34 cited in Rothstein (1992).
Tol, R.S.J. (2006). The Stern Review of economics of climate change: A comment. *Energy and Environment* 17(6): 977–981.
Weart, S. (2003). *The Discovery of Global Warming*. Cambridge, MA: Harvard University Press.
Weitzman, M.L. (2007). Review of the Stern Review on the economics of climate change. *Journal of Economic Literature* 45(3): 703–724.
Werksman, J. (1998). The Clean Development Mechanism: Unwrapping the 'Kyoto Surprise'. *Review of European Community & International Environmental Law* 7(2): 147–158.
Yohe, G. and D. Murphy (2007). On setting near-term climate policy while the dust begins to settle: The legacy of the Stern Review. *Energy & Environment* 18(5): 621.

Parliamentary Documents and Tax Acts

Committee statement (Utlåtande) 1895:8 2K TFU (No. 3) No. 16.
Committee statement (Utlåtande) 1899:2 2aK TFU (No. 4) No. 2.
Committee statement (Utlåtande) 2aK 1906.
Report (Betänkande) 1910 Angående åtgärder till förhindrande af utländska lottsedlars spridande i riket och förändrad lagstiftning om lotterier.
SFS 1957: 262 (General Energy Tax Act).
SFS 1990: 582 (Carbon Dioxide Tax Act).

Index